D0394813

Little Oxford Dictionary of
Quotations

Little Oxford Dictionary of

Quotations

THIRD EDITION

Edited by
Susan Ratcliffe

OXFORD
UNIVERSITY PRESS

OXFORD
UNIVERSITY PRESS

Great Clarendon Street, Oxford OX2 6DP

Oxford University Press is a department of the University of Oxford.
It furthers the University's objective of excellence in research, scholarship,
and education by publishing worldwide in

Oxford New York

Auckland Bangkok Buenos Aires Cape Town Chennai
Dar es Salaam Delhi Hong Kong Istanbul Karachi Kolkata
Kuala Lumpur Madrid Melbourne Mexico City Mumbai Nairobi
São Paulo Shanghai Taipei Tokyo Toronto

Oxford is a registered trade mark of Oxford University Press
in the UK and in certain other countries

Published in the United States
by Oxford University Press Inc., New York

British Library Cataloguing in Publication Data

Data available

Library of Congress Cataloging in Publication Data

Data available

ISBN 0–19–860998–1

10 9 8 7 6 5 4 3 2 1

Designed by Jane Stevenson
Typeset in Minion and Argo
by Interactive Sciences Limited, Gloucester
Printed and bound by
Legoprint SpA, Italy

Contents

Foreword to the Third Edition   vii

Foreword to the First Edition   ix

List of Subjects   xiii

Little Oxford Dictionary of Quotations   1

Index of Authors   439

Foreword to the Third Edition

'Studies serve for delight, for ornament, and for ability' said Francis Bacon, and so too do quotations. An apt or witty quotation can enhance our ability to make a point, it can provide an ornament for a speech or a presentation, and it can simply be a delight in itself. All these needs are fulfilled by the rich selection of quotations, on a variety of subjects, in this new edition of the *Little Oxford Dictionary of Quotations*.

Search here for quotations on special occasions such as **Birthdays**: 'Our birthdays are feathers in the broad wing of time' (Jean Paul Richter), **Examinations**: 'I evidently knew more about economics than my examiners' (John Maynard Keynes), and **Retirement**: 'The transition from Who's Who to Who's He' (Eddie George). Special people are here as well: **Lovers**: 'He's more myself than I am. Whatever our souls are made of his and mine are the same' (Emily Brontë) and **Babies** 'A baby is God's opinion that life should go on' (Carl Sandburg). Other new sections include many on lifestyle interests: **Tennis**: 'Do what you love and love what you do and everything else is detail' (Martina Navratilova), **Exercise**: 'Avoid running at all times' (Leroy 'Satchel' Paige), and **Railways**: 'The only way of catching a train I have ever discovered is to miss the train before' (G. K. Chesterton).

New quotations are continually being added to the Oxford database: some from old favourites such as Homer 'A gift though small is welcome' and Milton 'With thee conversing I forget all time', others newly minted in the twenty-first century such as Donald Rumsfeld on the 'known unknowns' and the 'unknown unknowns' and Joan Baez's opinion that 'I've never had a humble opinion. If you've got

Foreword to the Third Edition

an opinion, why be humble about it?'. Old hands such as Mark Twain advise 'Get your facts first, and then you can distort 'em as much as you please', while Bill Cosby reflects 'The heart of marriage is memories'.

On any occasion, 'A joyful and pleasant thing it is to be thankful', as the Bible tells us, and in this case thanks are due to Elizabeth Knowles, Publishing Manager, Quotations Dictionaries, for her manifold ideas and suggestions, to Jean Harker and Verity Mason for their contributions to the Reading Programme, and to Kim Allen for proofreading.

Look within for the wise and witty words of the great and the famous to express the events and emotions of everyday life: 'What oft was thought, but ne'er so well expressed'.

SUSAN RATCLIFFE

Oxford 2004

Foreword to the First Edition

The Little Oxford Dictionary of Quotations is a collection
which casts a fresh light on even the most familiar sayings.
It is organized by themes, such as **Action**, **Liberty**, and
Memory, and within each theme the quotations are
arranged in date order, so that the interplay of ideas down
the centuries becomes apparent. It is intended for the reader
who is searching for quotations on a specific subject, the
reader who remembers the sense of a quotation but not the
precise words, and, of course, the browser.

The themes have been chosen to reflect as wide a range of
subjects as possible, concentrating on the general rather
than the specific. A few themes have a slightly different
character: thus **People** and **Places** cover quotations about
many different individual people and places, while **Political
Comment** and **Wars** include quotations relevant to specific
events. The length of the sections reflects to some extent the
preoccupations of people throughout history, ranging from
short ones such as **Advice** to the many and varied comments
on **Life** and **Love**. Where subjects overlap, the reader is
directed to related themes at the head of the section; for
example, at **Death**: see also **Epitaphs**, **Last Words**, **Murder**.
An author index is provided to help readers wishing to trace
a particular quotation or seeking quotations from specific
individuals.

Within each theme, the aim is to take in a variety of
viewpoints, including both the most familiar quotations
and some less well-known or perhaps new material. So
within **News and Journalism**, along with C. P. Scott's classic
'Comment is free, but facts are sacred', we have Tom
Stoppard's gloss 'Comment is free but facts are on expenses'
and more recently Lord MacGregor on 'journalists dabbling

Foreword to the First Edition

their fingers in the stuff of other people's souls'. This book contains some one hundred quotations which have not previously appeared in any dictionary of quotations. These new quotations appear, for example, under the themes **Environment** ('...all that remains/For us will be concrete and tyres'), **Men and Women** ('Whereas nature turns girls into women, society has to make boys into men'), and **Science** ('The aim of science is not to open the door to infinite wisdom, but to set a limit to infinite error').

The chronological ordering within each theme enables the quotations to 'talk' to one another, shedding new light on each. Thus we have Samuel Johnson telling us 'Change is not made without inconvenience, even from worse to better', followed by Voltaire: 'If we do not find anything pleasant, at least we shall find something new'. Much of the cross-referencing required by an alphabetical arrangement of authors becomes redundant: Ralegh's line written on a window-pane 'Fain would I climb, yet fear I to fall' is now immediately followed by Elizabeth I's reply 'If thy heart fails thee, climb not at all.'

The quotations have been classified by their subject rather than by keywords in the text. For example, Tom Lehrer's 'It is sobering to consider that when Mozart was my age he had already been dead for a year' is essentially about **Achievement** rather than **Music** or **Death**, and has been placed accordingly. As far as possible each quotation has been included only once, but a few, such as Pope's 'To err is human, to forgive divine' plainly had a place in two sections.

A short source reference is given for each quotation, usually including its date. Where the date is uncertain or unknown, the author's date of death has been used to determine the order within a theme. The quotations themselves have been kept as short as possible: contextual information has occasionally been added to the source note, and related but less well-known and well-expressed versions have generally been excluded. Owing to constraints of space, foreign language originals have been given only where they are well-known or where translations differ. Such information, including full finding references, can be found in *The Oxford Dictionary of Quotations*.

We are always grateful to those readers who write to us with their comments, suggestions, and discoveries, and we hope this tradition will continue. *The Little Oxford Dictionary* draws largely on the work done for the fourth edition of *The Oxford Dictionary of Quotations*, and therefore owes a substantial debt to all those involved in the preparation of that volume. None the less, this book has its own identity, and the editor's chief pleasure as it took shape has been in listening to diffent voices speaking to each other across the ages: ' "What is the use of a book," thought Alice, "without pictures or conversations?" '

SUSAN RATCLIFFE

Oxford, March 1994

List of Subjects

A

Ability
Absence
Achievement
Acting
Action
Advertising
Advice
Ambition
Anger
Animals
Anxiety
Apology
Appearance
Architecture
Argument
The Army
Art
Australia
Autumn

B

Babies
Baseball
Beauty
Beginning
Behaviour
Belief
Bereavement
Biography
Birds

Birth
Birthdays
Boats
The Body
Books
Boredom
Boxing
Brevity
Britain
Bureaucracy
Business

C

Canada
Careers
Cars
Cats
Censorship
Certainty
Chance
Change
Character
Charity
Charm
Children
Choice
Christmas
The Church
The Cinema
Civilization
Class

Clothes
Computers
Conscience
Conversation
Cookery
Cooperation
The Country
Courage
Creativity
Cricket
Crime
Crises
Criticism
Cruelty
Custom
Cynicism

D

Dance
Danger
Day
Death
Debt
Deceit
Democracy
Despair
Determination
Diaries
Diplomacy
Discontent

List of Subjects

Discovery *see*
  Invention and
  Discovery
Dogs
Doubt
Drawing
Dreams
Drink
Drugs

E

The Earth
Eating
Economics
Education
Effort
Elections
Ending
Enemies
England
The Environment
Envy and Jealousy
Equality
Europe
Evil
Examinations
Exercise
Experience

F

Failure
Fame
The Family
Fashion

Fate
Fathers
Fear
Festivals
Fishing
Flight
Flowers
Food
Foolishness
Football
Forgiveness
France
Friendship
The Future

G

Gardens
The Generation Gap
Genius
Gifts
God
Golf
Good Looks
Goodness
Gossip
Government
Greatness

H

Habit
Happiness
Hatred
Health
The Heart

Heaven
Hell
Heroes
History
Home
Honour
Honours
Hope
Hospitality
Houses
Housework
The Human Race
Human Rights
Humour
Hypocrisy

I

Idealism
Ideas
Idleness
Ignorance
Imagination
Indifference
Intelligence
Invention and
  Discovery
Ireland

J

Jealousy *see* Envy
  and Jealousy
Journalism
Justice

List of Subjects

K

Knowledge

L

Language
Languages
The Law
Leadership
Leisure
Letters
Liberty
Libraries
Lies
Life
Life Sciences
Lifestyles
Literature
London
Love
Lovers
Luck

M

Madness
Management
Manners
Marriage
Mathematics
Meaning
Medicine
Meeting
Memory
Men

Men and Women
Middle Age
The Mind
Misfortune
Mistakes
Moderation
Money
Morality
Mothers
Mountains
Murder
Music

N

Names
Nature
Night

O

Old Age
Opinion
Optimism

P

Painting
Parents
Parting
The Past
Patriotism
Peace
Perfection
Pessimism
Philosophy

Photography
Planning
Pleasure
Poetry
Politicians
Politics
Pollution
Poverty
Power
Practicality
Praise
Prayer
Prejudice
The Present
The Presidency
Pride
Progress
Protest
Punishment

Q

Quotations

R

Race
Railways
Reading
Reality
Religion
Retirement
Revenge
Revolution
Royalty

Trust and Treachery

S

Satisfaction
Science
Scotland
Sculpture
The Sea
Secrecy
The Self
Self-Knowledge
Sex
Sickness
Silence
Singing
The Skies
Sleep
Society
Solitude
Sorrow
Speechmaking
Sport
Spring
Statistics
Style
Success
Suffering
Summer
The Supernatural
Sympathy

T

Taxes
Teaching
Technology
Television
Temptation
Tennis
Thanks
The Theatre
Thinking
Time
The Town
Transience
Travel
Trust and Treachery
Truth

U

The United States
The Universe

V

Violence

W

Wales
War
Wealth
Weather
Weddings
Winning
Winter
Woman's Role
Women
Words
Work
Writing

Y

Youth

Quotations

Natural abilities are like natural plants, that need pruning by study.
Francis Bacon 1561–1626

If a man write a better book, preach a better sermon, or make a better mouse-trap than his neighbour, tho' he build his house in the woods, the world will make a beaten path to his door.
Ralph Waldo Emerson 1803–82

This very remarkable man
Commends a most practical plan:
You can do what you want
If you don't think you can't,
So don't think you can't think you can.
Charles Inge 1868–1957, *on the French psychologist Émile Coué*

I'm usually called a jack of all trades by people who are scarcely jacks of one.
Jonathan Miller 1934–

DUMBLEDORE: It is our choices, Harry, that show what we truly are, far more than our abilities.
J. K. Rowling 1965–

MARLON BRANDO: I could have had class. I could have been a contender.
Budd Schulberg 1914–

Non omnia possumus omnes.
We can't all do everything.
Virgil 70–19 BC

These success encourages: they can because they think they can.
Virgil 70–19 BC

Absence

The Lord watch between me and thee, when we are absent one from another.
> **Bible**

The heart may think it knows better: the senses know that absence blots people out. We have really no absent friends.
> **Elizabeth Bowen** 1899–1973

The absent are always in the wrong.
> **Philippe Néricault Destouches** 1680–1754

Absence diminishes commonplace passions and increases great ones, as the wind extinguishes candles and kindles fire.
> **Duc de la Rochefoucauld** 1613–80

Absence makes the heart grow fonder.
> **Proverb**

Most of what matters in your life takes place in your absence.
> **Salman Rushdie** 1947–

Achievement ····▶ Ambition, Effort

That's one small step for a man, one giant leap for mankind.
> **Neil Armstrong** 1930– , *stepping onto the moon*

The desire accomplished is sweet to the soul.
> **Bible**

To those of you who received honours, awards and distinctions, I say well done. And to the C students, I say you, too, can be president of the United States.
> **George W. Bush** 1946–

Give us the tools and we will finish the job.
Winston Churchill 1874–1965

None climbs so high as he who knows not whither he is going.
Oliver Cromwell 1599–1658

There must be a beginning of any great matter, but the continuing unto the end until it be thoroughly finished yields the true glory.
Francis Drake c.1540–96

The distance is nothing; it is only the first step that is difficult.
Mme Du Deffand 1697–1780, *commenting on the legend that St Denis, carrying his head in his hands, walked two leagues*

Nothing great was ever achieved without enthusiasm.
Ralph Waldo Emerson 1803–82

Those who believe that they are exclusively in the right are generally those who achieve something.
Aldous Huxley 1894–1963

He has, indeed, done it very well; but it is a foolish thing well done.
Samuel Johnson 1709–84

It is sobering to consider that when Mozart was my age he had already been dead for a year.
Tom Lehrer 1928–

So little done, so much to do.
Cecil Rhodes 1853–1902

You have to motivate yourself with challenges. That's how you know you're still alive. Once you start doing only what you've proven you can do, you're on the road to death.
Jerry Seinfeld 1954–

Acting

To grasp the full significance of life is the actor's duty, to interpret it is his problem, and to express it his dedication.
Marlon Brando 1924-2004

The basic essential of a great actor is that he loves himself in acting.
Charlie Chaplin 1889-1977

Just say the lines and don't trip over the furniture.
Noël Coward 1899-1973

Actors are cattle.
Alfred Hitchcock 1899-1980

Acting is a masochistic form of exhibitionism. It is not quite the occupation of an adult.
Laurence Olivier 1907-89

She ran the whole gamut of the emotions from A to B.
Dorothy Parker 1893-1967

Acting is merely the art of keeping a large group of people from coughing.
Ralph Richardson 1902-83

Suit the action to the word, the word to the action.
William Shakespeare 1564-1616

O Lord, Sir—when a heroine goes mad she always goes into white satin.
Richard Brinsley Sheridan 1751-1816

They say an actor is only as good as his parts. Well, my parts have done me pretty well, darling.
Barbara Windsor 1937-

Action

But men must know, that in this theatre of man's life it is reserved only for God and angels to be lookers on.
Francis Bacon 1561–1626

Let's roll.
Todd Beamer 1968–2001, *as Beamer and other passengers were planning to storm the cockpit of the hijacked United Airlines Flight 93, 11 September 2001*

Better to light a candle than curse the darkness.
Peter Benenson 1921–

Enough of talking—it is time now to do.
Tony Blair 1953– , *taking office as Prime Minister*

The world can only be grasped by action, not by contemplation…The hand is the cutting edge of the mind.
Jacob Bronowski 1908–74

Action is consolatory. It is the enemy of thought and the friend of flattering illusions.
Joseph Conrad 1857–1924

Oh that thou hadst like others been all words,
And no performance.
Philip Massinger 1583–1640

They also serve who only stand and wait.
John Milton 1608–74

Think nothing done while aught remains to do.
Samuel Rogers 1763–1855

If it were done when 'tis done, then 'twere well
It were done quickly.
William Shakespeare 1564–1616

5

Advertising

A good poster is a visual telegram.
   A. M. Cassandre 1901-68

Advertising is the most fun you can have with your clothes on.
   Jerry Della Femina

Promise, large promise, is the soul of an advertisement.
   Samuel Johnson 1709-84

Society drives people crazy with lust and calls it advertising.
   John Lahr 1941-

Advertising may be described as the science of arresting human intelligence long enough to get money from it.
   Stephen Leacock 1869-1944

Half the money I spend on advertising is wasted, and the trouble is I don't know which half.
   Lord Leverhulme 1851-1925

The consumer isn't a moron; she is your wife.
   David Ogilvy 1911-

Advertising is the rattling of a stick inside a swill bucket.
   George Orwell 1903-50

Good wine needs no bush.
   Proverb

Advice

Don't panic.
   Douglas Adams 1952-2001, *on the cover of* The Hitch Hiker's Guide to the Galaxy

Books will speak plain when counsellors blanch.
   Francis Bacon 1561-1626

Well, if you knows of a better 'ole, go to it.
Bruce Bairnsfather 1888–1959

Advice is seldom welcome; and those who want it the most always like it the least.
Lord Chesterfield 1694–1773

Fools need advice most, but wise men only are the better for it.
Benjamin Franklin 1706–90

Get the advice of everybody whose advice is worth having—they are very few—and then do what you think best yourself.
Charles Stewart Parnell 1846–91

After all, when you seek advice from someone it's certainly not because you want them to give it. You just want them to be there while you talk to yourself.
Terry Pratchett 1948–

Look for what's missing. Many advisers can tell a president how to improve what's proposed, or what's gone amiss. Few are able to see what isn't there.
Donald Rumsfeld 1932–

I always pass on good advice. It is the only thing to do with it. It is never of any use to oneself.
Oscar Wilde 1854–1900

Ambition ····▶ Achievement, Effort

Aut Caesar, aut nihil.
Caesar or nothing.
Cesare Borgia 1476–1507

Ah, but a man's reach should exceed his grasp,
Or what's a heaven for?
Robert Browning 1812–89

Ambition

Well is it known that ambition can creep as well as soar.
Edmund Burke 1729-97

[I] had rather be first in a village than second at Rome.
Julius Caesar 100-44 BC

All ambitions are lawful except those which climb
upwards on the miseries or credulities of mankind.
Joseph Conrad 1857-1924

Ambition leads me not only farther than any other man
has been before me, but as far as I think it possible for
man to go.
James Cook 1728-79

At the age of six I wanted to be a cook. At seven I
wanted to be Napoleon. And my ambition has been
growing steadily ever since.
Salvador Dali 1904-89

Hitch your wagon to a star.
Ralph Waldo Emerson 1803-82

The worst fault of the working classes is telling their
children they're not going to succeed, saying: 'There is
life, but it's not for you.'
John Mortimer 1923-

Fain would I climb, yet fear I to fall.
Walter Ralegh c.1552-1618, *line written on a window-pane;
Queen Elizabeth I (1533-1603) replied 'If thy heart fails thee,
climb not at all'*

When that the poor have cried, Caesar hath wept;
Ambition should be made of sterner stuff.
William Shakespeare 1564-1616

The world continues to offer glittering prizes to those
who have stout hearts and sharp swords.
F. E. Smith 1872-1930

There is always room at the top.
Daniel Webster 1782–1852

Anger

Anger makes dull men witty, but it keeps them poor.
Francis Bacon 1561–1626

A soft answer turneth away wrath.
Bible

The tigers of wrath are wiser than the horses of instruction.
William Blake 1757–1827

Beware the fury of a patient man.
John Dryden 1631–1700

Anger is never without an argument, but seldom with a good one.
Lord Halifax 1633–95

Ira furor brevis est.
Anger is a short madness.
Horace 65–8 BC

When angry, count ten before you speak; if very angry a hundred.
Thomas Jefferson 1743–1826

Anger in its time and place
May assume a kind of grace.
It must have some reason in it
And not last beyond a minute.
Charles Lamb 1775–1834

When angry, count four; when very angry, swear.
Mark Twain 1835–1910

Animals ····▶ Cats, Dogs

All things bright and beautiful,
All creatures great and small,
All things wise and wonderful,
The Lord God made them all.
    Cecil Frances Alexander 1818–95

I'm not over-fond of animals. I am merely astounded by
them.
    David Attenborough 1926–

The question is not, Can they reason? nor, Can they talk?
but, Can they suffer?
    Jeremy Bentham 1748–1832

A righteous man regardeth the life of his beast: but the
tender mercies of the wicked are cruel.
    Bible

Tiger Tiger, burning bright,
In the forests of the night;
What immortal hand or eye,
Could frame thy fearful symmetry?
    William Blake 1757–1827

A four-legged friend, a four-legged friend,
He'll never let you down.
    J. Brooks

Wee, sleekit, cow'rin', tim'rous beastie,
O what a panic's in thy breastie!
    Robert Burns 1759–96, *on a mouse*

I am fond of pigs. Dogs look up to us. Cats look down
on us. Pigs treat us as equals.
    Winston Churchill 1874–1965

Animals, whom we have made our slaves, we do not like to consider our equal.
Charles Darwin 1809–82

Nature's great masterpiece, an elephant,
The only harmless great thing.
John Donne 1572–1631

Where in this wide world can man find nobility without
    pride,
Friendship without envy, or beauty without vanity?
Ronald Duncan 1914–82, *on the horse*

'Twould ring the bells of Heaven
The wildest peal for years,
If Parson lost his senses
And people came to theirs,
And he and they together
Knelt down with angry prayers
For tamed and shabby tigers
And dancing dogs and bears,
And wretched, blind, pit ponies,
And little hunted hares.
Ralph Hodgson 1871–1962

I hate a word like 'pets': it sounds so much
Like something with no living of its own.
Elizabeth Jennings 1926–2001

It ar'n't that I loves the fox less, but that I loves the
'ound more.
R. S. Surtees 1805–64

Anxiety

What's the use of worrying?
It never was worth while,
So, pack up your troubles in your old kit-bag,

Anxiety

And smile, smile, smile.
George Asaf 1880–1951

In trouble to be troubled
Is to have your trouble doubled.
Daniel Defoe 1660–1731

I'm not [biting my fingernails]. I'm biting my knuckles. I finished the fingernails months ago.
Joseph L. Mankiewicz 1909– , *while directing* Cleopatra

O polished perturbation! golden care!
William Shakespeare 1564–1616

What though care killed a cat, thou hast mettle enough in thee to kill care.
William Shakespeare 1564–1616

Neurosis is the way of avoiding non-being by avoiding being.
Paul Tillich 1886–1965

Apology

Very sorry can't come. Lie follows by post.
Lord Charles Beresford 1846–1919, *telegraphed message to the Prince of Wales, on being summoned to dine at the eleventh hour*

Never make a defence or apology before you be accused.
Charles I 1600–49

Never complain and never explain.
Benjamin Disraeli 1804–81

The most important thing a man can learn—the importance of three little words: 'I was wrong.' These words will get you much further than 'I love you.'
Charlton Heston 1924–

Several excuses are always less convincing than one.
Aldous Huxley 1894–1963

It is a good rule in life never to apologize. The right sort of people do not want apologies, and the wrong sort take a mean advantage of them.
P. G. Wodehouse 1881–1975

Appearance ····▶ The Body

Your cameraman might enjoy himself because my face looks like a wedding-cake left out in the rain.
W. H. Auden 1907–73

If everyone were cast in the same mould, there would be no such thing as beauty.
Charles Darwin 1809–82

I am the family face;
Flesh perishes, I live on.
Thomas Hardy 1840–1928

At 50, everyone has the face he deserves.
George Orwell 1903–50

Men seldom make passes
At girls who wear glasses.
Dorothy Parker 1893–1967

It costs a lot of money to look this cheap.
Dolly Parton 1946–

Had Cleopatra's nose been shorter, the whole face of the world would have changed.
Blaise Pascal 1623–62

Appearance

Anything which says it can magically take away your wrinkles is a scandalous lie.
Anita Roddick 1942-

There's no art
To find the mind's construction in the face.
William Shakespeare 1564-1616

Architecture

A monstrous carbuncle on the face of a much-loved and elegant friend.
Charles, Prince of Wales 1948- , *on the proposed extension to the National Gallery, London*

We shape our buildings, and afterwards our buildings shape us.
Winston Churchill 1874-1965

Light (God's eldest daughter) is a principal beauty in building.
Thomas Fuller 1608-61

Less is more.
Ludwig Mies van der Rohe 1886-1969

God is in the details.
Ludwig Mies van der Rohe 1886-1969

You should be able to read a building. It should be what it does.
Richard Rogers 1933-

Architecture in general is frozen music.
Friedrich von Schelling 1775-1854

Form follows function.
Louis Henri Sullivan 1856-1924

Well building hath three conditions. Commodity, firmness, and delight.
Henry Wotton 1568–1639

The physician can bury his mistakes, but the architect can only advise his client to plant vines—so they should go as far as possible from home to build their first buildings.
Frank Lloyd Wright 1867–1959

Argument

You cannot argue with someone who denies the first principles.
Auctoritates Aristotelis

It is better to dwell in a corner of the housetop, than with a brawling woman in a wide house.
Bible

It takes in reality only one to make a quarrel. It is useless for the sheep to pass resolutions in favour of vegetarianism, while the wolf remains of a different opinion.
Dean Inge 1860–1954

The Catholic and the Communist are alike in assuming that an opponent cannot be both honest and intelligent.
George Orwell 1903–50

Who can refute a sneer?
William Paley 1743–1805

The argument of the broken window pane is the most valuable argument in modern politics.
Emmeline Pankhurst 1858–1928

I am not arguing with you—I am telling you.
James McNeill Whistler 1834–1903

The Army

The Army ····▸ War

Lions led by donkeys.
Anonymous *associated with British forces during the First World War, but of earlier origin*

The sergeant is the army.
Dwight D. Eisenhower 1890–1969

Old soldiers never die,
They simply fade away.
J. Foley 1906–70

How do you ask a man to be the last man to die in Vietnam? How do you ask a man to be the last man to die for a mistake?
John Kerry 1943–

O it's Tommy this, an' Tommy that, an' 'Tommy, go away';
But it's 'Thank you, Mister Atkins,' when the band begins to play.
Rudyard Kipling 1865–1936

Remember that there is not one of you who does not carry in his cartridge-pouch the marshal's baton of the duke of Reggio; it is up to you to bring it forth.
Louis XVIII 1755–1824

When I was in the military, they gave me a medal for killing two men and a discharge for loving one.
Leonard Matlovich d. 1988

An army marches on its stomach.
Napoleon I 1769–1821

What passing-bells for these who die as cattle?
Only the monstrous anger of the guns.
Wilfred Owen 1893–1918

16

Wars may be fought with weapons, but they are won by men.

George S. Patton 1885–1945

A man who is good enough to shed his blood for the country is good enough to be given a square deal afterwards.

Theodore Roosevelt 1858–1919

They dashed on towards that thin red line tipped with steel.

William Howard Russell 1820–1907

      A soldier,
Full of strange oaths, and bearded like the pard,
Jealous in honour, sudden and quick in quarrel,
Seeking the bubble reputation
Even in the cannon's mouth.

William Shakespeare 1564–1616

When the military man approaches, the world locks up its spoons and packs off its womankind.

George Bernard Shaw 1856–1950

The British soldier can stand up to anything except the British War Office.

George Bernard Shaw 1856–1950

Theirs not to make reply,
Theirs not to reason why,
Theirs but to do and die:
Into the valley of Death
Rode the six hundred.

Alfred, Lord Tennyson 1809–92

Discipline is the soul of an army. It makes small numbers formidable; procures success to the weak and esteem to all.

George Washington 1732–99

The Army

I don't know what effect these men will have upon the enemy, but, by God, they frighten me.

Duke of Wellington 1769–1852, *popular version of Wellington's remark: 'As Lord Chesterfield said of the generals of his day, "I only hope that when the enemy reads the list of their names, he trembles as I do"'*

Art ····▶ Painting, Sculpture

Art is meant to disturb, science reassures.

Georges Braque 1882–1963

The history of art is the history of revivals.

Samuel Butler 1835–1902

A product of the untalented, sold by the unprincipled to the utterly bewildered.

Al Capp 1907–79, *on abstract art*

Art for art's sake, with no purpose, for any purpose perverts art. But art achieves a purpose which is not its own.

Benjamin Constant 1767–1834

Art is vice. You don't marry it legitimately, you rape it.

Edgar Degas 1834–1917

I always said God was against art and I still believe it.

Edward Elgar 1857–1934

The artist must be in his work as God is in creation, invisible and all-powerful; one must sense him everywhere but never see him.

Gustave Flaubert 1821–80

Art for Art's sake. Why not?
Art for Life's sake. Why not?
Art for Pleasure's sake. Why not?
What does it matter, as long as it is Art?

Paul Gauguin 1848–1903

In art the best is good enough.
  Johann Wolfgang von Goethe 1749–1832

The proletarian state must bring up thousands of
excellent 'mechanics of culture', 'engineers of the soul'.
  Maxim Gorky 1868–1936

Life is short, the art long.
  Hippocrates c.460–357 BC

It's clever, but is it Art?
  Rudyard Kipling 1865–1936

God help the Minister that meddles with art!
  Lord Melbourne 1779–1848

The true artist will let his wife starve, his children go
barefoot, his mother drudge for his living at seventy,
sooner than work at anything but his art.
  George Bernard Shaw 1856–1950

Australia

Who knows but that England may revive in New South
Wales when it has sunk in Europe.
  Joseph Banks 1743–1820

True patriots we; for be it understood,
We left our country for our country's good.
  Henry Carter d. 1806, *written for the opening of the
  Playhouse, Sydney, New South Wales, when the actors were
  principally convicts*

And her five cities, like teeming sores,
Each drains her: a vast parasite robber-state
Where second-hand Europeans pullulate
Timidly on the edge of alien shores.
  A. D. Hope 1907–

Australia

Australia is a lucky country run mainly by second-rate
people who share its luck.
Donald Richmond Horne 1921–

You would take Australia right back down the time
tunnel to the cultural cringe where you have always come
from.
Paul Keating 1944– , *addressing Australian Conservative
supporters of links with Great Britain*

Australia has a marvellous sky and air and blue clarity,
and a hoary sort of land beneath it, like a Sleeping
Princess on whom the dust of ages has settled.
D. H. Lawrence 1885–1930

In joyful strains then let us sing
Advance Australia fair.
P. D. McCormick c.1834–1916

What Great Britain calls the Far East is to us the near
north.
Robert Gordon Menzies 1894–1978

The crimson thread of kinship runs through us all.
Henry Parkes 1815–95, *on Australian federation*

Autumn

Coldly, sadly descends
The autumn evening. The Field
Strewn with its dank yellow drifts
Of withered leaves, and the elms,
Fade into dimness apace.
Matthew Arnold 1822–88

Early autumn—
rice field, ocean,
one green.
Matsuo Basho 1644–94

Now is the time for the burning of the leaves.
Laurence Binyon 1869–1943

Season of mists and mellow fruitfulness,
Close bosom-friend of the maturing sun;
Conspiring with him how to load and bless
With fruit the vines that round the thatch-eaves run.
John Keats 1795–1821

I want to go south, where there is no autumn, where the
cold doesn't crouch over one like a snow-leopard waiting
to pounce. The heart of the North is dead, and the
fingers of cold are corpse fingers.
D. H. Lawrence 1885–1930

O wild West Wind, thou breath of Autumn's being,
Thou, from whose unseen presence the leaves dead
Are driven, like ghosts from an enchanter fleeing.
Percy Bysshe Shelley 1792–1822

For man, autumn is a time of harvest, of gathering
together. For nature, it is a time of sowing, of scattering
abroad.
Edwin Way Teale 1899–1980

In…the fall, the whole country goes to glory.
Frances Trollope 1780–1863, *of North America*

Babies ····▶ Birth

There is no finer investment for any community than
putting milk into babies.
Winston Churchill 1874–1965

So for the mother's sake the child was dear,
And dearer was the mother for the child.
Samuel Taylor Coleridge 1772–1834

Babies

It is a pleasant thing to reflect upon, and furnishes a complete answer to those who contend for the general degeneration of the human species, that every baby born into the world is a finer one than the last.
Charles Dickens 1812-70

There never was a child so lovely but his mother was glad to get asleep.
Ralph Waldo Emerson 1803-82

Since you arrived, days have melted into night and back again and we are learning a new grammar, a long sentence whose punctuation marks are feeding and winding and nappy changing and these occasional moments of quiet.
Fergal Keane 1961-

A loud noise at one end and no sense of responsibility at the other.
Ronald Knox 1888-1957, *definition of a baby*

Yet does your young ambition burn?
Is industry your habit?
Ah, no—your present whole concern
Is one white woollen rabbit.
Phyllis McGinley 1905-78

It is only in our advanced and synthetic civilization that mothers no longer sing to the babies they are carrying.
Yehudi Menuhin 1916-99

A baby is God's opinion that life should go on.
Carl Sandburg 1878-1967

You know more than you think you do.
Benjamin Spock 1903-98, *opening words of* Baby and Child Care

Baseball

Think! How the hell are you gonna think and hit at the same time?
Yogi Berra 1925–

A ball player's got to be kept hungry to become a big leaguer. That's why no boy from a rich family ever made the big leagues.
Joe DiMaggio 1914–99

Baseball is very big with my people. It figures. It's the only way we can get to shake a bat at a white man without starting a riot.
Dick Gregory 1932–

Take me out to the ball game,
Take me out with the crowd.
Buy me some peanuts and cracker-jack—
I don't care if I never get back.
Jack Norworth 1879–1959

All you have to do is keep the five players who hate your guts away from the five who are undecided.
Casey Stengel 1891–1975

Baseball, it is said, is only a game. True. And the Grand Canyon is only a hole in Arizona. Not all holes, or games, are created equal.
George F. Will 1941–

Beauty ····▶ Good Looks

There is no excellent beauty that hath not some strangeness in the proportion.
Francis Bacon 1561–1626

Beauty

Consider the lilies of the field, how they grow; they toil
not, neither do they spin:
And yet I say unto you, That even Solomon in all his
glory was not arrayed like one of these.
       Bible

If you get simple beauty and naught else,
You get about the best thing God invents.
       Robert Browning 1812–89

I never saw an ugly thing in my life: for let the form of an
object be what it may,—light, shade, and perspective will
always make it beautiful.
       John Constable 1776–1837

Beauty is mysterious as well as terrible. God and devil are
fighting there, and the battlefield is the heart of man.
       Fedor Dostoevsky 1821–81

He was afflicted by the thought that where Beauty was,
nothing ever ran quite straight, which, no doubt, was why
so many people looked on it as immoral.
       John Galsworthy 1867–1933

All things counter, original, spare, strange;
Whatever is fickle, freckled (who knows how?)
With swift, slow; sweet, sour; adazzle, dim;
He fathers-forth whose beauty is past change:
Praise him.
       Gerard Manley Hopkins 1844–89

Beauty is no quality in things themselves. It exists merely
in the mind which contemplates them.
       David Hume 1711–76

'Beauty is truth, truth beauty,'—that is all
Ye know on earth, and all ye need to know.
       John Keats 1795–1821

A thing of beauty is a joy for ever:
Its loveliness increases; it will never
Pass into nothingness.
    John Keats 1795–1821

At some point in life the world's beauty becomes enough.
You don't need to photograph, paint or even remember
it. It is enough.
    Toni Morrison 1931–

Remember that the most beautiful things in the world are
the most useless; peacocks and lilies for instance.
    John Ruskin 1819–1900

Beauty is all very well at first sight; but who ever looks at
it when it has been in the house three days?
    George Bernard Shaw 1856–1950

Beginning ····▸ Ending

In the beginning God created the heaven and the earth.
And the earth was without form, and void; and darkness
was upon the face of the deep.
    Bible

'Begin at the beginning,' the King said, gravely, 'and go
on till you come to the end: then stop.'
    Lewis Carroll 1832–98

What we call the beginning is often the end
And to make an end is to make a beginning.
The end is where we start from.
    T. S. Eliot 1888–1965

All this will not be finished in the first 100 days. Nor will
it be finished in the first 1,000 days, nor in the life of this
Administration, nor even perhaps in our lifetime on this
planet. But let us begin.
    John F. Kennedy 1917–63

Beginning

Are you sitting comfortably? Then I'll begin.
Julia Lang 1921–

A tower of nine storeys begins with a heap of earth.
The journey of a thousand *li* starts from where one
stands.
Lao Tzu c.604–c.531 BC

Behaviour ····▸ Manners

When I go to Rome, I fast on Saturday, but here [Milan]
I do not. Do you also follow the custom of whatever
church you attend, if you do not want to give or receive
scandal.
St Ambrose c.339–97, *usually quoted as 'When in Rome, do as
the Romans do'*

Private faces in public places
Are wiser and nicer
Than public faces in private places.
W. H. Auden 1907–73

In necessary things, unity; in doubtful things, liberty; in
all things, charity.
Richard Baxter 1615–91

When people are on their best behaviour they aren't
always at their best.
Alan Bennett 1934–

Caesar's wife must be above suspicion.
Julius Caesar 100–44 BC

He only does it to annoy,
Because he knows it teases.
Lewis Carroll 1832–98

He was a verray, parfit gentil knyght.
Geoffrey Chaucer c.1343–1400

Take the tone of the company that you are in.
Lord Chesterfield 1694–1773

O tempora, O mores!
Oh, the times! Oh, the manners!
Cicero 106–43 BC

I get too hungry for dinner at eight.
I like the theatre, but never come late.
I never bother with people I hate.
That's why the lady is a tramp.
Lorenz Hart 1895–1943

They [the *Letters* of Lord Chesterfield] teach the morals
of a whore, and the manners of a dancing master.
Samuel Johnson 1709–84

Be a good animal, true to your instincts.
D. H. Lawrence 1885–1930

Go directly—see what she's doing, and tell her she
mustn't.
Punch

The basis of all good human behaviour is kindness.
Eleanor Roosevelt 1884–1962

Tout comprendre rend très indulgent.
To be totally understanding makes one very indulgent.
Mme de Staël 1766–1817

Belief

The Sea of Faith
Was once, too, at the full, and round earth's shore
Lay like the folds of a bright girdle furled.
But now I only hear
Its melancholy, long, withdrawing roar.
Matthew Arnold 1822–88

Belief

For what a man would like to be true, that he more readily believes.
   Francis Bacon 1561–1626

Every time a child says 'I don't believe in fairies' there is a little fairy somewhere that falls down dead.
   J. M. Barrie 1860–1937

A faith is something you die for; a doctrine is something you kill for: there is all the difference in the world.
   Tony Benn 1925–

Lord, I believe; help thou mine unbelief.
   Bible

Of course not, but I am told it works even if you don't believe in it.
   Niels Bohr 1885–1962, *when asked whether he really believed a horseshoe hanging over his door would bring him luck*

Why, sometimes I've believed as many as six impossible things before breakfast.
   Lewis Carroll 1832–98

I do not believe…I know.
   Carl Gustav Jung 1875–1961

Credulity is the man's weakness, but the child's strength.
   Charles Lamb 1775–1834

The dust of exploded beliefs may make a fine sunset.
   Geoffrey Madan 1895–1947

Que sais-je?
What do I know?
   Montaigne 1533–92

We can believe what we choose. We are answerable for what we choose to believe.
   Cardinal Newman 1801–90

It is necessary to the happiness of man that he be mentally faithful to himself. Infidelity does not consist in believing, or in disbelieving, it consists in professing to believe what one does not believe.

Thomas Paine 1737–1809

Man is a credulous animal, and must believe *something*; in the absence of good grounds for belief, he will be satisfied with bad ones.

Bertrand Russell 1872–1970

There lives more faith in honest doubt,
Believe me, than in half the creeds.

Alfred, Lord Tennyson 1809–92

Certum est quia impossibile est.
It is certain because it is impossible.

Tertullian AD c.160–c.225, *often quoted as* 'Credo quia impossibile [*I believe because it is impossible*]'

Bereavement ····▸ Sorrow

Do not stand at my grave and weep:
I am not there. I do not sleep.
I am a thousand winds that blow.
I am the diamond glints on snow…
Do not stand at my grave and cry;
I am not there, I did not die.

Anonymous *quoted in letter left by British soldier Stephen Cummins when killed by the IRA; origin uncertain*

You can shed tears that she is gone or you can smile because she has lived.

Anonymous *preface to the Order of Service at the funeral of Queen Elizabeth the Queen Mother*

Bereavement

He was my North, my South, my East and West,
My working week and my Sunday rest,
My noon, my midnight, my talk, my song;
I thought that love would last for ever: I was wrong.
  W. H. Auden 1907–73

Blessed are they that mourn: for they shall be comforted.
  Bible

Bereavement is a universal and integral part of our
experience of love. It follows marriage as normally as
marriage follows courtship or as autumn follows summer.
  C. S. Lewis 1898–1963

A man's dying is more the survivors' affair than his own.
  Thomas Mann 1875–1955

Time does not bring relief; you all have lied
Who told me time would ease me of my pain!
I miss him in the weeping of the rain;
I want him at the shrinking of the tide.
  Edna St Vincent Millay 1892–1950

I can't think of a more wonderful thanksgiving for the
life I have had than that everyone should be jolly at my
funeral.
  Lord Mountbatten 1900–79

The spring has gone out of the year.
  Pericles c.495–429 BC, *funeral oration*

Widow. The word consumes itself.
  Sylvia Plath 1932–63

How often are we to die before we go quite off this stage?
In every friend we lose a part of ourselves, and the best
part.
  Alexander Pope 1688–1744

Biography

I come to bury Caesar, not to praise him.
The evil that men do lives after them,
The good is oft interrèd with their bones.
William Shakespeare 1564–1616

Beloved, come to me often in my dreams. No, not that.
Live in my dreams.
Marina Tsvetaeva 1892–1941

Even memory is not necessary for love. There is a land of
the living and a land of the dead and the bridge is love,
the only survival, the only meaning.
Thornton Wilder 1897–1975

He first deceased; she for a little tried
To live without him: liked it not, and died.
Henry Wotton 1568–1639

Biography

The Art of Biography
Is different from Geography.
Geography is about Maps,
But Biography is about Chaps.
Edmund Clerihew Bentley 1875–1956

A well-written Life is almost as rare as a well-spent one.
Thomas Carlyle 1795–1881

An autobiography is an obituary in serial form with the
last instalment missing.
Quentin Crisp 1908–99

It's an excellent life of somebody else. But I've really lived
inside myself, and she can't get in there.
Robertson Davies 1913–95, *on a biography of himself*

There is properly no history; only biography.
Ralph Waldo Emerson 1803–82

Biography

Nobody can write the life of a man, but those who have eat and drunk and lived in social intercourse with him.
Samuel Johnson 1709–84

Lives of great men all remind us
We can make our lives sublime,
And, departing, leave behind us
Footprints on the sands of time.
Henry Wadsworth Longfellow 1807–82

To write one's memoirs is to speak ill of everybody except oneself.
Marshal Pétain 1856–1951

Biography is the mesh through which real life escapes.
Tom Stoppard 1937–

Discretion is not the better part of biography.
Lytton Strachey 1880–1932

Then there is my noble and biographical friend who has added a new terror to death.
Charles Wetherell 1770–1846, *on Lord Campbell's* Lives of the Lord Chancellors *being written without the consent of heirs or executors*

Every great man nowadays has his disciples, and it is always Judas who writes the biography.
Oscar Wilde 1854–1900

Birds

That's the wise thrush; he sings each song twice over,
Lest you should think he never could recapture
The first fine careless rapture!
Robert Browning 1812–89

The bisy larke, messager of day.
Geoffrey Chaucer c.1343–1400

It was the Rainbow gave thee birth,
And left thee all her lovely hues.
W. H. Davies 1871–1940, *of the kingfisher*

I caught this morning morning's minion, kingdom of
   daylight's dauphin, dapple-dawn-drawn Falcon.
Gerard Manley Hopkins 1844–89

Oh, a wondrous bird is the pelican!
His beak holds more than his belican.
He takes in his beak
Food enough for a week.
But I'll be darned if I know how the helican.
Dixon Lanier Merritt 1879–1972

Alone and warming his five wits,
The white owl in the belfry sits.
Alfred, Lord Tennyson 1809–92

I once had a sparrow alight upon my shoulder for a
moment while I was hoeing in a village garden, and I felt
that I was more distinguished by that circumstance than I
should have been by any epaulette I could have worn.
Henry David Thoreau 1817–62

Birth ····▸ Babies

It doesn't matter about being born in a duckyard, as long
as you're hatched from a swan's egg!
Hans Christian Andersen 1805–75

In sorrow thou shalt bring forth children.
Bible

Birth

No phallic hero, no matter what he does to himself or to
another to prove his courage, ever matches the solitary,
existential courage of the woman who gives birth.
Andrea Dworkin 1946-

I am not yet born; O fill me
With strength against those who would freeze my
humanity.
Louis MacNeice 1907-63

Death and taxes and childbirth! There's never any
convenient time for any of them.
Margaret Mitchell 1900-49

Men should be bewailed at their birth, and not at their
death.
Montesquieu 1689-1755

Good work, Mary. We all knew you had it in you.
Dorothy Parker 1893-1967, *telegram to Mrs Sherwood on the
arrival of her baby*

Love set you going like a fat gold watch.
The midwife slapped your footsoles, and your bald cry
Took its place among the elements.
Sylvia Plath 1932-63

What you say of the pride of giving life to an immortal
soul is very fine, dear, but I own I can not enter into that;
I think much more of our being like a cow or a dog at
such moments; when our poor nature becomes so very
animal and unecstatic.
Queen Victoria 1819-1901

Our birth is but a sleep and a forgetting…
Not in entire forgetfulness,
And not in utter nakedness,
But trailing clouds of glory do we come.
William Wordsworth 1770-1850

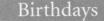
Birthdays

A diplomat is a man who always remembers a woman's birthday but never remembers her age.

Robert Frost 1874–1963

You know you're getting old when the candles cost more than the cake.

Bob Hope 1903–2003

Natalis grate numeras?
Do you count your birthdays thankfully?

Horace 65–8 BC

One of the sadder things, I think,
Is how our birthdays slowly sink:
Presents and parties disappear,
The cards grow fewer year by year.

Philip Larkin 1922–85

Believing, hear, what you deserve to hear:
Your birthday as my own to me is dear…
But yours gives most; for mine did only lend
Me to the world; yours gave to me a friend.

Martial AD c.40–c.104

EEYORE: But after all, what *are* birthdays? Here today and gone tomorrow.

A. A. Milne 1882–1956

Our birthdays are feathers in the broad wing of time.

Jean Paul Richter 1763–1825

Boats

Jolly boating weather,
And a hay harvest breeze,
Blade on the feather,

35

Boats

Shade off the trees
Swing, swing together
With your body between your knees.
William Cory 1823-92

A wet sheet and a flowing sea,
A wind that follows fast
And fills the white and rustling sail
And bends the gallant mast.
Allan Cunningham 1784-1842

There is *nothing*—absolutely nothing—half so much
worth doing as simply messing about in boats.
Kenneth Grahame 1859-1932

When you are up there, it's like trying to hang on to a
telegraph pole in an earthquake.
Ellen MacArthur 1977- , *90 feet up the mast of her boat*
Kingfisher

Quinquireme of Nineveh from distant Ophir
Rowing home to haven in sunny Palestine,
With a cargo of ivory,
And apes and peacocks,
Sandalwood, cedarwood, and sweet white wine.
John Masefield 1878-1967

The Body ····> Appearance

Entrails don't care for travel,
Entrails don't care for stress:
Entrails are better kept folded inside you
For outside, they make a mess.
Connie Bensley 1929-

I will give thanks unto thee, for I am fearfully and
wonderfully made.
Bible

A woman watches her body uneasily, as though it were an unreliable ally in the battle for love.
Leonard Cohen 1934–

i like my body when it is with your
body. It is so quite new a thing.
Muscles better and nerves more.
e. e. cummings 1894–1962

The leg, a source of much delight,
which carries weight and governs height.
Ian Dury 1942–2000

Anatomy is destiny.
Sigmund Freud 1856–1939

I'm fat, but I'm thin inside. Has it ever struck you that there's a thin man inside every fat man, just as they say there's a statue inside every block of stone?
George Orwell 1903–50

Our body is a machine for living. It is organized for that, it is its nature. Let life go on in it unhindered and let it defend itself.
Leo Tolstoy 1828–1910

I sing the body electric.
Walt Whitman 1819–92

You can never be too rich or too thin.
Duchess of Windsor 1896–1986

Books ····➤ Libraries, Reading

Some books are undeservedly forgotten; none are undeservedly remembered.
W. H. Auden 1907–73

Books

Some books are to be tasted, others to be swallowed, and some few to be chewed and digested.
   Francis Bacon 1561–1626

Books say: she did this because. Life says: she did this. Books are where things are explained to you; life is where things aren't.
   Julian Barnes 1946–

Of making many books there is no end; and much study is a weariness of the flesh.
   Bible

What literature can and should do is change the people who teach the people who don't read the books.
   A. S. Byatt 1936–

A great book is like great evil.
   Callimachus c.305–c.240 BC

'What is the use of a book', thought Alice, 'without pictures or conversations?'
   Lewis Carroll 1832–98

The greatest masterpiece in literature is only a dictionary out of order.
   Jean Cocteau 1889–1963

Another damned, thick, square book! Always scribble, scribble, scribble! Eh! Mr Gibbon?
   Duke of Gloucester 1743–1805

Far too many relied on the classic formula of a beginning, a muddle, and an end.
   Philip Larkin 1922–85, *of novels entered for the Booker Prize*

A good book is the precious life-blood of a master spirit.
   John Milton 1608–74

There is no book so bad that some good cannot be got out of it.
   Pliny the Elder AD 23–79

The principle of procrastinated rape is said to be the ruling one in all the great best-sellers.
    V. S. Pritchett 1900–97

No furniture so charming as books.
    Sydney Smith 1771–1845

The shelf life of the modern hardback writer is somewhere between the milk and the yoghurt.
    Calvin Trillin 1935–

A good book is the best of friends, the same to-day and for ever.
    Martin Tupper 1810–89

'*Classic.*' A book which people praise and don't read.
    Mark Twain 1835–1910

Publish and be damned.
    Duke of Wellington 1769–1852, *replying to a blackmail threat*

This is an important book, the critic assumes, because it deals with war. This is an insignificant book because it deals with the feelings of women in a drawing-room.
    Virginia Woolf 1882–1941

Boredom

Nothing happens, nobody comes, nobody goes, it's awful!
    Samuel Beckett 1906–89

Life, friends, is boring. We must not say so…
And moreover my mother taught me as a boy
(repeatedly) 'Ever to confess you're bored
means you have no
Inner Resources.'
    John Berryman 1914–72

Boredom

Everyone is a bore to someone. That is unimportant. The thing to avoid is being a bore to oneself.
Gerald Brenan 1894–1987

What's wrong with being a boring kind of guy?
George Bush 1924–

Millions long for immortality who don't know what to do with themselves on a rainy Sunday afternoon.
Susan Ertz 1894–1985

Nothing, like something, happens anywhere.
Philip Larkin 1922–85

Waiting is still an occupation. It's having nothing to wait for that is terrible.
Cesare Pavese 1908–50

Boredom is…a vital problem for the moralist, since half the sins of mankind are caused by the fear of it.
Bertrand Russell 1872–1970

A healthy male adult bore consumes *each year* one and a half times his own weight in other people's patience.
John Updike 1932–

The secret of being a bore…is to tell everything.
Voltaire 1694–1778

Boxing

Float like a butterfly, sting like a bee.
Muhammad Ali 1942– , *summary of his boxing strategy*

I'm the greatest.
Muhammad Ali 1942–

Boxing's just showbusiness with blood.
Frank Bruno 1961–

Honey, I just forgot to duck.
> **Jack Dempsey** 1895-1983, *to his wife, on losing the World Heavyweight title*

The bigger they are, the further they have to fall.
> **Robert Fitzsimmons** 1862-1917, *prior to a boxing match*

We was robbed!
> **Joe Jacobs** 1896-1940, *after Jack Sharkey beat Max Schmeling (of whom Jacobs was manager) in a heavyweight title fight*

He can run. But he can't hide.
> **Joe Louis** 1914-81, *of Billy Conn, his opponent*

I fight for money, but I am not greedy. How many steaks can one man eat?
> **Laszlo Papp** 1926-2003

My main objective is to be professional but kill him.
> **Mike Tyson** 1966- , *of his opponent Lennox Lewis*

Brevity

It is a foolish thing to make a long prologue, and to be short in the story itself.
> **Bible**

I strive to be brief, and I become obscure.
> **Horace** 65-8 BC

I have made this [letter] longer than usual, only because I have not had the time to make it shorter.
> **Blaise Pascal** 1623-62

Words are like leaves; and where they most abound,
Much fruit of sense beneath is rarely found.
> **Alexander Pope** 1688-1744

Brevity

If there is anywhere a thing said in two sentences that could have been as clearly and as engagingly said in one, then it's amateur work.
Robert Louis Stevenson 1850–94

Britain

Great Britain has lost an empire and has not yet found a role.
Dean Acheson 1893–1971

The British nation is unique in this respect. They are the only people who like to be told how bad things are, who like to be told the worst.
Winston Churchill 1874–1965

Britain will be honoured by historians more for the way she disposed of an empire than for the way in which she acquired it.
Lord Harlech 1918–85

Britain is no longer totally a white place where people ride horses, wear long frocks and drink tea. The national dish is no longer fish and chips, it's curry.
Marianne Jean-Baptiste

What is our task? To make Britain a fit country for heroes to live in.
David Lloyd George 1863–1945

Fifty years on from now, Britain will still be the country of long shadows on county [cricket] grounds, warm beer, invincible green suburbs, dog lovers, and—as George Orwell said—old maids bicycling to Holy Communion through the morning mist.
John Major 1943–

Rule, Britannia, rule the waves;
Britons never will be slaves.
    James Thomson 1700–48

Other nations use 'force'; we Britons alone use 'Might'.
    Evelyn Waugh 1903–66

Bureaucracy ····➤ Management

A memorandum is written not to inform the reader but
to protect the writer.
    Dean Acheson 1893–1971

It is an inevitable defect, that bureaucrats will care more
for routine than for results.
    Walter Bagehot 1826–77

Guidelines for bureaucrats: (1) When in charge, ponder.
(2) When in trouble, delegate. (3) When in doubt,
mumble.
    James H. Boren 1925–

Give a civil servant a good case and he'll wreck it with
clichés, bad punctuation, double negatives and convoluted
apology.
    Alan Clark 1928–99

The Civil Service is profoundly deferential—'Yes,
Minister! No, Minister! If you wish it, Minister!'
    Richard Crossman 1907–74

Whatever was required to be done, the Circumlocution
Office was beforehand with all the public departments in
the art of perceiving—HOW NOT TO DO IT.
    Charles Dickens 1812–70

Bureaucracy

The truth in these matters may be stated as a scientific law: 'The persistence of public officials varies inversely with the importance of the matter on which they are persisting.'
Bernard Levin 1928-2004

The man who is denied the opportunity of taking decisions of importance begins to regard as important the decisions he is allowed to take.
C. Northcote Parkinson 1909-93

Back in the East you can't do much without the right papers, but *with* the right papers you can do *anything*. They *believe* in papers. Papers are power.
Tom Stoppard 1937-

Business

There is nothing more requisite in business than dispatch.
Joseph Addison 1672-1719

A Company for carrying on an undertaking of Great Advantage, but no one to know what it is.
Anonymous *The South Sea Company prospectus*

A merchant shall hardly keep himself from doing wrong.
Bible (Apocrypha)

They [corporations] cannot commit treason, nor be outlawed, nor excommunicate, for they have no souls.
Edward Coke 1552-1634

Here's the rule for bargains: 'Do other men, for they would do you.' That's the true business precept.
Charles Dickens 1812-70

Remember that time is money.
Benjamin Franklin 1706-90

Necessity never made a good bargain.
Benjamin Franklin 1706-90

If business always made the right decisions, business wouldn't be business.
J. Paul Getty 1892-1976

Only the paranoid survive.
Andrew Grove 1936-

Accountants are the witch-doctors of the modern world and willing to turn their hands to any kind of magic.
Lord Justice Harman 1894-1970

The best of all monopoly profits is a quiet life.
J. R. Hicks 1904-

I liked it so much, I bought the company!
Victor Kiam 1926-2001, *advertisement for Remington Shavers, spoken by the company's new owner*

He's a man way out there in the blue, riding on a smile and a shoeshine. And when they start not smiling back—that's an earthquake…A salesman is got to dream, boy. It comes with the territory.
Arthur Miller 1915-

We even sell a pair of earrings for under £1, which is cheaper than a prawn sandwich from Marks & Spencers. But I have to say the earrings probably won't last as long.
Gerald Ratner 1949-

The customer is never wrong.
César Ritz 1850-1918

I think that business practices would improve immeasurably if they were guided by 'feminine' principles—qualities like love and care and intuition.
Anita Roddick 1942-

Business

People of the same trade seldom meet together, even for merriment and diversion, but the conversation ends in a conspiracy against the public, or in some contrivance to raise prices.

Adam Smith 1723-90

Deals are my art form. Other people paint beautifully on canvas or write wonderful poetry. I like making deals, preferably big deals. That's how I get my kicks.

Donald Trump 1946-

The public be damned! I'm working for my stockholders.

William H. Vanderbilt 1821-85

[Commercialism is] doing well that which should not be done at all.

Gore Vidal 1925-

There is only one boss. The customer. And he can fire everybody in the company from the chairman on down, simply by spending his money somewhere else.

Sam Walton 1919-92

You cannot be a success in any business without believing that it is the greatest business in the world…You have to put your heart in the business and the business in your heart.

Thomas Watson Snr. 1874-1956

Canada

North of the 49th parallel we value equality; south of it, they treasure freedom.

Michael Adams

Dusty, cobweb-covered, maimed, and set at naught,
Beauty crieth in an attic, and no man regardeth.
O God! O Montreal!

Samuel Butler 1835-1902

I am rather inclined to believe that this is the land God gave to Cain.
Jacques Cartier 1491–1557

Some say that no one ever leaves Montreal, for that city, like Canada itself, is designed to preserve the past, a past that happened somewhere else.
Leonard Cohen 1934–

I see Canada as a country torn between a very northern, rather extraordinary, mystical spirit which it fears and its desire to present itself to the world as a Scotch banker.
Robertson Davies 1913–95

Vive Le Québec Libre.
Long Live Free Quebec.
Charles de Gaulle 1890–1970

Canada is ten independent personalities, united only by a common suspicion of Ottawa.
Allan Fotheringham 1932–

If some countries have too much history, we have too much geography.
William Lyon Mackenzie King 1874–1950

The nineteenth century was the century of the United States. I think we can claim that it is Canada that shall fill the twentieth century.
Wilfrid Laurier 1841–1919

Mon pays ce n'est pas un pays, c'est l'hiver.
My country is not a country, it is winter.
Gilles Vigneault 1928–

These two nations have been at war over a few acres of snow near Canada, and…they are spending on this fine struggle more than Canada itself is worth.
Voltaire 1694–1778

Canada

O Canada! Our home and native land!
True patriot love in all thy sons command.
With glowing hearts we see thee rise,
The True North strong and free!
Robert Stanley Weir 1856–1926

Careers ····▶ Work

I will undoubtedly have to seek what is happily known as
gainful employment, which I am glad to say does not
describe holding public office.
Dean Acheson 1893–1971

For promotion cometh neither from the east, nor from
the west: nor yet from the south.
Bible

McJob: A low-pay, low-prestige, low-dignity, low benefit,
no-future job in the service sector.
Douglas Coupland 1961–

To do nothing and get something, formed a boy's ideal of
a manly career.
Benjamin Disraeli 1804–81

By working faithfully eight hours a day, you may
eventually get to be a boss and work twelve hours a day.
Robert Frost 1874–1963

It is wonderful, when a calculation is made, how little the
mind is actually employed in the discharge of any
profession.
Samuel Johnson 1709–84

I didn't get where I am today without….
David Nobbs 1935– , *catchphrase used by Reginald Perrin's
manager C. J.*

I have that normal male thing of valuing myself
according to the job I do. When I can't tell someone in
one word what I am, then something is missing. I don't
represent anything any more.
   Michael Portillo 1953-

Thou art not for the fashion of these times,
Where none will sweat but for promotion.
   William Shakespeare 1564-1616

The test of a vocation is the love of the drudgery it
involves.
   Logan Pearsall Smith 1865-1946

Cars

A car standing alone can be a beautiful and emotive
object, but wherever two or three are gathered together,
in my view, you have ugliness.
   Rowan Atkinson 1955-

I think that cars today are almost the exact equivalent of
the great Gothic cathedrals: I mean the supreme creation
of an era.
   Roland Barthes 1915-80

[There are] only two classes of pedestrians in these days
of reckless motor traffic—the quick, and the dead.
   Lord Dewar 1864-1930

The poetry of motion! The *real* way to travel! The *only*
way to travel! Here today—in next week tomorrow!
   Kenneth Grahame 1859-1932

There is no class of person more moved by hatred than
the motorist and the policeman is a convenient receptacle
for his feeling.
   C. W. Hewitt

Cars

Cyclists see motorists as tyrannical and uncaring.
Motorists believe cyclists are afflicted by a perversion.
  Boris Johnson 1964-

What good is speed if the brain has oozed out on the way?
  Karl Kraus 1874-1936

The car has become an article of dress without which we feel uncertain, unclad and incomplete in the urban compound.
  Marshall McLuhan 1911-80

Beneath this slab
John Brown is stowed.
He watched the ads,
And not the road.
  Ogden Nash 1902-71

You have your own company, your own temperature control, your own music—and don't have to put up with dreadful human beings sitting alongside you.
  Steven Norris 1945- , *on cars compared to public transport*

No other man-made device since the shields and lances of ancient knights fulfils a man's ego like an automobile.
  Lord Rootes 1894-1964

Cats

Macavity, Macavity, there's no one like Macavity,
There never was a Cat of such deceitfulness and suavity.
He always has an alibi, and one or two to spare:
At whatever time the deed took place—MACAVITY WASN'T THERE!
  T. S. Eliot 1888-1965

He walked by himself, and all places were alike to him.
  Rudyard Kipling 1865-1936

Censorship

Cats seem to go on the principle that it never does any
harm to ask for what you want.
Joseph Wood Krutch 1893–1970

If a fish is the movement of water embodied, given shape,
then cat is a diagram and pattern of subtle air.
Doris Lessing 1919–

When I play with my cat, who knows whether she isn't
amusing herself with me more than I am with her?
Montaigne 1533–92

The trouble with a kitten is
THAT
Eventually it becomes a
CAT.
Ogden Nash 1902–71

For I will consider my Cat Jeoffry…
For he counteracts the powers of darkness by his
   electrical skin and glaring eyes.
For he counteracts the Devil, who is death, by brisking
   about the life.
Christopher Smart 1722–71

Censorship

The reading or non-reading a book—will never keep
down a single petticoat.
Lord Byron 1788–1824

One does not put Voltaire in the Bastille.
Charles de Gaulle 1890–1970, *when asked to arrest Sartre*

Is it a book you would even wish your wife or your
servants to read?
Mervyn Griffith-Jones 1909–79, *of D. H. Lawrence's* Lady
Chatterley's Lover

Censorship

Wherever books will be burned, men also, in the end, are burned.
   Heinrich Heine 1797–1856

One has to multiply thoughts to the point where there aren't enough policemen to control them.
   Stanislaw Lec 1909–66

Those whom books will hurt will not be proof against events. Events, not books, should be forbid.
   Herman Melville 1819–91

The power of the press is very great, but not so great as the power of suppress.
   Lord Northcliffe 1865–1922

If these writings of the Greeks agree with the book of God, they are useless and need not be preserved; if they disagree, they are pernicious and ought to be destroyed.
   Caliph Omar d. 644, *on burning the library of Alexandria*

Don't you see that the whole aim of Newspeak is to narrow the range of thought? In the end we shall make thoughtcrime literally impossible, because there will be no words in which to express it.
   George Orwell 1903–50

It is obvious that 'obscenity' is not a term capable of exact legal definition; in the practice of the Courts, it means 'anything that shocks the magistrate'.
   Bertrand Russell 1872–1970

If decade after decade the truth cannot be told, each person's mind begins to roam irretrievably. One's fellow countrymen become harder to understand than Martians.
   Alexander Solzhenitsyn 1918–

The state has no place in the nation's bedrooms.
   Pierre Trudeau 1919–2000

I disapprove of what you say, but I will defend to the
death your right to say it.
Voltaire 1694–1778, *a later summary of his attitude towards*
Helvétius following the burning of the latter's De l'esprit

The Khomeini cry for the execution of Rushdie is an
infantile cry. From the beginning of time we have seen
that. To murder the thinker does not murder the thought.
Arnold Wesker 1932–

Certainty ····▶ Doubt

My mind is not a bed to be made and re-made.
James Agate 1877–1947

If a man will begin with certainties, he shall end in
doubts; but if he will be content to begin with doubts, he
shall end in certainties.
Francis Bacon 1561–1626

I was very confident we would find them. I have to accept
we have not found them. I have to accept we may not
find them.
Tony Blair 1953– , *on weapons of mass destruction in Iraq*

The archbishop is usually to be found nailing his colours
to the fence.
Frank Field 1942– , *of Archbishop Runcie*

What, never?
No, never!
What, *never*?
Hardly ever!
W. S. Gilbert 1836–1911

I'll give you a definite maybe.
Sam Goldwyn 1882–1974

Certainty

I wish I was as cocksure of anything as Tom Macaulay is
of everything.
Lord Melbourne 1779–1848

Ah, what a dusty answer gets the soul
When hot for certainties in this our life!
George Meredith 1828–1909

Minds like beds always made up,
(more stony than a shore)
unwilling or unable.
William Carlos Williams 1883–1963

Chance ····▶ Luck

Cast thy bread upon the waters: for thou shalt find it
after many days.
Bible

But for the grace of God there goes John Bradford.
John Bradford c.1510–55, *on seeing a group of criminals being
led to their execution; usually quoted as 'There but for the grace
of God go I'*

The best laid schemes o' mice an' men
Gang aft a-gley.
Robert Burns 1759–96

The chapter of knowledge is a very short, but the chapter
of accidents is a very long one.
Lord Chesterfield 1694–1773

At this moment he was unfortunately called out by a
person on business from Porlock.
Samuel Taylor Coleridge 1772–1834, *preliminary note to
'Kubla Khan', explaining why the poem remained unfinished*

Accidents will occur in the best-regulated families.
Charles Dickens 1812–70

If an army of monkeys were strumming on typewriters they *might* write all the books in the British Museum.
  Arthur Eddington 1882–1944

I am convinced that *He* [God] does not play dice.
  Albert Einstein 1879–1955

Mr Bond, they have a saying in Chicago: 'Once is happenstance. Twice is coincidence. The third time it's enemy action.'
  Ian Fleming 1908–64, *Goldfinger to James Bond*

The chance of winning the lottery jackpot is less than that of being struck by lightning. I have never bought a ticket and plan to buy an insulating rubber helmet with the money I save. It will increase my life expectancy by precisely one fourteen-millionth.
  Steve Jones 1944–

Predictability: Does the flap of a butterfly's wings in Brazil set off a tornado in Texas?
  Edward N. Lorenz 1917–

O! many a shaft, at random sent,
Finds mark the archer little meant!
And many a word, at random spoken,
May soothe or wound a heart that's broken.
  Sir Walter Scott 1771–1832

There is a tide in the affairs of men,
Which, taken at the flood, leads on to fortune.
  William Shakespeare 1564–1616

Change ····▶ Beginning, Ending

He that will not apply new remedies must expect new evils; for time is the greatest innovator.
  Francis Bacon 1561–1626

Change

Can the Ethiopian change his skin, or the leopard his spots?
Bible

And now for something completely different.
Graham Chapman 1941–89 et al. *catchphrase* in Monty Python's Flying Circus

Variety's the very spice of life,
That gives it all its flavour.
William Cowper 1731–1800

Change is inevitable in a progressive country. Change is constant.
Benjamin Disraeli 1804–81

When it is not necessary to change, it is necessary not to change.
Lucius Cary, Viscount Falkland 1610–43

Most of the change we think we see in life
Is due to truths being in and out of favour.
Robert Frost 1874–1963

You can't step twice into the same river.
Heraclitus c.540–c.480 BC

Consistency is contrary to nature, contrary to life. The only completely consistent people are the dead.
Aldous Huxley 1894–1963

Change is not made without inconvenience, even from worse to better.
Samuel Johnson 1709–84

Plus ça change, plus c'est la même chose.
The more things change, the more they are the same.
Alphonse Karr 1808–90

If we want things to stay as they are, things will have to change.
Giuseppe di Lampedusa 1896–1957

It is best not to swap horses when crossing streams.
Abraham Lincoln 1809-65

Change and decay in all around I see;
O Thou, who changest not, abide with me.
Henry Francis Lyte 1793-1847

Tomorrow to fresh woods, and pastures new.
John Milton 1608-74

God, give us the serenity to accept what cannot be
  changed;
Give us the courage to change what should be changed;
Give us the wisdom to distinguish one from the other.
Reinhold Niebuhr 1892-1971

          Forward, forward let us range,
Let the great world spin for ever down the ringing
  grooves of change.
Alfred, Lord Tennyson 1809-92

If we do not find anything pleasant, at least we shall find
something new.
Voltaire 1694-1778

All changed, changed utterly:
A terrible beauty is born.
W. B. Yeats 1865-1939

Character

It is not in the still calm of life, or the repose of a pacific
station, that great characters are formed…Great
necessities call out great virtues.
Abigail Adams 1744-1818

A thick skin is a gift from God.
Konrad Adenauer 1876-1967

Character

It is the nature, and the advantage, of strong people that they can bring out the crucial questions and form a clear opinion about them. The weak always have to decide between alternatives that are not their own.
Dietrich Bonhoeffer 1906–45

My parents were convinced that I would one day become Mr Average, but almost 30 years on I am still an A1 freak.
Boy George 1961–

If you have bright plumage, people will take pot shots at you.
Alan Clark 1928–99

Claudia's the sort of person who goes through life holding on to the sides.
Alice Thomas Ellis 1932–

Talent develops in quiet places, character in the full current of human life.
Johann Wolfgang von Goethe 1749–1832

Those who stand for nothing fall for anything.
Alex Hamilton 1936–

A man's character is his fate.
Heraclitus c.540–c.480 BC

If you can fill the unforgiving minute
With sixty seconds' worth of distance run,
Yours is the Earth and everything that's in it,
And—which is more—you'll be a Man, my son!
Rudyard Kipling 1865–1936

I see the better things, and approve; I follow the worse.
Ovid 43 BC–AD c.17

He's so wet you could shoot snipe off him.
Anthony Powell 1905–2000

You can tell a lot about a fellow's character by his way of eating jellybeans.
Ronald Reagan 1911–2004

> My nature is subdued
> To what it works in, like the dyer's hand.
William Shakespeare 1564–1616

If you can't stand the heat, get out of the kitchen.
Harry Vaughan *associated with Harry S. Truman*

Charity ····▸ Gifts

God loveth a cheerful giver.
Bible

CHAIRMAN: What is service?
CANDIDATE: The rent we pay for our room on earth.
Tubby Clayton 1885–1972, *admission ceremony of Toc H*

People often feed the hungry so that nothing may disturb their own enjoyment of a good meal.
W. Somerset Maugham 1874–1965

Do good by stealth, and blush to find it fame.
Alexander Pope 1688–1744

He gives the poor man twice as much good who gives quickly.
Publilius Syrus 1st century BC

The Christian usually tries to give away his own money, whilst the philosopher usually tries to give away the money of someone else.
Lord Salisbury 1830–1903

'Tis not enough to help the feeble up,
But to support him after.
William Shakespeare 1564–1616

Charity

Thy necessity is yet greater than mine.

> **Philip Sidney** 1554–86, *on giving his water-bottle to a dying soldier on the battle-field of Zutphen; commonly quoted as 'thy need is greater than mine'*

No one would remember the Good Samaritan if he'd only had good intentions. He had money as well.

> **Margaret Thatcher** 1925–

Friends, I have lost a day.

> **Titus** AD 39–81, *on reflecting that he had done nothing to help anybody all day*

Behold, I do not give lectures or a little charity,
When I give I give myself.

> **Walt Whitman** 1819–92

Charm

Charm…it's a sort of bloom on a woman. If you have it, you don't need to have anything else; and if you don't have it, it doesn't much matter what else you have.

> **J. M. Barrie** 1860–1937

You know what charm is: a way of getting the answer yes without having asked any clear question.

> **Albert Camus** 1913–60

All charming people have something to conceal, usually their total dependence on the appreciation of others.

> **Cyril Connolly** 1903–74

Oozing charm from every pore,
He oiled his way around the floor.

> **Alan Jay Lerner** 1918–86

What is charm then? The free giving of a grace, the spending of something given by nature in her role of spendthrift…something extra, superfluous, unnecessary,

essentially a power thrown away.
   Doris Lessing 1919–

Children ····▶ Babies, The Family, Youth

Children sweeten labours, but they make misfortunes more bitter.
   Francis Bacon 1561–1626

Quality time? There's always another load of washing.
   Julian Barnes 1946–

Suffer the little children to come unto me, and forbid them not: for of such is the kingdom of God.
   Bible

When I was a child, I spake as a child, I understood as a child, I thought as a child: but when I became a man, I put away childish things.
   Bible

There is no such thing as other people's children.
   Hillary Rodham Clinton 1947–

Alas, regardless of their doom,
The little victims play!
No sense have they of ills to come,
Nor care beyond to-day.
   Thomas Gray 1716–71

Oh, for an hour of Herod!
   Anthony Hope 1863–1933, *at the first night of* Peter Pan

If there is anything that we wish to change in the child, we should first examine it and see whether it is not something that could better be changed in ourselves.
   Carl Gustav Jung 1875–1961

Children

A child is owed the greatest respect; if you ever have
something disgraceful in mind, don't ignore your son's
tender years.
    Juvenal AD c.60–c.130

Literature is mostly about having sex and not much
about having children. Life is the other way round.
    David Lodge 1935–

It should be noted that children at play are not playing
about; their games should be seen as their most serious-
minded activity.
    Montaigne 1533–92

But all children matures,
Maybe even yours.
    Ogden Nash 1902–71

The affection you get back from children is sixpence
given as change for a sovereign.
    Edith Nesbit 1858–1924

Behold the child, by Nature's kindly law
Pleased with a rattle, tickled with a straw.
    Alexander Pope 1688–1744

A child is not a vase to be filled, but a fire to be lit.
    François Rabelais c.1494–c.1553

Any man who hates dogs and babies can't be all bad.
    Leo Rosten 1908–97, *of W. C. Fields, and often attributed
to him*

Grown-ups never understand anything for themselves,
and it is tiresome for children to be always and forever
explaining things to them.
    Antoine de Saint-Exupéry 1900–44

      At first the infant,
Mewling and puking in the nurse's arms.
And then the whining schoolboy, with his satchel,

And shining morning face, creeping like snail
Unwillingly to school.
William Shakespeare 1564–1616

The summer that I was ten—
Can it be there was only one
summer that I was ten? It must
have been a long one then.
May Swenson 1919–89

You will find as the children grow up that as a rule
children are a bitter disappointment—their greatest object
being to do precisely what their parents do not wish and
have anxiously tried to prevent.
Queen Victoria 1819–1901

I have four sons and three stepsons. I have learnt what it
is like to step on Lego with bare feet.
Fay Weldon 1931–

The Child is father of the Man.
William Wordsworth 1770–1850

Choice

White shall not neutralize the black, nor good
Compensate bad in man, absolve him so:
Life's business being just the terrible choice.
Robert Browning 1812–89

The die is cast.
Julius Caesar 100–44 BC, *at the crossing of the Rubicon*

Any customer can have a car painted any colour that he
wants so long as it is black.
Henry Ford 1863–1947, *of the Model T Ford*

Choice

Two roads diverged in a wood, and I—
I took the one less travelled by,
And that has made all the difference.
    Robert Frost 1874–1963

How happy could I be with either,
Were t'other dear charmer away!
    John Gay 1685–1732

Which do you want? A whipping and no turnips or
turnips and no whipping?
    Toni Morrison 1931–

You pays your money and you takes your choice.
    Punch

I'll make him an offer he can't refuse.
    Mario Puzo 1920–99

To be, or not to be: that is the question.
    William Shakespeare 1564–1616

Take care to get what you like or you will be forced to
like what you get.
    George Bernard Shaw 1856–1950

There is no real alternative.
    Margaret Thatcher 1925–

Between two evils, I always pick the one I never tried
before.
    Mae West 1892–1980

Christmas

Christmas won't be Christmas without any presents.
    Louisa May Alcott 1832–88

I'm dreaming of a white Christmas,
Just like the ones I used to know.
    Irving Berlin 1888–1989

And girls in slacks remember Dad,
And oafish louts remember Mum,
And sleepless children's hearts are glad,
And Christmas-morning bells say 'Come!'
    John Betjeman 1906–84

She brought forth her firstborn son, and wrapped him in
swaddling clothes, and laid him in a manger; because
there was no room for them in the inn.
    Bible

Yes, Virginia, there is a Santa Claus.
    Francis Pharcellus Church 1839–1906, *newspaper editorial*
    replying to a letter from eight-year-old Virginia O'Hanlon

Christmas is the Disneyfication of Christianity.
    Don Cupitt 1934–

'Bah,' said Scrooge. 'Humbug!'
    Charles Dickens 1812–70, *responding to the greeting 'Merry*
    Christmas'

A lovely thing about Christmas is that it's compulsory,
like a thunderstorm, and we all go through it together.
    Garrison Keillor 1942–

But, oh! Father Christmas, if you love me at all,
Bring me a big, red India-rubber ball!
    A. A. Milne 1882–1956

'Twas the night before Christmas, when all through the
    house
Not a creature was stirring, not even a mouse;
The stockings were hung by the chimney with care,
In hopes that St Nicholas soon would be there.
    Clement C. Moore 1779–1863

But I heard him exclaim, ere he drove out of sight,
'Happy Christmas to all and to all a good night.'
    Clement C. Moore 1779–1863

Christmas

Still xmas is a good time with all those presents and good food and i hope it will never die out or at any rate not until i am grown up and hav to pay for it all.
Geoffrey Willans 1911–58 and **Ronald Searle** 1920–

The Church ····▶ Religion

The nearer the Church the further from God.
Bishop Lancelot Andrewes 1555–1626

We must recall that the Church is always 'one generation away from extinction.'
George Carey 1935–

He cannot have God for his father who has not the church for his mother.
St Cyprian AD c.200–258

And of all plagues with which mankind are curst, Ecclesiastic tyranny's the worst.
Daniel Defoe 1660–1731

Our cathedrals are like abandoned computers now, but they used to be prayer factories once.
Lawrence Durrell 1912–90

I want to throw open the windows of the Church so that we can see out and the people can see in.
Pope John XXIII 1881–1963

We are an Easter people and Alleluia is our song.
Pope John Paul II 1920–

'The Church is an anvil which has worn out many hammers', and the story of the first collision is, in essentials, the story of all.
Alexander Maclaren 1826–1910

The Church [of England] should go forward along the path of progress and be no longer satisfied only to represent the Conservative Party at prayer.
Maude Royden 1876–1956

The Church can no longer contain the fizzy, explosive stuff that the true wine of the bottle ought to be.
Donald Soper 1903–98

I never saw, heard, nor read, that the clergy were beloved in any nation where Christianity was the religion of the country. Nothing can render them popular, but some degree of persecution.
Jonathan Swift 1667–1745

As often as we are mown down by you, the more we grow in numbers; the blood of Christians is the seed.
Tertullian AD c.160–c.225, *traditionally 'The blood of the martyrs is the seed of the Church'*

I look upon all the world as my parish.
John Wesley 1703–91

The Catholic Church has never really come to terms with women. What I object to is being treated either as Madonnas or Mary Magdalenes.
Shirley Williams 1930–

The Cinema ····▸ Acting

WILLIAM HOLDEN: You used to be in pictures. You used to be big.
GLORIA SWANSON: I am big. It's the pictures that got small.
Charles Brackett 1892–1969 and **Billy Wilder** 1906–2002

There are no rules in film-making. Only sins. And the cardinal sin is dullness.
Frank Capra 1897–1991

The Cinema

All I need to make a comedy is a park, a policeman and a pretty girl.

Charlie Chaplin 1889–1977

Bring on the empty horses!

Michael Curtiz 1888–1962, *while directing* The Charge of the Light Brigade

GEORGES FRANJU: Movies should have a beginning, a middle and an end.

GODARD: Certainly, but not necessarily in that order.

Jean-Luc Godard 1930–

Photography is truth. The cinema is truth 24 times per second.

Jean-Luc Godard 1930–

Pictures are for entertainment, messages should be delivered by Western Union.

Sam Goldwyn 1882–1974

Why should people go out and pay to see bad movies when they can stay at home and see bad television for nothing?

Sam Goldwyn 1882–1974

If I made Cinderella, the audience would immediately be looking for a body in the coach.

Alfred Hitchcock 1899–1980

If you gave him a good script, actors and technicians, Mickey Mouse could direct a movie.

Nicholas Hytner 1956–

We've got more stars than there are in the heavens, all of them except for that damned Mouse over at Disney.

Louis B. Mayer 1885–1957

The trouble, Mr Goldwyn, is that you are only interested in art and I am only interested in money.

George Bernard Shaw 1856–1950

This is the biggest electric train a boy ever had!
Orson Welles 1915–85, *of the RKO studios*

It is like writing history with lightning. And my only
regret is that it is all so terribly true.
Woodrow Wilson 1856–1924, *on seeing D. W. Griffith's film*
The Birth of a Nation

Civilization

The three great elements of modern civilization,
Gunpowder, Printing, and the Protestant Religion.
Thomas Carlyle 1795–1881

Civilization and profits go hand in hand.
Calvin Coolidge 1872–1933

JOURNALIST: Mr Gandhi, what do you think of modern
   civilization?
GANDHI: That would be a good idea.
Mahatma Gandhi 1869–1948

The lamps are going out all over Europe; we shall not see
them lit again in our lifetime.
Lord Grey of Fallodon 1862–1933, *on the eve of the First
World War*

If a nation expects to be ignorant and free, in a state of
civilization, it expects what never was and never will be.
Thomas Jefferson 1743–1826

Whenever I hear the word culture…I release the safety-
catch of my Browning!
Hanns Johst 1890–1978, *often attributed to Hermann Goering,
and quoted as 'Whenever I hear the word culture, I reach for my
pistol!'*

If civilization had been left in female hands, we would
still be living in grass huts.
Camille Paglia 1947–

Civilization

You can't say civilization don't advance, however, for in every war they kill you in a new way.
Will Rogers 1879–1935

Civilization has made the peasantry its pack animal. The bourgeoisie in the long run only changed the form of the pack.
Leon Trotsky 1879–1940

In Italy for thirty years under the Borgias they had warfare, terror, murder, bloodshed—they produced Michelangelo, Leonardo da Vinci and the Renaissance. In Switzerland they had brotherly love, five hundred years of democracy and peace and what did that produce...? The cuckoo clock.
Orson Welles 1915–85

Class

The rich man in his castle,
The poor man at his gate,
God made them, high or lowly,
And ordered their estate.
Cecil Frances Alexander 1818–95

Il faut épater le bourgeois.
One must astonish the bourgeois.
Charles Baudelaire 1821–67

Like many of the Upper Class
He liked the Sound of Broken Glass.
Hilaire Belloc 1870–1953

Just because I have made a point of never losing my accent it doesn't mean I am an eel-and-pie yob.
Michael Caine 1933–

The Stately Homes of England,
How beautiful they stand,
To prove the upper classes
Have still the upper hand.
        Noël Coward 1899–1973

O let us love our occupations,
Bless the squire and his relations,
Live upon our daily rations,
And always know our proper stations.
        Charles Dickens 1812–70

The proletarians have nothing to lose but their chains.
They have a world to win. WORKING MEN OF ALL
COUNTRIES, UNITE!
        Karl Marx 1818–83 and **Friedrich Engels** 1820–95, *commonly*
        rendered 'Workers of the world, unite!'

We of the sinking middle class…may sink without further
struggles into the working class where we belong, and
probably when we get there it will not be so dreadful as
we feared, for, after all, we have nothing to lose but our
aitches.
        George Orwell 1903–50

First you take their faces from 'em by calling 'em the
masses and then you accuse 'em of not having any faces.
        J. B. Priestley 1894–1984

When Adam dalfe and Eve spane…
Where was than the pride of man?
        Richard Rolle de Hampole c.1290–1349, *taken in the form*
        'When Adam delved and Eve span, who was then the
        gentleman?' by John Ball as the text of his revolutionary sermon
        on the outbreak of the Peasants' Revolt, 1381

The State is an instrument in the hands of the ruling
class, used to break the resistance of the adversaries of
that class.
        Joseph Stalin 1879–1953

Class

The French want no-one to be their *superior*. The English want *inferiors*. The Frenchman constantly raises his eyes above him with anxiety. The Englishman lowers his beneath him with satisfaction.
Alexis de Tocqueville 1805–59

Clothes

It is totally impossible to be well dressed in cheap shoes.
Hardy Amies 1909–2003

From the cradle to the grave, underwear first, last and all the time.
Bertolt Brecht 1898–1956

No perfumes, but very fine linen, plenty of it, and country washing.
Beau Brummell 1778–1840

The sense of being well-dressed gives a feeling of inward tranquillity which religion is powerless to bestow.
Miss C. F. Forbes 1817–1911

A sweet disorder in the dress
Kindles in clothes a wantonness.
Robert Herrick 1591–1674

You should never have your best trousers on when you go out to fight for freedom and truth.
Henrik Ibsen 1828–1906

His socks compelled one's attention without losing one's respect.
Saki 1870–1916

The apparel oft proclaims the man.
William Shakespeare 1564–1616

Beware of all enterprises that require new clothes.
Henry David Thoreau 1817–62

Life is an adventure, so I make clothes to have adventures in.
Vivienne Westwood 1941–

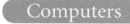

Computers

To err is human but to really foul things up requires a computer.
Anonymous

A modern computer hovers between the obsolescent and the nonexistent.
Sydney Brenner 1927–

The Internet is an elite organisation; most of the population of the world has never even made a phone call.
Noam Chomsky 1928–

The symbol of the atomic age, which tended to centralise power, was a nucleus with electrons held in tight orbit; the symbol of the digital age is the Web, with countless centres of power all equally networked.
Walter Isaacson 1952–

The PC is the LSD of the '90s.
Timothy Leary 1920–96

The Analytical Engine weaves algebraic patterns just as the Jacquard loom weaves flowers and leaves.
Ada Lovelace 1815–52, *of Babbage's early 19th century mechanical computer*

On the Internet, nobody knows you're a dog.
Peter Steiner 1940– , *cartoon caption*

We used to have lots of questions to which there were no answers. Now with the computer there are lots of answers to which we haven't thought up the questions.
Peter Ustinov 1921–2004

Computers

We've all heard that a million monkeys banging on a million typewriters will eventually reproduce the entire works of Shakespeare. Now, thanks to the Internet, we know this is not true.
   Robert Wilensky 1951–

Conscience

We have erred, and strayed from thy ways like lost sheep. We have followed too much the devices and desires of our own hearts.
   Book of Common Prayer 1662

Conscience is thoroughly well-bred and soon leaves off talking to those who do not wish to hear it.
   Samuel Butler 1835–1902

O dignitosa coscienza e netta,
Come t'è picciol fallo amaro morso!

O pure and noble conscience, how bitter a sting to thee is
   a little fault!
   Dante Alighieri 1265–1321

I cannot and will not cut my conscience to fit this year's fashions.
   Lillian Hellman 1905–84

Conscience: the inner voice which warns us that someone may be looking.
   H. L. Mencken 1880–1956

Thus conscience doth make cowards of us all.
   William Shakespeare 1564–1616

Corporations have neither bodies to be punished, nor souls to be condemned, they therefore do as they like.
   Edward, 1st Baron Thurlow 1731–1806, *usually quoted as 'Did you ever expect a corporation to have a conscience, when it has*

no soul to be damned, and no body to be kicked?'

Conversation ····➤ Speechmaking

On every formal visit a child ought to be of the party, by way of provision for discourse.
Jane Austen 1775–1817

Although there exist many thousand subjects for elegant conversation, there are persons who cannot meet a cripple without talking about feet.
Ernest Bramah 1868–1942

'The time has come,' the Walrus said,
'To talk of many things:
Of shoes—and ships—and sealing wax—
Of cabbages—and kings.'
Lewis Carroll 1832–98

Religion is by no means a proper subject of conversation in a mixed company.
Lord Chesterfield 1694–1773

Too much agreement kills a chat.
Eldridge Cleaver 1935–98

And, when you stick on conversation's burrs,
Don't strew your pathway with those dreadful *urs*.
Oliver Wendell Holmes 1809–94

A…sharp tongue is the only edged tool that grows keener with constant use.
Washington Irving 1783–1859

Questioning is not the mode of conversation among gentlemen. It is assuming a superiority.
Samuel Johnson 1709–84

Must I always be a mere listener?
Juvenal AD c.60–c.130

Conversation

The opposite of talking isn't listening. The opposite of talking is waiting.
Fran Lebowitz 1946–

Ah! Would I had the common sense
To sit demurely on a fence
And let who will be vocal.
Phyllis McGinley 1905–78

Speech is civilisation itself. The word, even the most contradictory word, preserves contact—it is silence which isolates.
Thomas Mann 1875–1955

With thee conversing I forget all time.
John Milton 1608–74

The feast of reason and the flow of soul.
Alexander Pope 1688–1744

He never knew what to say. If life was a party, he wasn't even in the kitchen.
Terry Pratchett 1948–

I am not bound to please thee with my answer.
William Shakespeare 1564–1616

Cookery ····▶ Eating, Food

Anyone who tells a lie has not a pure heart, and cannot make a good soup.
Ludwig van Beethoven 1770–1827

Be content to remember that those who can make omelettes properly can do nothing else.
Hilaire Belloc 1870–1953

Cooking is the most ancient of the arts, for Adam was
born hungry.
Anthelme Brillat-Savarin 1755–1826

Good food is always a trouble and its preparation should
be regarded as a labour of love.
Elizabeth David 1913–92

Heaven sends us good meat, but the Devil sends cooks.
David Garrick 1717–79

Kissing don't last: cookery do!
George Meredith 1828–1909

I never see any home cooking. All I get is fancy stuff.
Prince Philip 1921–

The cook was a good cook, as cooks go; and as cooks go,
she went.
Saki 1870–1916

I want to focus on my salad.
Martha Stewart 1941– , *when questioned about insider trading
during her cookery spot on CBS* The Early Show

Cooperation

If a house be divided against itself, that house cannot
stand.
Bible

When bad men combine, the good must associate; else
they will fall, one by one, an unpitied sacrifice in a
contemptible struggle.
Edmund Burke 1729–97

All for one, one for all.
Alexandre Dumas 1802–70

Cooperation

We must indeed all hang together, or, most assuredly, we shall all hang separately.
  Benjamin Franklin 1706–90

If someone claps his hand a sound arises. Listen to the sound of the single hand!
  Hakuin 1686–1769

If we cannot end now our differences, at least we can help make the world safe for diversity.
  John F. Kennedy 1917–63

We must learn to live together as brothers or perish together as fools.
  Martin Luther King 1929–68

When Hitler attacked the Jews I was not a Jew, therefore, I was not concerned. And when Hitler attacked the Catholics, I was not a Catholic, and therefore, I was not concerned. And when Hitler attacked the unions and the industrialists, I was not a member of the unions and I was not concerned. Then, Hitler attacked me and the Protestant church—and there was nobody left to be concerned.
  Martin Niemöller 1892–1984

Government and co-operation are in all things the laws of life; anarchy and competition the laws of death.
  John Ruskin 1819–1900

The Country ····▶ Environment

'Tis distance lends enchantment to the view,
And robes the mountain in its azure hue.
  Thomas Campbell 1777–1844

God made the country, and man made the town.
  William Cowper 1731–1800

It is my belief, Watson, founded upon my experience, that the lowest and vilest alleys in London do not present a more dreadful record of sin than does the smiling and beautiful countryside.

Arthur Conan Doyle 1859–1930

Green belts should be the start of the countryside, not a ditch between Subtopias.

Hugh Gaitskell 1906–63

Our salvation can only come through the farmer. Neither the lawyers, nor the doctors, nor the rich landlords are going to secure it.

Mahatma Gandhi 1869–1948

Agriculture is the foundation of manufactures; since the productions of nature are the materials of art.

Edward Gibbon 1737–94

There is nothing good to be had in the country, or if there is, they will not let you have it.

William Hazlitt 1778–1830

The Farmer will never be happy again;
He carries his heart in his boots;
For either the rain is destroying his grain
Or the drought is destroying his roots.

A. P. Herbert 1890–1971

Oh, give me land, lots of land under starry skies above,
Don't fence me in.

Cole Porter 1891–1964

I have no relish for the country; it is a kind of healthy grave.

Sydney Smith 1771–1845

Anybody can be good in the country.

Oscar Wilde 1854–1900

Courage

No coward soul is mine,
No trembler in the world's storm-troubled sphere:
I see Heaven's glories shine,
And faith shines equal, arming me from fear.
Emily Brontë 1818–48

Courage is rightly esteemed the first of human qualities
because as has been said, it is the quality which
guarantees all others.
Winston Churchill 1874–1965

De l'audace, et encore de l'audace, et toujours de l'audace!
Boldness, and again boldness, and always boldness!
Georges Jacques Danton 1759–94

Courage is the price that Life exacts for granting peace,
The soul that knows it not, knows no release
From little things.
Amelia Earhart 1898–1937

Grace under pressure.
Ernest Hemingway 1899–1961, *when asked what he meant by 'guts'*

Tender-handed stroke a nettle,
And it stings you for your pains;
Grasp it like a man of mettle,
And it soft as silk remains.
Aaron Hill 1685–1750

Courage is not simply *one* of the virtues but the form of
every virtue at the testing point.
C. S. Lewis 1898–1963

As to moral courage, I have very rarely met with two
o'clock in the morning courage: I mean instantaneous
courage.
Napoleon I 1769–1821

All men would be cowards if they durst.
John Wilmot, Earl of Rochester 1647–80

Cowards die many times before their deaths;
The valiant never taste of death but once.
William Shakespeare 1564–1616

Audentis Fortuna iuvat.
Fortune assists the bold.
Virgil 70–19 BC, *often quoted as 'Fortune favours the brave'*

Creativity

Think before you speak is criticism's motto; speak before
you think creation's.
E. M. Forster 1879–1970

Poems are made by fools like me,
But only God can make a tree.
Joyce Kilmer 1886–1918

Nothing can be created out of nothing.
Lucretius c.94–55 BC

Why does my Muse only speak when she is unhappy?
She does not, I only listen when I am unhappy
When I am happy I live and despise writing
For my Muse this cannot but be dispiriting.
Stevie Smith 1902–71

The worst crime is to leave a man's hands empty.
Men are born makers, with that primal simplicity
In every maker since Adam.
Derek Walcott 1930–

Urge and urge and urge,
Always the procreant urge of the world.
Walt Whitman 1819–92

Cricket

Cricket

Bowl fast, bowl faster. When you play Test cricket you don't give Englishmen an inch. Play it tough, all the way. Grind them into the dust.
Don Bradman 1908–2001

I couldn't bat for the length of time required to score 500. I'd get bored and fall over.
Denis Compton 1918–

Never read print, it spoils one's eye for the ball.
W. G. Grace 1848–1915, *habitual advice to his players*

It's more than a game. It's an institution.
Thomas Hughes 1822–96

Cricket—a game which the English, not being a spiritual people, have invented in order to give themselves some conception of eternity.
Lord Mancroft 1914–87

Cricket civilizes people and creates good gentlemen. I want everyone to play cricket in Zimbabwe; I want ours to be a nation of gentlemen.
Robert Mugabe 1924–

There's a breathless hush in the Close to-night—
Ten to make and the match to win—
A bumping pitch and a blinding light,
An hour to play and the last man in.
Henry Newbolt 1862–1938

Personally, I have always looked on cricket as organized loafing.
William Temple 1881–1944

Crime ····▸ Justice, Murder, Punishment

Labour is the party of law and order in Britain today.
Tough on crime and tough on the causes of crime.
Tony Blair 1953-

Once in the racket you're always in it.
Al Capone 1899-1947

Crime isn't a disease, it's a symptom. Cops are like a
doctor that gives you aspirin for a brain tumour.
Raymond Chandler 1888-1959

Thieves respect property. They merely wish the property
to become their property that they may more perfectly
respect it.
G. K. Chesterton 1874-1936

Thou shalt not steal; an empty feat,
When it's so lucrative to cheat.
Arthur Hugh Clough 1819-61

Singularity is almost invariably a clue. The more
featureless and commonplace a crime is, the more
difficult is it to bring it home.
Arthur Conan Doyle 1859-1930

For de little stealin' dey gits you in jail soon or late. For
de big stealin' dey makes you Emperor and puts you in
de Hall o' Fame when you croaks.
Eugene O'Neill 1888-1953

A clever theft was praiseworthy amongst the Spartans;
and it is equally so amongst Christians, provided it be on
a sufficiently large scale.
Herbert Spencer 1820-1903

Crises

Crises

Comin' in on a wing and a pray'r.
Harold Adamson 1906–80

Crisis? What Crisis?
Anonymous Sun *headline, summarizing James Callaghan on the winter of discontent: 'I don't think other people in the world would share the view [that] there is mounting chaos'*

Go in, stay in, tune in.
Anonymous *British government advice on preparing for emergencies, 2004*

We do not experience and thus we have no measure of the disasters we prevent.
J. K. Galbraith 1908–

Swimming for his life, a man does not see much of the country through which the river winds.
W. E. Gladstone 1809–98

The illustrious bishop of Cambrai was of more worth than his chambermaid, and there are few of us that would hesitate to pronounce, if his palace were in flames, and the life of only one of them could be preserved, which of the two ought to be preferred.
William Godwin 1756–1836

For it is your business, when the wall next door catches fire.
Horace 65–8 BC

If you can keep your head when all about you
Are losing theirs and blaming it on you.
Rudyard Kipling 1865–1936

We're eyeball to eyeball, and I think the other fellow just blinked.
Dean Rusk 1909–

I myself have always deprecated…in crisis after crisis, appeals to the Dunkirk spirit as an answer to our problems.
Harold Wilson 1916–95

I'm at my best in a messy, middle-of-the-road muddle.
Harold Wilson 1916–95

Criticism

A man must serve his time to every trade
Save censure—critics all are ready made.
Lord Byron 1788–1824

Whom the gods wish to destroy they first call promising.
Cyril Connolly 1903–74

Everything must be like something, so what is this like?
E. M. Forster 1879–1970

No theoretician, no writer on art, however interesting he or she might be, could be as interesting as Picasso. A good writer on art may give you an insight to Picasso, but, after all, Picasso was there first.
David Hockney 1937–

Parodies and caricatures are the most penetrating of criticisms.
Aldous Huxley 1894–1963

I don't care anything about reasons, but I know what I like.
Henry James 1843–1916

This will never do.
Francis, Lord Jeffrey 1773–1850, *on Wordsworth's* The Excursion

Criticism

You *may* abuse a tragedy, though you cannot write one.
You may scold a carpenter who has made you a bad
table, though you cannot make a table. It is not your
trade to make tables.
   Samuel Johnson 1709–84, *on literary criticism*

I cry all the way to the bank.
   Liberace 1919–87, *on bad reviews*

People who like this sort of thing will find this the sort of
thing they like.
   Abraham Lincoln 1809–65, *judgement of a book*

One should look long and carefully at oneself before one
considers judging others.
   Molière 1622–73

I am sitting in the smallest room of my house. I have
your review before me. In a moment it will be
behind me.
   Max Reger 1873–1916, *responding to a savage review*

If you are not criticized, you may not be doing much.
   Donald Rumsfeld 1932–

Remember, a statue has never been set up in honour of a
critic!
   Jean Sibelius 1865–1957

I never read a book before reviewing it; it prejudices a
man so.
   Sydney Smith 1771–1845

As learned commentators view
In Homer more than Homer knew.
   Jonathan Swift 1667–1745

A critic is a man who knows the way but can't drive the
car.
   Kenneth Tynan 1927–80

I maintain that two and two would continue to make four, in spite of the whine of the amateur for three, or the cry of the critic for five.
James McNeill Whistler 1834–1903

Cruelty

Boys throw stones at frogs for fun, but the frogs don't die for 'fun', but in sober earnest.
Bion c.325–c.255 BC

A robin red breast in a cage
Puts all Heaven in a rage.
William Blake 1757–1827

The wish to hurt, the momentary intoxication with pain, is the loophole through which the pervert climbs into the minds of ordinary men.
Jacob Bronowski 1908–74

It is cruel to break people's legs, even if the statement is made by someone in the habit of breaking their arms.
Brigid Brophy 1929–

Man's inhumanity to man
Makes countless thousands mourn!
Robert Burns 1759–96

The healthy man does not torture others—generally it is the tortured who turn into torturers.
Carl Gustav Jung 1875–1961

Our language lacks words to express this offence, the demolition of a man.
Primo Levi 1919–87, *of a year spent in Auschwitz*

Cruelty

Death may be inevitable but cruelty is not. If we must eat meat, then we must ensure that the animals we kill for our food live the best possible lives before they die.
Desmond Morris 1928–

The infliction of cruelty with a good conscience is a delight to moralists. That is why they invented Hell.
Bertrand Russell 1872–1970

I must be cruel only to be kind.
William Shakespeare 1564–1616

This was the most unkindest cut of all.
William Shakespeare 1564–1616

Custom

One can't carry one's father's corpse about everywhere.
Guillaume Apollinaire 1880–1918, *on tradition*

Custom reconciles us to everything.
Edmund Burke 1729–97

Tradition means giving votes to the most obscure of all classes, our ancestors. It is the democracy of the dead.
G. K. Chesterton 1874–1936

Actions receive their tincture from the times,
And as they change are virtues made or crimes.
Daniel Defoe 1660–1731

If one were to order all mankind to choose the best set of rules in the world, each group would, after due consideration, choose its own customs; each group regards its own as being by far the best.
Herodotus c.485–c.425 BC

Custom, then, is the great guide of human life.
David Hume 1711–76

Cynicism

The tradition of all the dead generations weighs like a
nightmare on the brain of the living.
Karl Marx 1818–83

Everyone calls barbarism what is not customary to him.
Molière 1622–73

But to my mind,—though I am native here,
And to the manner born,—it is a custom
More honoured in the breach than the observance.
William Shakespeare 1564–1616

Laws are sand, customs are rock. Laws can be evaded and
punishment escaped, but an openly transgressed custom
brings sure punishment.
Mark Twain 1835–1910

Cynicism

Kill them all; God will recognize his own.
Arnald-Amaury d. 1225, *when asked how the true Catholics
could be distinguished from the heretics at the massacre of
Béziers*

Never glad confident morning again!
Robert Browning 1812–89

What makes all doctrines plain and clear?
About two hundred pounds a year.
And that which was proved true before,
Prove false again? Two hundred more.
Samuel Butler 1612–80

To get practice in being refused.
Diogenes 404–323 BC, *reply when asked why he was begging
for alms from a statue*

Cynicism

Pathos, piety, courage—they exist, but are identical, and so is filth. Everything exists, nothing has value.

E. M. Forster 1879–1970

Cynicism is an unpleasant way of saying the truth.

Lillian Hellman 1905–84

Paris is well worth a mass.

Henri IV 1553–1610

Cynicism is our shared common language, the Esperanto that actually caught on.

Nick Hornby 1957–

A man who knows the price of everything and the value of nothing.

Oscar Wilde 1854–1900, *definition of a cynic*

Dance

A dance is a measured pace, as a verse is a measured speech.

Francis Bacon 1561–1626

There may be trouble ahead,
But while there's moonlight and music and love and
   romance,
Let's face the music and dance.

Irving Berlin 1888–1989

On with the dance! let joy be unconfined;
No sleep till morn, when Youth and Pleasure meet
To chase the glowing Hours with flying feet.

Lord Byron 1788–1824

This wondrous miracle did Love devise,
For dancing is love's proper exercise.

Sir John Davies 1569–1626

The truest expression of a people is in its dances and its music. Bodies never lie.
Agnes de Mille 1908–93

Dance is the hidden language of the soul.
Martha Graham 1894–1991

Come, and trip it as ye go
On the light fantastic toe.
John Milton 1608–74

[Dancing is] a perpendicular expression of a horizontal desire.
George Bernard Shaw 1856–1950

Everyone knows that the real business of a ball is either to look out for a wife, to look after a wife, or to look after somebody else's wife.
R. S. Surtees 1805–64

Danger

You can put up a sign on the door, 'beware of the dog', without having a dog.
Hans Blix 1928–

Dangers by being despised grow great.
Edmund Burke 1729–97

When there is no peril in the fight, there is no glory in the triumph.
Pierre Corneille 1606–84

In skating over thin ice, our safety is in our speed.
Ralph Waldo Emerson 1803–82

Out of this nettle, danger, we pluck this flower, safety.
William Shakespeare 1564–1616

Day

Day ····▶ Night

Awake! for Morning in the bowl of night
Has flung the stone that puts the stars to flight.
Edward Fitzgerald 1809–83

Summer afternoon—summer afternoon...the two most
beautiful words in the English language.
Henry James 1843–1916

What are days for?
Days are where we live.
Philip Larkin 1922–85

I have a horror of sunsets, they're so romantic, so
operatic.
Marcel Proust 1871–1922

Night's candles are burnt out, and jocund day
Stands tiptoe on the misty mountain tops.
William Shakespeare 1564–1616

Death ····▶ Bereavement

It's not that I'm afraid to die. I just don't want to be
there when it happens.
Woody Allen 1935-

Revenge triumphs over death; love slights it; honour
aspireth to it; grief flieth to it.
Francis Bacon 1561–1626

To die will be an awfully big adventure.
J. M. Barrie 1860–1937

For dust thou art, and unto dust shalt thou return.
Bible

O death, where is thy sting? O grave, where is thy victory?
Bible

In the midst of life we are in death.
Book of Common Prayer 1662

Forasmuch as it hath pleased Almighty God of his great
mercy to take unto himself the soul of our dear brother
here departed, we therefore commit his body to the
ground; earth to earth, ashes to ashes, dust to dust; in
sure and certain hope of the Resurrection to eternal life.
Book of Common Prayer 1662

If I should die, think only this of me:
That there's some corner of a foreign field
That is for ever England.
Rupert Brooke 1887–1915

This parrot is no more! It has ceased to be! It's expired
and gone to meet its maker! This is a late parrot! It's a
stiff! Bereft of life it rests in peace—if you hadn't nailed
it to the perch it would be pushing up the daisies! It's
rung down the curtain and joined the choir invisible!
THIS IS AN EX–PARROT!
Graham Chapman 1941–89 et al.

However many ways there may be of being alive, it is
certain that there are vastly more ways of being dead.
Richard Dawkins 1941–

Any man's death diminishes me, because I am involved in
Mankind; And therefore never send to know for whom
the bell tolls; it tolls for thee.
John Donne 1572–1631

Death be not proud, though some have called thee
Mighty and dreadful, for thou art not so.
John Donne 1572–1631

The bodies of those that made such a noise and tumult
when alive, when dead, lie as quietly among the graves of
their neighbours as any others.
Jonathan Edwards 1703–58

Death

Webster was much possessed by death
And saw the skull beneath the skin.
>   **T. S. Eliot** 1888–1965

Death, therefore, the most awful of evils, is nothing to us, seeing that, when we are death is not come, and when death is come, we are not.
>   **Epicurus** 341–271 BC

Death is nothing if one can approach it as such. I was just a tiny night-light, suffocated in its own wax, and on the point of expiring.
>   **E. M. Forster** 1879–1970

Death is nothing at all; it does not count. I have only slipped away into the next room.
>   **Henry Scott Holland** 1847–1918

I would rather be tied to the soil as another man's serf, even a poor man's, who hadn't much to live on himself, than be King of all these the dead and destroyed.
>   **Homer** 8th century BC

Non omnis moriar.
I shall not altogether die.
>   **Horace** 65–8 BC

Depend upon it, Sir, when a man knows he is to be hanged in a fortnight, it concentrates his mind wonderfully.
>   **Samuel Johnson** 1709–84

Now more than ever seems it rich to die,
To cease upon the midnight with no pain.
>   **John Keats** 1795–1821

Dying is a very dull, dreary affair. And my advice to you is to have nothing whatever to do with it.
>   **W. Somerset Maugham** 1874–1965

And all our calm is in that balm—
Not lost but gone before.
  Caroline Norton 1808–77

Die, my dear Doctor, that's the last thing I shall do!
  Lord Palmerston 1784–1865

Guns aren't lawful;
Nooses give;
Gas smells awful;
You might as well live.
  Dorothy Parker 1893–1967

We shall die alone.
  Blaise Pascal 1623–62

Abiit ad plures.
He's gone to join the majority [the dead].
  Petronius d. AD 65

Deception is not as creative as truth. We do best in life if
we look at it with clear eyes, and I think that applies to
coming up to death as well.
  Cicely Saunders 1916– , *of the Hospice movement*

Anyone can stop a man's life, but no one his death; a
thousand doors open on to it.
  Seneca ('the Younger') c.4 BC–AD 65

        Nothing in his life
Became him like the leaving it.
  William Shakespeare 1564–1616

I care not; a man can die but once; we owe God a death.
  William Shakespeare 1564–1616

        To die, to sleep;
To sleep: perchance to dream: ay, there's the rub;
For in that sleep of death what dreams may come
When we have shuffled off this mortal coil,

Death

Must give us pause.
William Shakespeare 1564–1616

Death must be distinguished from dying, with which it is
often confused.
Sydney Smith 1771–1845

If there wasn't death, I think you couldn't go on.
Stevie Smith 1902–71

One death is a tragedy, a million deaths a statistic.
Joseph Stalin 1879–1953

For though from out our bourne of time and place
The flood may bear me far,
I hope to see my pilot face to face
When I have crossed the bar.
Alfred, Lord Tennyson 1809–92

Though lovers be lost love shall not;
And death shall have no dominion.
Dylan Thomas 1914–53

I know death hath ten thousand several doors
For men to take their exits.
John Webster c.1580–c.1625

　　　　　The good die first,
And they whose hearts are dry as summer dust
Burn to the socket.
William Wordsworth 1770–1850

Nor dread nor hope attend
A dying animal;
A man awaits his end
Dreading and hoping all.
W. B. Yeats 1865–1939

Debt

I don't borrow on credit cards because it is too expensive.
Matt Barrett 1944- , *view of the chief executive of Barclays Bank*

Be not made a beggar by banqueting upon borrowing.
Bible

The human species, according to the best theory I can form of it, is composed of two distinct races, *the men who borrow*, and *the men who lend*.
Charles Lamb 1775–1834

Should we really let our people starve so we can pay our debts?
Julius Nyerere 1922–99

You can't put your VISA bill on your American Express card.
P. J. O'Rourke 1947-

Neither a borrower, nor a lender be.
William Shakespeare 1564–1616

Deceit ·····► Lies

Propaganda is a soft weapon: hold it in your hands too long, and it will move about like a snake, and strike the other way.
Jean Anouilh 1910–87

An open foe may prove a curse,
But a pretended friend is worse.
John Gay 1685–1732

It was beautiful and simple as all truly great swindles are.
O. Henry 1862–1910

Deceit

You may fool all the people some of the time; you can even fool some of the people all the time; but you can't fool all of the people all the time.
    Abraham Lincoln 1809–65

O what a tangled web we weave,
When first we practise to deceive!
    Sir Walter Scott 1771–1832

A deception that elevates us is dearer than a host of low truths.
    Marina Tsvetaeva 1892–1941

Democracy ····▶ Politics, Voting

The cure for the ills of Democracy is more Democracy.
    John Adams 1735–1826

After each war there is a little less democracy to save.
    Brooks Atkinson 1894–1984

Democracy means government by discussion, but it is only effective if you can stop people talking.
    Clement Attlee 1883–1967

One man shall have one vote.
    John Cartwright 1740–1824

Democracy is the worst form of Government except all those other forms that have been tried from time to time.
    Winston Churchill 1874–1965

As for our majority…one is enough.
    Benjamin Disraeli 1804–81

So Two cheers for Democracy: one because it admits variety and two because it permits criticism. Two cheers are quite enough: there is no occasion to give three. Only Love the Beloved Republic deserves that.
    E. M. Forster 1879–1970

All the world over, I will back the masses against the classes.
W. E. Gladstone 1809–98

We here highly resolve that the dead shall not have died in vain, that this nation, under God, shall have a new birth of freedom; and that government of the people, by the people, and for the people, shall not perish from the earth.
Abraham Lincoln 1809–65

I never could believe that Providence had sent a few men into the world, ready booted and spurred to ride, and millions ready saddled and bridled to be ridden.
Richard Rumbold c.1622–85

Democracy substitutes election by the incompetent many for appointment by the corrupt few.
George Bernard Shaw 1856–1950

If one must serve, I hold it better to serve a well-bred lion, who is naturally stronger than I am, than two hundred rats of my own breed.
Voltaire 1694–1778

The world must be made safe for democracy.
Woodrow Wilson 1856–1924

Despair ····▶ Hope, Pessimism

My God, my God, look upon me; why hast thou forsaken me?
Bible

There is no despair so absolute as that which comes with the first moments of our first great sorrow, when we have not yet known what it is to have suffered and be healed, to have despaired and have recovered hope.
George Eliot 1819–80

Despair

In a real dark night of the soul it is always three o'clock in the morning.
> **F. Scott Fitzgerald** 1896–1940

Not, I'll not, carrion comfort, Despair, not feast on thee;
Not untwist—slack they may be—these last strands
of man
In me or, most weary, cry *I can no more.* I can;
Can something, hope, wish day come, not choose not
to be.
> **Gerard Manley Hopkins** 1844–89

Human life begins on the far side of despair.
> **Jean-Paul Sartre** 1905–80

Determination

Ils ne passeront pas.

They shall not pass.
> **Anonymous** slogan of the French army at the defence of Verdun, 1916

Nil carborundum illegitimi.
> **Anonymous** cod Latin for 'Don't let the bastards grind you down', in circulation during the Second World War, though possibly of earlier origin

Thought shall be the harder, heart the keener, courage the greater, as our might lessens.
> **The Battle of Maldon** c.1000

I can only go one way. I've not got a reverse gear.
> **Tony Blair** 1953–

I was ever a fighter, so—one fight more,
The best and the last!
I would hate that death bandaged my eyes, and forbore,
And bade me creep past.
> **Robert Browning** 1812–89

Determination

Obstinacy, Sir, is certainly a great vice…It happens,
however, very unfortunately, that almost the whole line of
the great and masculine virtues, constancy, gravity,
magnanimity, fortitude, fidelity, and firmness are closely
allied to this disagreeable quality.
    Edmund Burke 1729–97

I will fight for what I believe in until I drop dead. And
that's what keeps you alive.
    Barbara Castle 1910–2002

Say not the struggle naught availeth,
The labour and the wounds are vain,
The enemy faints not, nor faileth,
And as things have been, things remain.
    Arthur Hugh Clough 1819–61

Nothing in the world can take the place of persistence.
Talent will not; nothing is more common than
unsuccessful men with talent. Genius will not;
unrewarded genius is almost a proverb. Education will
not; the world is full of educated derelicts. Persistence and
determination are omnipotent. The slogan 'press on' has
solved and always will solve the problems of the human
race.
    Calvin Coolidge 1872–1933

Pick yourself up,
Dust yourself off,
Start all over again.
    Dorothy Fields 1905–74

The best way out is always through.
    Robert Frost 1874–1963

Under the bludgeonings of chance
My head is bloody, but unbowed.
    W. E. Henley 1849–1903

Determination

When the going gets tough, the tough get going.
Joseph P. Kennedy 1888–1969

The drop of rain maketh a hole in the stone, not by violence, but by oft falling.
Hugh Latimer c.1485–1555

With malice toward none; with charity for all; with firmness in the right, as God gives us to see the right, let us strive on to finish the work we are in.
Abraham Lincoln 1809–65

> Perseverance, dear my lord,
> Keeps honour bright.
William Shakespeare 1564–1616

One man that has a mind and knows it can always beat ten men who haven't and don't.
George Bernard Shaw 1856–1950

Do not underestimate the determination of a quiet man.
Iain Duncan Smith 1954–

'Tis known by the name of perseverance in a good cause,—and of obstinacy in a bad one.
Laurence Sterne 1713–68

> That which we are, we are;
> One equal temper of heroic hearts,
> Made weak by time and fate, but strong in will
> To strive, to seek, to find, and not to yield.
Alfred, Lord Tennyson 1809–92

We shall not be diverted from our course. To those waiting with bated breath for that favourite media catch-phrase, the U-turn, I have only this to say. 'You turn if you want; the lady's not for turning.'
Margaret Thatcher 1925–

What is the victory of a cat on a hot tin roof?—I wish I knew…Just staying on it, I guess, as long as she can.
Tennessee Williams 1911–83

Diaries

What is more dull than a discreet diary? One might just as well have a discreet soul.
Henry 'Chips' Channon 1897–1958

I want to go on living even after death!
Anne Frank 1929–45

To be a good diarist one must have a little snouty, sneaky mind.
Harold Nicolson 1886–1968

One need not write in a diary what one is to remember for ever.
Sylvia Townsend Warner 1893–1978

I always say, keep a diary and some day it'll keep you.
Mae West 1892–1980

I never travel without my diary. One should always have something sensational to read in the train.
Oscar Wilde 1854–1900

Diplomacy

In things that are tender and unpleasing, it is good to break the ice by some whose words are of less weight, and to reserve the more weighty voice to come in as by chance.
Francis Bacon 1561–1626

To jaw-jaw is always better than to war-war.
Winston Churchill 1874–1965

Diplomacy

Treaties, you see, are like girls and roses: they last while they last.
    Charles de Gaulle 1890–1970

I feel happier now that we have no allies to be polite to and to pamper.
    George VI 1895–1952

Let us never negotiate out of fear. But let us never fear to negotiate.
    John F. Kennedy 1917–63

One of the things I learnt when I was negotiating was that until I changed myself I could not change others.
    Nelson Mandela 1918–

We are prepared to go to the gates of Hell—but no further.
    Pope Pius VII 1742–1823, *attempting to reach an agreement with Napoleon*

I'm afraid you've got a bad egg, Mr Jones.
Oh no, my Lord, I assure you! Parts of it are excellent!
    Punch

Speak softly and carry a big stick; you will go far.
    Theodore Roosevelt 1858–1919

You can no more make an agreement with those leaders of Colombia than you can nail currant jelly to the wall. And the failure to nail currant jelly to the wall is not due to the nail. It's due to the currant jelly.
    Theodore Roosevelt 1858–1919

By indirections find directions out.
    William Shakespeare 1564–1616

An ambassador is an honest man sent to lie abroad for the good of his country.
    Henry Wotton 1568–1639

Discontent .....> Satisfaction

When you don't have any money, the problem is food. When you have money, it's sex. When you have both it's health.
 J. P. Donleavy 1926–

We loathe our manna, and we long for quails.
 John Dryden 1631–1700

It is an uneasy lot at best, to be what we call highly taught and yet not to enjoy: to be present at this great spectacle of life and never to be liberated from a small hungry shivering self.
 George Eliot 1819–80

He who thinks to realize when he is older the hopes and desires of youth is always deceiving himself, for every decade of a man's life possesses its own kind of happiness, its own hopes and prospects.
 Johann Wolfgang von Goethe 1749–1832

   It is a flaw
In happiness, to see beyond our bourn—
It forces us in summer skies to mourn:
It spoils the singing of the nightingale.
 John Keats 1795–1821

It is better to be a human being dissatisfied than a pig satisfied; better to be Socrates dissatisfied than a fool satisfied.
 John Stuart Mill 1806–73

'Tis just like a summer birdcage in a garden; the birds that are without despair to get in, and the birds that are within despair, and are in a consumption, for fear they shall never get out.
 John Webster c.1580–c.1625

Discontent

He spoke with a certain what-is-it in his voice, and I could see that, if not actually disgruntled, he was far from being gruntled.

P. G. Wodehouse 1881–1975

Discovery ····▶ Invention and Discovery

Dogs

The great pleasure of a dog is that you may make a fool of yourself with him and not only will he not scold you, but he will make a fool of himself too.

Samuel Butler 1835–1902

Near this spot are deposited the remains of one who possessed beauty without vanity, strength without insolence, courage without ferocity, and all the virtues of Man, without his vices.

Lord Byron 1788–1824, *epitaph on his Newfoundland dog*

Brothers and Sisters, I bid you beware
Of giving your heart to a dog to tear.

Rudyard Kipling 1865–1936

A door is what a dog is perpetually on the wrong side of.

Ogden Nash 1902–71

I am his Highness' dog at Kew;
Pray, tell me sir, whose dog are you?

Alexander Pope 1688–1744, *engraved on the collar of a dog*

A dog in the home is a piece of moving furniture.

Philippe de Rothschild 1902–88

That indefatigable and unsavoury engine of pollution, the dog.

John Sparrow 1906–92

The more one gets to know of men, the more one values dogs.

A. Toussenel 1803–85, *attributed to Mme Roland in the form 'The more I see of men, the more I like dogs'*

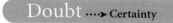

Doubt ····▸ Certainty

Oh! let us never, never doubt
What nobody is sure about!
Hilaire Belloc 1870–1953

How long halt ye between two opinions?
Bible

I am too much of a sceptic to deny the possibility of anything.
T. H. Huxley 1825–95

I respect faith but doubt is what gets you an education.
Wilson Mizner 1876–1933

Ten thousand difficulties do not make one doubt.
John Henry Newman 1801–90

Now, the melancholy god protect thee, and the tailor make thy doublet of changeable taffeta, for thy mind is a very opal.
William Shakespeare 1564–1616

I must have a prodigious quantity of mind; it takes me as much as a week, sometimes, to make it up.
Mark Twain 1835–1910

Life is doubt,
And faith without doubt is nothing but death.
Miguel de Unamuno 1864–1937

Drawing

Not a day without a line.
Apelles fl. 325 BC, *proverbial summary of his philosophy*

A picture equals a movement in space.
Emily Carr 1871–1945

Treat nature in terms of the cylinder, the sphere, the cone, all in perspective.
Paul Cézanne 1839–1906

I rarely draw what I see—I draw what I feel in my body.
Barbara Hepworth 1903–75

Le dessin est la probité de l'art.
Drawing is the true test of art.
J. A. D. Ingres 1780–1867

An active line on a walk, moving freely without a goal. A walk for walk's sake.
Paul Klee 1879–1940

When I was the age of these children I could draw like Raphael: it took me many years to learn how to draw like these children.
Pablo Picasso 1881–1973, *visiting an exhibition of childen's drawings*

Dreams

Have you noticed…there is never any third act in a nightmare? They bring you to a climax of terror and then leave you there. They are the work of poor dramatists.
Max Beerbohm 1872–1956

The armoured cars of dreams, contrived to let us do so many a dangerous thing.
Elizabeth Bishop 1911–79

That children dream not in the first half year, that men dream not in some countries, are to me sick men's dreams, dreams out of the ivory gate, and visions before midnight.

Sir Thomas Browne 1605–82

All the things one has forgotten scream for help in dreams.

Elias Canetti 1905–94

When we dream that we are dreaming, the moment of awakening is at hand.

J. M. Coetzee 1940–

The interpretation of dreams is the royal road to a knowledge of the unconscious activities of the mind.

Sigmund Freud 1856–1939

The dream of reason produces monsters.

Goya 1746–1828

Was it a vision, or a waking dream?
Fled is that music:—do I wake or sleep?

John Keats 1795–1821

O God! I could be bounded in a nut-shell, and count myself a king of infinite space, were it not that I have bad dreams.

William Shakespeare 1564–1616

      The quick Dreams,
The passion-wingèd Ministers of thought.

Percy Bysshe Shelley 1792–1822

Drink

One reason why I don't drink is because I wish to know when I am having a good time.

Nancy Astor 1879–1964

Drink

When the wine is in, the wit is out.
Thomas Becon 1512–67

Wine is a mocker, strong drink is raging.
Bible

Freedom and Whisky gang thegither!
Robert Burns 1759–96

I have taken more out of alcohol than alcohol has taken out of me.
Winston Churchill 1874–1965

A man shouldn't fool with booze until he's fifty; then he's a damn fool if he doesn't.
William Faulkner 1897–1962

I often wonder what the Vintners buy
One half so precious as the Goods they sell.
Edward Fitzgerald 1809–83

And malt does more than Milton can
To justify God's ways to man.
A. E. Housman 1859–1936

You're not drunk if you can lie on the floor without holding on.
Dean Martin 1917–95

Candy
Is dandy
But liquor
Is quicker.
Ogden Nash 1902–71

Wine is for drinking and enjoying, talking about it is deadly dull.
Jancis Robinson 1950–

I'm only a beer teetotaller, not a champagne teetotaller.
George Bernard Shaw 1856–1950

I'm not so think as you drunk I am.
J. C. Squire 1884–1958

The lips that touch liquor must never touch mine.
George W. Young 1846–1919

Drugs

Death is the final penalty, but the life of a sportsman on drugs is a perpetual living penalty because he is offending against himself.
Christopher Brasher 1928–2003

I'll die young, but it's like kissing God.
Lenny Bruce 1925–66, *on his drug addiction*

Junk is the ideal product…the ultimate merchandise. No sales talk necessary. The client will crawl through a sewer and beg to buy.
William S. Burroughs 1914–97

I experimented with marijuana a time or two. And I didn't like it, and I didn't inhale.
Bill Clinton 1946–

Thou hast the keys of Paradise, oh just, subtle, and mighty opium!
Thomas De Quincey 1785–1859

Drugs is like getting up and having a cup of tea in the morning.
Noel Gallagher 1967–

In this country, don't forget, a habit is no damn private hell. There's no solitary confinement outside of jail. A habit is hell for those you love.
Billie Holiday 1915–59

Drugs

Every form of addiction is bad, no matter whether the narcotic be alcohol or morphine or idealism.

Carl Gustav Jung 1875-1961

Sure thing, man. I used to be a laboratory myself once.

Keith Richards 1943- , *on being asked to autograph a fan's school chemistry book*

The Earth

The earth is the Lord's, and all that therein is: the compass of the world, and they that dwell therein.

Bible

Topography displays no favourites; North's as near as West.
More delicate than the historians' are the map-makers' colours.

Elizabeth Bishop 1911-79

How inappropriate to call this planet Earth when it is clearly Ocean.

Arthur C. Clarke 1917-

Now there is one outstandingly important fact regarding Spaceship Earth, and that is that no instruction book came with it.

R. Buckminster Fuller 1895-1983

To me, it underscores our responsibility to deal more kindly with one another, and to preserve and cherish the pale blue dot, the only home we've ever known.

Carl Sagan 1934-96, *of Earth as photographed by Voyager 1*

We have a beautiful
mother
Her green lap
immense
Her brown embrace

eternal
Her blue body
everything
we know.
  Alice Walker 1944–

Need for a knowledge of geography is greater than the
need of gardens for water after the stars have failed to
fulfil their promise of rain.
  Yāqūt d. 1229

Eating ····▶ Cookery, Food

Tell me what you eat and I will tell you what you are.
  Anthelme Brillat-Savarin 1755–1826

Some have meat and cannot eat,
Some cannot eat that want it:
But we have meat and we can eat,
Sae let the Lord be thankit.
  Robert Burns 1759–96

Hunger is the best sauce in the world.
  Cervantes 1547–1616

It's a very odd thing—
As odd as can be—
That whatever Miss T eats
Turns into Miss T.
  Walter de la Mare 1873–1956

Gluttony is an emotional escape, a sign something is
eating us.
  Peter De Vries 1910–93

ANTHONY HOPKINS: I do wish we could chat longer, but
I'm having an old friend for dinner.
  Thomas Harris 1940– and **Ted Tally** 1952–

Eating

Time for a little something.
A. A. Milne 1882–1956

One should eat to live, and not live to eat.
Molière 1622–73

The appetite grows by eating.
François Rabelais c.1494–c.1553

Now good digestion wait on appetite,
And health on both!
William Shakespeare 1564–1616

We each day dig our graves with our teeth.
Samuel Smiles 1812–1904

He sows hurry and reaps indigestion.
Robert Louis Stevenson 1850–94

I'll fill hup the chinks wi' cheese.
R. S. Surtees 1805–64

MICHAEL DOUGLAS: Lunch? You gotta be kidding. Lunch is for wimps.
Stanley Weiser and **Oliver Stone** 1946–

Economics

There's no such thing as a free lunch.
Anonymous

There is enough in the world for everyone's need, but not enough for everyone's greed.
Frank Buchman 1878–1961

Capitalism is using its money; we socialists throw it away.
Fidel Castro 1927–

Inflation is the one form of taxation that can be imposed without legislation.
Milton Friedman 1912–

Trickle-down theory—the less than elegant metaphor that if one feeds the horse enough oats, some will pass through to the road for the sparrows.
J. K. Galbraith 1908–

Finance is, as it were, the stomach of the country, from which all the other organs take their tone.
W. E. Gladstone 1809–98

Rising unemployment and the recession have been the price that we've had to pay to get inflation down. [Labour shouts] That is a price well worth paying.
Norman Lamont 1942–

The green shoots of economic spring are appearing once again.
Norman Lamont 1942– , *often quoted as 'the green shoots of recovery'*

Every year the international finance system kills more people than the second world war. But at least Hitler was mad, you know.
Ken Livingstone 1945–

If the policy isn't hurting, it isn't working.
John Major 1943– , *on controlling inflation*

We have always known that heedless self-interest was bad morals; we know now that it is bad economics.
Franklin D. Roosevelt 1882–1945

Call a thing immoral or ugly, soul-destroying or a degradation of man, a peril to the peace of the world or to the well-being of future generations: as long as you have not shown it to be 'uneconomic' you have not really questioned its right to exist, grow, and prosper.
E. F. Schumacher 1911–77

It's a recession when your neighbour loses his job; it's a depression when you lose yours.
Harry S. Truman 1884–1972

Economics

What a country calls its vital economic interests are not the things which enable its citizens to live, but the things which enable it to make war.
Simone Weil 1909-43

Greed—for lack of a better word—is good. Greed is right. Greed works.
Stanley Weiser and **Oliver Stone** 1946-

It is not that pearls fetch a high price *because* men have dived for them; but on the contrary, men dive for them because they fetch a high price.
Richard Whately 1787-1863

Education ····➤ Examinations, Teaching

What one knows is, in youth, of little moment; they know enough who know how to learn.
Henry Brooks Adams 1838-1918

Give me a child for the first seven years, and you may do what you like with him afterwards.
Anonymous *attributed as a Jesuit maxim*

I said...how, and why, young children, were sooner allured by love, than driven by beating, to attain good learning.
Roger Ascham 1515-68

Studies serve for delight, for ornament, and for ability.
Francis Bacon 1561-1626

The dread of beatings! Dread of being late!
And, greatest dread of all, the dread of games!
John Betjeman 1906-84

Ask me my three main priorities for Government, and I tell you: education, education and education.
Tony Blair 1953-

And gladly wolde he lerne and gladly teche.
Geoffrey Chaucer c.1343–1400

That lyf so short, the craft so long to lerne.
Geoffrey Chaucer c.1343–1400

In education there should be no class distinction.
Confucius 551–479 BC

C-l-e-a-n, clean, verb active, to make bright, to scour.
W-i-n, win, d-e-r, der, winder, a casement. When the boy
knows this out of the book, he goes and does it.
Charles Dickens 1812–70

A University should be a place of light, of liberty, and of
learning.
Benjamin Disraeli 1804–81

Study as if you were to live for ever; live as if you were to
die tomorrow.
St Edmund of Abingdon c.1175–1240

You send your child to the schoolmaster, but 'tis the
schoolboys who educate him.
Ralph Waldo Emerson 1803–82

The proper study of mankind is books.
Aldous Huxley 1894–1963

A millionbillionwillion miles from home
Waiting for the bell to go. (To go where?)
Why are they all so big, other children?
So noisy?
Roger McGough 1937– , *of the first day at school*

If you educate a man you educate one person, but if you
educate a woman you educate a family.
Ruby Manikan

Universities never reform themselves; everyone knows
that.
Lord Melbourne 1779–1848

Education

My spelling is Wobbly. It's good spelling but it Wobbles, and the letters get in the wrong places.
A. A. Milne 1882–1956

Know then thyself, presume not God to scan;
The proper study of mankind is man.
Alexander Pope 1688–1744

I would I had bestowed that time in the tongues that I have in fencing, dancing, and bear-baiting. O! had I but followed the arts!
William Shakespeare 1564–1616

Education is what survives when what has been learned has been forgotten.
B. F. Skinner 1904–90

What does education often do? It makes a straight-cut ditch of a free, meandering brook.
Henry David Thoreau 1817–62

The best thing for being sad…is to learn something.
T. H. White 1906–64

Effort

We're number two. We try harder.
Anonymous *advertising slogan for Avis car rentals*

Madam, if a thing is possible, consider it done; the impossible? that will be done.
Charles Alexandre de Calonne 1734–1802

Now, *here*, you see, it takes all the running *you* can do, to keep in the same place. If you want to get somewhere else, you must run at least twice as fast as that!
Lewis Carroll 1832–98

Oh, how I am tired of the struggle!
Johann Wolfgang von Goethe 1749–1832

Between us and excellence, the gods have placed the sweat of our brows.
   Hesiod fl. c.700 BC

Parturient montes, nascetur ridiculus mus.

Mountains will go into labour, and a silly little mouse will be born.
   Horace 65–8 BC

I had done all that I could; and no man is well pleased to have his all neglected, be it ever so little.
   Samuel Johnson 1709–84

Our salvation is in striving to achieve what we know we'll never achieve.
   Ryszard Kapuscinski 1932–

Superhuman effort isn't worth a damn unless it achieves results.
   Ernest Shackleton 1874–1922

Things won are done; joy's soul lies in the doing.
   William Shakespeare 1564–1616

Elections ••••▸ Democracy

Elections are won by men and women chiefly because most people vote against somebody rather than for somebody.
   Franklin P. Adams 1881–1960

Vote early and vote often.
   Anonymous *US election slogan, already current by 1858*

The accursed power which stands on Privilege
(And goes with Women, and Champagne, and Bridge)
Broke—and Democracy resumed her reign:
(Which goes with Bridge, and Women and Champagne).
   Hilaire Belloc 1870–1953, *on an election*

Elections

An election is coming. Universal peace is declared, and the foxes have a sincere interest in prolonging the lives of the poultry.
George Eliot 1819–80

Hell, I never vote *for* anybody. I always vote *against*.
W. C. Fields 1880–1946

I always voted at my party's call,
And I never thought of thinking for myself at all.
W. S. Gilbert 1836–1911

To give victory to the right, not bloody bullets, but peaceful ballots only, are necessary.
Abraham Lincoln 1809–65, *usually quoted as 'The ballot is stronger than the bullet'*

If voting changed anything, they'd abolish it.
Ken Livingstone 1945–

One of the nuisances of the ballot is that when the oracle has spoken you never know what it means.
Lord Salisbury 1830–1903

It's not the voting that's democracy, it's the counting.
Tom Stoppard 1937–

Ending

It ain't over till it's over.
Yogi Berra 1925–

Better is the end of a thing than the beginning thereof.
Bible

Now this is not the end. It is not even the beginning of the end. But it is, perhaps, the end of the beginning.
Winston Churchill 1874–1965, *on the Battle of Egypt*

The party's over, it's time to call it a day.
Betty Comden 1919– and **Adolph Green** 1915–

Enemies

The opera ain't over 'til the fat lady sings.
Proverb

This is the way the world ends
Not with a bang but a whimper.
T. S. Eliot 1888–1965

In my end is my beginning.
Mary, Queen of Scots 1542–87

The rest is silence.
William Shakespeare 1564–1616

This is the beginning of the end.
Charles-Maurice de Talleyrand 1754–1838, *on the
announcement of Napoleon's Pyrrhic victory at Borodino, 1812*

They think it's all over—it is now.
Kenneth Wolstenholme 1920–2002

Enemies

He who has a thousand friends has not a friend to spare,
And he who has one enemy will meet him everywhere.
Ali ibn-Abi-Talib c.602–661

Not while I'm alive 'e ain't!
Ernest Bevin 1881–1951, *reply to the observation that Nye Bevan
was sometimes his own worst enemy*

Love your enemies, do good to them which hate you.
Bible

Fidel Castro is right. You do not quieten your enemy by
talking with him like a priest, but by burning him.
Nicolae Ceauşescu 1918–89

An injury is much sooner forgotten than an insult.
Lord Chesterfield 1694–1773

Enemies

You can calculate the worth of a man by the number of his enemies, and the importance of a work of art by the harm that is spoken of it.
   Gustave Flaubert 1821–80

Better to have him inside the tent pissing out, than outside pissing in.
   Lyndon Baines Johnson 1908–73, *of J. Edgar Hoover*

People wish their enemies dead—but I do not; I say give them the gout, give them the stone!
   Lady Mary Wortley Montagu 1689–1762

The enemies of my enemies are my friends.
   Proverb

There is nothing in the whole world so painful as feeling that one is not liked. It always seems to me that people who hate me must be suffering from some strange form of lunacy.
   Sei Shōnagon c.966–c.1013

England ····▶ Britain, London

I will not cease from mental fight,
Nor shall my sword sleep in my hand,
Till we have built Jerusalem,
In England's green and pleasant land.
   William Blake 1757–1827

Oh, to be in England
Now that April's there.
   Robert Browning 1812–89

The Thames is liquid history.
   John Burns 1858–1943, *to an American, who had compared the Thames disparagingly with the Mississippi*

England

In England there are sixty different religions, and only one sauce.
Francesco Caracciolo 1752–99

Mad dogs and Englishmen
Go out in the midday sun.
Noël Coward 1899–1973

What should they know of England who only England know?
Rudyard Kipling 1865–1936

Let not England forget her precedence of teaching nations how to live.
John Milton 1608–74

England is a nation of shopkeepers.
Napoleon I 1769–1821

England expects that every man will do his duty.
Horatio, Lord Nelson 1758–1805, *at the battle of Trafalgar*

There'll always be an England
While there's a country lane,
Wherever there's a cottage small
Beside a field of grain.
Ross Parker 1914–74 and **Hugh Charles** 1907–

Ask any man what nationality he would prefer to be, and ninety-nine out of a hundred will tell you that they would prefer to be Englishmen.
Cecil Rhodes 1853–1902

This royal throne of kings, this sceptred isle,
This earth of majesty, this seat of Mars...
This blessèd plot, this earth, this realm, this England.
William Shakespeare 1564–1616

England

Englishmen never will be slaves: they are free to do whatever the Government and public opinion allow them to do.
George Bernard Shaw 1856–1950

A soggy little island huffing and puffing to keep up with Western Europe.
John Updike 1932–

You never find an Englishman among the under-dogs—except in England, of course.
Evelyn Waugh 1903–66

The English country gentleman galloping after a fox—the unspeakable in full pursuit of the uneatable.
Oscar Wilde 1854–1900

We must be free or die, who speak the tongue
That Shakespeare spake; the faith and morals hold
Which Milton held.
William Wordsworth 1770–1850

The Environment ····▶ Country, Pollution

Come, friendly bombs, and fall on Slough!
It isn't fit for humans now,
There isn't grass to graze a cow.
Swarm over, Death!
John Betjeman 1906–84

Woe unto them that join house to house, that lay field to field, till there be no place.
Bible

And was Jerusalem builded here
Among these dark Satanic mills?
William Blake 1757–1827

O all ye Green Things upon the Earth, bless ye the Lord.
    Book of Common Prayer 1662

I do not know of any environmental group in any
country that does not view its government as an
adversary.
    Gro Harlem Brundtland 1939-

What would the world be, once bereft
Of wet and wildness? Let them be left,
O let them be left, wildness and wet;
Long live the weeds and the wilderness yet.
    Gerard Manley Hopkins 1844-89

I am I plus my surroundings and if I do not preserve the
latter, I do not preserve myself.
    José Ortega y Gasset 1883-1955

The parks are the lungs of London.
    William Pitt 1708-78

Consult the genius of the place in all.
    Alexander Pope 1688-1744

Small is beautiful.
    E. F. Schumacher 1911-77

If I were a Brazilian without land or money or the means
to feed my children, I would be burning the rain forest
too.
    Sting 1951-

Envy and Jealousy

Thou shalt not covet thy neighbour's house, thou shalt
not covet thy neighbour's wife.
    Bible

Envy and Jealousy

Jealousy is no more than feeling alone against smiling enemies.
Elizabeth Bowen 1899–1973

The danger chiefly lies in acting well;
No crime's so great as daring to excel.
Charles Churchill 1731–64

Thou shalt not covet; but tradition
Approves all forms of competition.
Arthur Hugh Clough 1819–61

Some folks rail against other folks, because other folks have what some folks would be glad of.
Henry Fielding 1707–54

To jealousy, nothing is more frightful than laughter.
Françoise Sagan 1935–

O! beware, my lord, of jealousy;
It is the green-eyed monster which doth mock
The meat it feeds on.
William Shakespeare 1564–1616

Equality ····▶ Human Rights

He maketh his sun to rise on the evil and on the good, and sendeth rain on the just and on the unjust.
Bible

A man's a man for a' that.
Robert Burns 1759–96

When every one is somebodee,
Then no one's anybody.
W. S. Gilbert 1836–1911

Your levellers wish to level *down* as far as themselves; but they cannot bear levelling *up* to themselves.
Samuel Johnson 1709–84

I have a dream that one day on the red hills of Georgia the sons of former slaves and the sons of former slave owners will be able to sit down together at the table of brotherhood.
    Martin Luther King 1929–68

All animals are equal but some animals are more equal than others.
    George Orwell 1903–50

Hath not a Jew eyes? hath not a Jew hands, organs, dimensions, senses, affections, passions?...If you prick us, do we not bleed? if you tickle us, do we not laugh? if you poison us, do we not die? and if you wrong us, shall we not revenge?
    William Shakespeare 1564–1616

Make all men equal today, and God has so created them that they shall all be unequal tomorrow.
    Anthony Trollope 1815–82

Europe

Qui parle Europe a tort, notion géographique.
Whoever speaks of Europe is wrong, [it is] a geographical concept.
    Otto von Bismarck 1815–98

Fog in Channel—Continent isolated.
    Russell Brockbank 1913– , *newspaper placard in cartoon*

The age of chivalry is gone.—That of sophisters, economists, and calculators, has succeeded; and the glory of Europe is extinguished for ever.
    Edmund Burke 1729–97, *on the French Revolution*

Europe

You ask if they were happy. This is not a characteristic of a European. To be contented—that's for the cows.
Coco Chanel 1883–1971

From Stettin in the Baltic to Trieste in the Adriatic an iron curtain has descended across the Continent.
Winston Churchill 1874–1965

Without Britain Europe would remain only a torso.
Ludwig Erhard 1897–1977

It means the end of a thousand years of history.
Hugh Gaitskell 1906–63, *on a European federation*

The policy of European integration is in reality a question of war and peace in the 21st century.
Helmut Kohl 1930–

I want the whole of Europe to have one currency; it will make trading much easier.
Napoleon I 1769–1821

Roll up that map; it will not be wanted these ten years.
William Pitt 1759–1806, *of a map of Europe, on hearing of Napoleon's victory at Austerlitz*

You're thinking of Europe as Germany and France. I don't. I think that's old Europe. If you look at the entire Nato Europe today, the centre of gravity is shifting to the east.
Donald Rumsfeld 1932–

Better fifty years of Europe than a cycle of Cathay.
Alfred, Lord Tennyson 1809–92

In my lifetime all our problems have come from mainland Europe and all the solutions have come from the English-speaking nations of the world.
Margaret Thatcher 1925–

Evil ····▶ Goodness

The fearsome, word-and-thought-defying *banality of evil*.
Hannah Arendt 1906-75

I and the public know
What all schoolchildren learn,
Those to whom evil is done
Do evil in return.
W. H. Auden 1907-73

With love for mankind and hatred of sins.
St Augustine of Hippo AD 354-430, *often quoted as 'Love the sinner but hate the sin'*

There is no peace, saith the Lord, unto the wicked.
Bible

It is necessary only for the good man to do nothing for evil to triumph.
Edmund Burke 1729-97

The face of 'evil' is always the face of total need.
William S. Burroughs 1914-97

As soon as men decide that all means are permitted to fight an evil, then their good becomes indistinguishable from the evil that they set out to destroy.
Christopher Dawson 1889-1970

Vice came in always at the door of necessity, not at the door of inclination.
Daniel Defoe 1660-1731

What we call evil is simply ignorance bumping its head in the dark.
Henry Ford 1863-1947

Evil

But if he does really think that there is no distinction between virtue and vice, why, Sir, when he leaves our houses, let us count our spoons.
Samuel Johnson 1709–84

No one ever suddenly became depraved.
Juvenal AD c.60–c.130

Farewell remorse! All good to me is lost;
Evil, be thou my good.
John Milton 1608–74

An orgy looks particularly alluring seen through the mists of righteous indignation.
Malcolm Muggeridge 1903–90

      By the pricking of my thumbs,
Something wicked this way comes.
William Shakespeare 1564–1616

Examinations

Examinations are formidable even to the best prepared, for the greatest fool may ask more than the wisest man can answer.
Charles Caleb Colton c.1780–1832

I evidently knew more about economics than my examiners.
John Maynard Keynes 1883–1946, *explaining why he performed badly in the Civil Service examinations*

These are not statistics, these are people's futures.
Estelle Morris 1952– , *on queries over A-level grades*

If we have to have an exam at 11, let us make it one for humour, sincerity, imagination, character—and where is the examiner who could test such qualities.
A. S. Neill 1883–1973

In examinations those who do not wish to know ask questions of those who cannot tell.
  Walter Raleigh 1861–1922

Do not on any account attempt to write on both sides of the paper at once.
  W. C. Sellar 1898–1951 and **R. J. Yeatman** 1898–1968

Had silicon been a gas, I would have been a major-general by now.
  James McNeill Whistler 1834–1903, *having been found 'deficient in chemistry' in a West Point examination*

Exercise ····▶ Health

I sometimes think that running has given me a glimpse of the greatest freedom a man can ever know, because it results in the simultaneous liberation of both body and mind.
  Roger Bannister 1929–

If you walk hard enough, you probably don't need any other God.
  Bruce Chatwin 1940–89

The wise, for cure, on exercise depend;
God never made his work for man to mend.
  John Dryden 1631–1700

Exercise is the yuppie version of bulimia.
  Barbara Ehrenreich 1941–

Exercise is bunk. If you are healthy, you don't need it: if you are sick you shouldn't take it.
  Henry Ford 1863–1947

The sovereign invigorator of the body is exercise, and of all the exercises, walking is best.
  Thomas Jefferson 1743–1826

Exercise

The only exercise I take is walking behind the coffins of
friends who took exercise.
Peter O'Toole 1932–

Avoid running at all times.
Leroy ('Satchel') Paige 1906–82

Those who do not find time for exercise will have to find
time for illness.
Proverb

Experience

All experience is an arch to build upon.
Henry Brooks Adams 1838–1918

You should make a point of trying every experience once,
excepting incest and folk-dancing.
Anonymous

Experience isn't interesting till it begins to repeat itself—
in fact, till it does that, it hardly *is* experience.
Elizabeth Bowen 1899–1973

Experience is the child of Thought, and Thought is the
child of Action. We cannot learn men from books.
Benjamin Disraeli 1804–81

The courtiers who surround him [Louis XVIII] have
forgotten nothing and learnt nothing.
General Dumouriez 1739–1823

We had the experience but missed the meaning.
T. S. Eliot 1888–1965

Experience is not what happens to a man; it is what a
man does with what happens to him.
Aldous Huxley 1894–1963

We took risks, we knew we took them; things have come out against us, and therefore we have no cause for complaint.
Robert Falcon Scott 1868–1912

Education is when you read the fine print; experience is what you get when you don't.
Pete Seeger 1919–

Experto credite.
Trust one who has gone through it.
Virgil 70–19 BC

Experience is the name everyone gives to their mistakes.
Oscar Wilde 1854–1900

Failure ····▸ Success

History to the defeated
May say Alas but cannot help or pardon.
W. H. Auden 1907–73

Ever tried. Ever failed. No matter. Try again. Fail again. Fail better.
Samuel Beckett 1906–89

She knows there's no success like failure
And that failure's no success at all.
Bob Dylan 1941–

Vae victis.
Down with the defeated!
Livy 59 BC–AD 17

There is only one step from the sublime to the ridiculous.
Napoleon I 1769–1821

Failure

Failure is human, after all, and you grow up by making mistakes. I've made a ton of them, but as long as I keep on failing better, I don't mind.
Joely Richardson 1965-

We fail!
But screw your courage to the sticking-place,
And we'll not fail.
William Shakespeare 1564–1616

Fame

Seven wealthy towns contend for HOMER dead
Through which the living HOMER begged his bread.
Anonymous

Fame is like a river, that beareth up things light and swollen, and drowns things weighty and solid.
Francis Bacon 1561–1626

There's no such thing as bad publicity except your own obituary.
Brendan Behan 1923-64

A prophet is not without honour, save in his own country, and in his own house.
Bible

I awoke one morning and found myself famous.
Lord Byron 1788–1824

The deed is all, the glory nothing.
Johann Wolfgang von Goethe 1749–1832

Far from the madding crowd's ignoble strife,
Their sober wishes never learned to stray;
Along the cool sequestered vale of life
They kept the noiseless tenor of their way.
Thomas Gray 1716–71

Exegi monumentum aere perennius.
I have erected a monument more lasting than bronze.
> **Horace** 65–8 BC

Kids want to be famous. They don't want to be good at anything any more.
> **Ronan Keating** 1977–

The best fame is a writer's fame: it's enough to get a table at a good restaurant, but not enough that you get interrupted when you eat.
> **Fran Lebowitz** 1946–

We're more popular than Jesus now; I don't know which will go first—rock 'n' roll or Christianity.
> **John Lennon** 1940–80, *of the Beatles*

Fame is the spur that the clear spirit doth raise
(That last infirmity of noble mind)
To scorn delights, and live laborious days.
> **John Milton** 1608–74

Famous men have the whole earth as their memorial.
> **Pericles** c.495–429 BC

So long as men can breathe, or eyes can see,
So long lives this, and this gives life to thee.
> **William Shakespeare** 1564–1616

You always hide just in the middle of the limelight.
> **George Bernard Shaw** 1856–1950, *to T. E. Lawrence, who had complained of Press attention*

Celebrity is a mask that eats into the face.
> **John Updike** 1932–

In the future everybody will be world famous for fifteen minutes.
> **Andy Warhol** 1927–87

The Family ····➤ Children, Parents

He that hath wife and children hath given hostages to
fortune; for they are impediments to great enterprises,
either of virtue or mischief.
    Francis Bacon 1561–1626

Thy wife shall be as the fruitful vine: upon the walls of
thine house.
Thy children like the olive-branches: round about thy
table.
    Bible

We begin our public affections in our families. No cold
relation is a zealous citizen.
    Edmund Burke 1729–97

[It is] time to turn our attention to pressing challenges
like…how to make American families more like the
Waltons and a little bit less like the Simpsons.
    George Bush 1924–

Believe me, family solidarity is after all the only good
thing. I have been deprived of it, so I know.
    Marie Curie 1867–1934

Men love women, women love children; children love
hamsters—it's quite hopeless.
    Alice Thomas Ellis 1932–

The truth is that it is not the sins of the fathers that
descend unto the third generation, but the sorrows of the
mothers.
    Marilyn French 1929–

One would be in less danger
From the wiles of the stranger
If one's own kin and kith
Were more fun to be with.
    Ogden Nash 1902–71

Human relationships don't belong to engineering, mathematics, chess, which offer problems that can be perfectly solved. Human relationships grow, like trees.
J. B. Priestley 1894–1984

I want to spend more time with my family, but I'm not sure they want to spend more time with me.
Esther Rantzen 1940–

A little more than kin, and less than kind.
William Shakespeare 1564–1616

If a man's character is to be abused, say what you will, there's nobody like a relation to do the business.
William Makepeace Thackeray 1811–63

All happy families resemble one another, but each unhappy family is unhappy in its own way.
Leo Tolstoy 1828–1910

It is no use telling me that there are bad aunts and good aunts. At the core, they are all alike. Sooner or later, out pops the cloven hoof.
P. G. Wodehouse 1881–1975

Fashion

A little of what you call frippery is very necessary towards looking like the rest of the world.
Abigail Adams 1744–1818

Fashion isn't made to be canned. Fashion in cans becomes quickly obsolete.
Coco Chanel 1883–1971

One had as good be out of the world, as out of the fashion.
Colley Cibber 1671–1757

Fashion

Sometimes fashion moves from the moment to the moment to the moment. But where is the integrity in design?
Donna Karan 1948-

Haute Couture should be fun, foolish and almost unwearable.
Christian Lacroix 1951-

Hip is the sophistication of the wise primitive in a giant jungle.
Norman Mailer 1923-

Fashion is more usually a gentle progression of revisited ideas.
Bruce Oldfield 1950-

You cannot be both fashionable and first-rate.
Logan Pearsall Smith 1865-1946

I like to dress egos. If you haven't got an ego today, you can forget it.
Gianni Versace 1949-96

It is charming to totter into vogue.
Horace Walpole 1717-97

Fate

Must it be? It must be.
Ludwig van Beethoven 1770-1827

Canst thou bind the sweet influences of Pleiades, or loose the bands of Orion?
Bible

Fate is not an eagle, it creeps like a rat.
Elizabeth Bowen 1899-1973

Nothing have I found stronger than Necessity.
Euripides c.485–c.406 BC

There once was an old man who said, 'Damn!
It is borne in upon me I am
An engine that moves
In determinate grooves,
I'm not even a bus, I'm a tram.'
Maurice Evan Hare 1886–1967

What we call fate does not come into us from the
outside, but emerges from us.
Rainer Maria Rilke 1875–1926

If it be now, 'tis not to come; if it be not to come, it will
be now; if it be not now, yet it will come: the readiness is
all.
William Shakespeare 1564–1616

We are merely the stars' tennis-balls, struck and bandied
Which way please them.
John Webster c.1580–c.1625

Every bullet has its billet.
William III 1650–1702

Fathers

I'm a father, that's what matters most. Nothing matters
more.
Gordon Brown 1951–

There must be many fathers around the country who
have experienced the cruellest, most crushing rejection of
all: their children have ended up supporting the wrong
team.
Nick Hornby 1957–

Fathers

If I'm more of an influence to your son as a rapper than you are as a father...you got to look at yourself as a parent.
   Ice Cube 1970-

My father was a management genius. But what I really wanted was a dad.
   Michael Jackson 1958-

After God comes my Papa—that was ever the motto, the axiom of my childhood and I cling to it still!
   Wolfgang Amadeus Mozart 1756-91

Being a father
Is quite a bother,
But I like it, rather.
   Ogden Nash 1902-71

I can do one of two things. I can be president of the United States or I can control Alice. I cannot possibly do both.
   Theodore Roosevelt 1858-1919

The fundamental defect of fathers, in our competitive society, is that they want their children to be a credit to them.
   Bertrand Russell 1872-1970

It doesn't matter who my father was; it matters who I remember he was.
   Anne Sexton 1928-74

It is a wise father that knows his own child.
   William Shakespeare 1564-1616

Fatherhood is a mirror in which we catch glimpses of ourselves as we really are.
   Hugo Williams 1942-

Fear

We must travel in the direction of our fear.
John Berryman 1914-72

No passion so effectually robs the mind of all its powers
of acting and reasoning as fear.
Edmund Burke 1729-97

If hopes were dupes, fears may be liars.
Arthur Hugh Clough 1819-61

Be afraid. Be very afraid.
David Cronenberg 1943-

Fear is my main point of reference. Causing fear is what
constitutes evil.
Marguerite Duras 1914-96

I will show you fear in a handful of dust.
T. S. Eliot 1888-1965

There is no terror in a bang, only in the anticipation
of it.
Alfred Hitchcock 1899-1980

Terror...often arises from a pervasive sense of
disestablishment; that things are in the unmaking.
Stephen King 1947-

The only thing we have to fear is fear itself.
Franklin D. Roosevelt 1882-1945

Only the unknown frightens men. But once a man has
faced the unknown, that terror becomes known.
Antoine de Saint-Exupéry 1900-44

Present fears
Are less than horrible imaginings.
William Shakespeare 1564-1616

Fear

In time we hate that which we often fear.
William Shakespeare 1564–1616

Our deepest fear is not that we are inadequate. Our deepest fear is that we are powerful beyond measure. It is our light, not our darkness, that most frightens us.
Marianne Williamson 1953–

Festivals

Hogmanay, like all festivals, being but a bank from which we can only draw what we put in.
J. M. Barrie 1860–1937

Never ask the children to tell the class what they did for Easter or Christmas or Confirmation or St Patrick's Day…Nothing points up the inequality of people's lives more starkly than asking innocent children to tell you how they spent what was meant to be a festival.
Maeve Binchy 1940–

Hurrah for the fun!
Is the pudding done?
Hurrah for the pumpkin pie!
Lydia Maria Child 1802–80

The true essentials of a feast are only fun and feed.
Oliver Wendell Holmes 1809–94

The holiest of all holidays are those
Kept by ourselves in silence and apart;
The secret anniversaries of the heart.
Henry Wadsworth Longfellow 1807–82

Time has no divisions to mark its passage, there is never a thunderstorm or blare of trumpets to announce the beginning of a new month or year. Even when a new

century begins it is only we mortals who ring bells and
fire off pistols.
    Thomas Mann 1875–1955

Tonight's December thirty-first,
Something is about to burst…
Hark, it's midnight, children dear.
Duck! Here comes another year!
    Ogden Nash 1902–71

Ring out the old, ring in the new,
Ring, happy bells, across the snow:
The year is going, let him go;
Ring out the false, ring in the true.
    Alfred, Lord Tennyson 1809–92

April 1. This is the day upon which we are reminded of
what we are on the other three hundred and sixty-four.
    Mark Twain 1835–1910

Seasons pursuing each other the indescribable
crowd is gathered, it is the fourth of Seventh-
month, (what salutes of cannon and small-arms!)
    Walt Whitman 1819–92

Fishing

If fishing is a religion, fly fishing is high church.
    Tom Brokaw 1940–

I love fishing. It's like transcendental meditation with a
punch-line.
    Billy Connolly 1942–

Fishing is unquestionably a form of madness but, happily,
for the once-bitten there is no cure.
    Lord Home 1903–95

Fishing

Fly fishing may be a very pleasant amusement; but angling or float fishing I can only compare to a stick and a string, with a worm at one end and a fool at the other.
Samuel Johnson 1709–84

As no man is born an artist, so no man is born an angler.
Izaak Walton 1593–1683

Flight

Would you *mind* if I flew the Atlantic?
Amelia Earhart 1898–1937, *to her husband George Putnam*

Had I been a man I might have explored the Poles, or climbed Mount Everest, but as it was, my spirit found outlet in the air.
Amy Johnson 1903–41

I feel about airplanes the way I feel about diets. It seems to me that they are wonderful things for other people to go on.
Jean Kerr 1923–2003

I was astonished at the effect my successful landing in France had on the nations of the world. To me, it was like a match lighting a bonfire.
Charles Lindbergh 1902–74

Oh! I have slipped the surly bonds of earth
And danced the skies on laughter-silvered wings;…
And, while with silent lifting mind I've trod
The high, untrespassed sanctity of space,
Put out my hand and touched the face of God.
John Gillespie Magee 1922–41

I did not fully understand the dread term 'terminal illness' until I saw Heathrow for myself.
Dennis Potter 1935–94

There are only two emotions in a plane: boredom and terror.
   Orson Welles 1915–85

Flowers

Unkempt about those hedges blows
An English unofficial rose.
   Rupert Brooke 1887–1915

Flowers…are a proud assertion that a ray of beauty
outvalues all the utilities of the world.
   Ralph Waldo Emerson 1803–82

I sometimes think that never blows so red
The rose as where some buried Caesar bled.
   Edward Fitzgerald 1809–83

Hey, buds below, up is where to grow,
Up with which below can't compare with.
Hurry! It's lovely up here! *Hurry*!
   Alan Jay Lerner 1918–86

The rose of all the world is not for me.
I want for my part
Only the little white rose of Scotland
That smells sharp and sweet—and breaks the heart.
   Hugh MacDiarmid 1892–1978

Flowers. Those free gifts laid out
on Mother Nature's perfume counter.
   Roger McGough 1937–

People from a planet without flowers would think we
must be mad with joy the whole time to have such things
about us.
   Iris Murdoch 1919–99

Flowers

Daffodils,
That come before the swallow dares, and take
The winds of March with beauty.
William Shakespeare 1564–1616

I wandered lonely as a cloud
That floats on high o'er vales and hills,
When all at once I saw a crowd,
A host, of golden daffodils;
Beside the lake, beneath the trees,
Fluttering and dancing in the breeze.
William Wordsworth 1770–1850

To me the meanest flower that blows can give
Thoughts that do often lie too deep for tears.
William Wordsworth 1770–1850

Food ····➤ Cookery, Eating

Shake and shake
The catsup bottle.
None will come,
And then a lot'll.
Richard Armour 1906–89

I'm President of the United States, and I'm not going to
eat any more broccoli!
George Bush 1924–

Doubtless God could have made a better berry, but
doubtless God never did.
William Butler 1535–1618, *on the strawberry*

Take away that pudding—it has no theme.
Winston Churchill 1874–1965

Please, sir, I want some more.
Charles Dickens 1812–70

Cheese, milk's leap toward immortality.
  Clifton Fadiman 1904-

A cucumber should be well sliced, and dressed with pepper and vinegar, and then thrown out, as good for nothing.
  Samuel Johnson 1709-84

All you have to do is eat breakfast three times a day.
  W. Somerset Maugham *to a friend who had said that he hated English food*

It is said that the effect of eating too much lettuce is 'soporific'.
  Beatrix Potter 1866-1943

I am a great eater of beef, and I believe that does harm to my wit.
  William Shakespeare 1564-1616

A hen's egg is, quite simply, a work of art, a masterpiece of design and construction with, it has to be said, brilliant packaging.
  Delia Smith

Serenely full, the epicure would say,
Fate cannot harm me, I have dined to-day.
  Sydney Smith 1771-1845

Many's the long night I've dreamed of cheese—toasted, mostly.
  Robert Louis Stevenson 1850-94

Cauliflower is nothing but cabbage with a college education.
  Mark Twain 1835-1910

I discovered that dinners follow the order of creation—fish first, then entrées, then joints, lastly the apple as dessert. The soup is chaos.
  Sylvia Townsend Warner 1893-1978

Food

What moistens the lip and what brightens the eye?
What calls back the past, like the rich pumpkin pie?
    John Greenleaf Whittier 1807-92

Foolishness

The world is full of fools, and he who would not see it
should live alone and smash his mirror.
    Anonymous

There's a sucker born every minute.
    Phineas T. Barnum 1810-91

Answer not a fool according to his folly, lest thou also be
like unto him.
Answer a fool according to his folly, lest he be wise in his
own conceit.
    Bible

For ye suffer fools gladly, seeing ye yourselves are wise.
    Bible

Never give a sucker an even break.
    W. C. Fields 1880-1946

Misce stultitiam consiliis brevem:
Dulce est desipere in loco.

Mix a little foolishness with your prudence: it's good to
    be silly at the right moment.
    Horace 65-8 BC

A knowledgeable fool is a greater fool than an ignorant
fool.
    Molière 1622-73

Fools rush in where angels fear to tread.
    Alexander Pope 1688-1744

The follies which a man regrets most, in his life, are those which he didn't commit when he had the opportunity.
Helen Rowland 1875–1950

The ultimate result of shielding men from the effects of folly, is to fill the world with fools.
Herbert Spencer 1820–1903

Let us be thankful for the fools. But for them the rest of us could not succeed.
Mark Twain 1835–1910

Be wise with speed;
A fool at forty is a fool indeed.
Edward Young 1683–1765

Football

The great fallacy is that the game is first and last about winning. It is nothing of the kind. The game is about glory, it is about doing things in style and with a flourish, about going out and beating the lot, not waiting for them to die of boredom.
Danny Blanchflower 1926–93

Football, wherein is nothing but beastly fury, and extreme violence, whereof proceedeth hurt, and consequently rancour and malice do remain with them that be wounded.
Thomas Elyot 1499–1546

Football is an art more central to our culture than anything the Arts Council deigns to recognize.
Germaine Greer 1939–

What makes a sane and rational person subject himself to such humiliation? Why on earth does anyone want to become a football referee?
Roy Hattersley 1932–

Football

The natural state of the football fan is bitter
disappointment, no matter what the score.
Nick Hornby 1957–

Oh, he's football crazy, he's football mad
And the football it has robbed him o' the wee bit sense
he had.
And it would take a dozen skivvies, his clothes to wash
and scrub,
Since our Jock became a member of that terrible football
club.
Jimmie McGregor 1932–

The goal was scored a little bit by the hand of God,
another bit by head of Maradona.
Diego Maradona 1960– , *on his controversial goal against
England in the 1986 World Cup*

Football? It's the beautiful game.
Pelé 1940–

To say that these men paid their shillings to watch
twenty-two hirelings kick a ball is merely to say that a
violin is wood and catgut, that *Hamlet* is so much paper
and ink. For a shilling the Bruddersford United AFC
offered you Conflict and Art.
J. B. Priestley 1894–1984

Some people think football is a matter of life and
death…I can assure them it is much more serious than
that.
Bill Shankly 1914–81

Football and cookery are the two most important subjects
in the country.
Delia Smith

Forgiveness

Her sins, which are many, are forgiven; for she loved much.
Bible

I shall be an autocrat: that's my trade. And the good Lord will forgive me: that's his.
Empress Catherine the Great 1729–96

After such knowledge, what forgiveness?
T. S. Eliot 1888–1965

God may pardon you, but I never can.
Elizabeth I 1533–1603

Every one says forgiveness is a lovely idea, until they have something to forgive.
C. S. Lewis 1898–1963

True reconciliation does not consist in merely forgetting the past.
Nelson Mandela 1918–

We read that we ought to forgive our enemies; but we do not read that we ought to forgive our friends.
Cosimo de' Medici 1389–1464

To err is human; to forgive, divine.
Alexander Pope 1688–1744

Youth, which is forgiven everything, forgives itself nothing: age, which forgives itself everything, is forgiven nothing.
George Bernard Shaw 1856–1950

The stupid neither forgive nor forget; the naïve forgive and forget; the wise forgive but do not forget.
Thomas Szasz 1920–

France

Everything ends this way in France. Weddings, christenings, duels, burials, swindlings, affairs of state—everything is a pretext for a good dinner.
Jean Anouilh 1910–87

France was long a despotism tempered by epigrams.
Thomas Carlyle 1795–1881

How can you govern a country which has 246 varieties of cheese?
Charles de Gaulle 1890–1970

France, mère des arts, des armes et des lois.
France, mother of arts, of warfare, and of laws.
Joachim Du Bellay 1522–60

Vive la différence, mais vive l'entente cordiale.
Long live the difference, but long live the Entente Cordiale.
Elizabeth II 1926–

The French soul is stronger than the French mind, and Voltaire shatters against Joan of Arc.
Victor Hugo 1802–85

Ce qui n'est pas clair n'est pas français.
What is not clear is not French.
Antoine de Rivarol 1753–1801

That sweet enemy, France.
Philip Sidney 1554–86

They order, said I, this matter better in France.
Laurence Sterne 1713–68

If the French noblesse had been capable of playing cricket with their peasants, their chateaux would never have been burnt.

G. M. Trevelyan 1876–1962

Oh, the comfort—the inexpressible comfort of feeling safe with a person, having neither to weigh thoughts, nor measure words, but pouring them all out, just as they are, chaff and grain together; knowing that a faithful hand will take and sift them—keep what is worth keeping—and with the breath of kindness blow the rest away.

Anonymous *often attributed to George Eliot or Dinah Mulock Craik*

One soul inhabiting two bodies.

Aristotle 384–322 BC, *definition of a friend*

A crowd is not company, and faces are but a gallery of pictures, and talk but a tinkling cymbal, where there is no love.

Francis Bacon 1561–1626

Champagne for my real friends, real pain for my sham friends.

Francis Bacon 1909–92

Friendship is one of the most tangible things in a world which offers fewer and fewer supports.

Kenneth Branagh 1960–

Love is like the wild rose-briar;
Friendship like the holly-tree:
The holly is dark when the rose-briar blooms,
But which will bloom most constantly?

Emily Brontë 1818–48

Friendship

There is no man so friendless but what he can find a
friend sincere enough to tell him disagreeable truths.
Edward Bulwer-Lytton 1803–73

Should auld acquaintance be forgot
And never brought to mind?
Robert Burns 1759–96

Give me the avowed, erect and manly foe;
Firm I can meet, perhaps return the blow;
But of all plagues, good Heaven, thy wrath can send,
Save me, oh, save me, from the candid friend.
George Canning 1770–1827

A woman can become a man's friend only in the
following stages—first an acquaintance, next a mistress,
and only then a friend.
Anton Chekhov 1860–1904

The only reward of virtue is virtue; the only way to have
a friend is to be one.
Ralph Waldo Emerson 1803–82

HUMPHREY BOGART: Louis, I think this is the beginning
of a beautiful friendship.
Julius J. Epstein 1909–2001 et al.

If a man does not make new acquaintance as he advances
through life, he will soon find himself left alone. A man,
Sir, should keep his friendship in constant repair.
Samuel Johnson 1709–84

Oh I get by with a little help from my friends,
Mm, I get high with a little help from my friends.
John Lennon 1940–80 and **Paul McCartney** 1942–

To like and dislike the same things, that is indeed true
friendship.
Sallust 86–35 BC

Friendship is constant in all other things
Save in the office and affairs of love.
William Shakespeare 1564–1616

I do not believe that friends are necessarily the people
you like best, they are merely the people who got there
first.
Peter Ustinov 1921–2004

The Future

'We are always doing', says he, 'something for Posterity,
but I would fain see Posterity do something for us.'
Joseph Addison 1672–1719

Some of the jam we thought was for tomorrow, we've
already eaten.
Tony Benn 1925–

The future ain't what it used to be.
Yogi Berra 1925–

Predictions can be very difficult—especially about the
future.
Niels Bohr 1885–1962

You can never plan the future by the past.
Edmund Burke 1729–97

The empires of the future are the empires of the mind.
Winston Churchill 1874–1965

I never think of the future. It comes soon enough.
Albert Einstein 1879–1955

You cannot fight against the future. Time is on our side.
W. E. Gladstone 1809–98

The Future

We have trained them [men] to think of the Future as a promised land which favoured heroes attain—not as something which everyone reaches at the rate of sixty minutes an hour, whatever he does, whoever he is.
C. S. Lewis 1898–1963

If you want a picture of the future, imagine a boot stamping on a human face—for ever.
George Orwell 1903–50

Lord! we know what we are, but know not what we may be.
William Shakespeare 1564–1616

Gardens

I value my garden more for being full of blackbirds than of cherries, and very frankly give them fruit for their songs.
Joseph Addison 1672–1719

Nothing is more pleasant to the eye than green grass kept finely shorn.
Francis Bacon 1561–1626

And the Lord God planted a garden eastward in Eden.
Bible

A garden is a lovesome thing, God wot!
T. E. Brown 1830–97

What is a weed? A plant whose virtues have not been discovered.
Ralph Waldo Emerson 1803–82

He that plants trees loves others beside himself.
Thomas Fuller 1654–1734

Sowe Carrets in your Gardens, and humbly praise God
for them, as for a singular and great blessing.
  Richard Gardiner b. c.1533

The kiss of the sun for pardon,
The song of the birds for mirth,
One is nearer God's Heart in a garden
Than anywhere else on earth.
  Dorothy Frances Gurney 1858–1932

But though an old man, I am but a young gardener.
  Thomas Jefferson 1743–1826

Our England is a garden, and such gardens are not made
By singing:—'Oh, how beautiful!' and sitting in the shade,
While better men than we go out and start their working
 lives
At grubbing weeds from gravel paths with broken dinner-
 knives.
  Rudyard Kipling 1865–1936

A garden was the primitive prison till man with
Promethean felicity and boldness luckily sinned himself
out of it.
  Charles Lamb 1775–1834

Annihilating all that's made
To a green thought in a green shade.
  Andrew Marvell 1621–78

There can be no other occupation like gardening in
which, if you were to creep behind someone at their
work, you would find them smiling.
  Mirabel Osler

Come into the garden, Maud,
I am here at the gate alone.
  Alfred, Lord Tennyson 1809–92

The Generation Gap ····▶ Youth

Each year brings new problems of Form and Content,
new foes to tug with: at Twenty I tried to
vex my elders, past Sixty it's the young whom
I hope to bother.
    W. H. Auden 1907-73

Come mothers and fathers,
Throughout the land
And don't criticize
What you can't understand.
    Bob Dylan 1941-

Si jeunesse savait; si vieillesse pouvait.
If youth knew; if age could.
    Henri Estienne 1531-98

Praise youth for pulling things apart,
Toppling the idols, breaking leases;
Then from the upset apple-cart
Praise oldsters picking up the pieces.
    Phyllis McGinley 1905-78

Every generation revolts against its fathers and makes
friends with its grandfathers.
    Lewis Mumford 1895-1982

Crabbed age and youth cannot live together:
Youth is full of pleasance, age is full of care.
    William Shakespeare 1564-1616

It's all that the young can do for the old, to shock them
and keep them up to date.
    George Bernard Shaw 1856-1950

Hope I die before I get old.
    Pete Townshend 1945-

When I was a boy of 14, my father was so ignorant I could hardly stand to have the old man around. But when I got to be 21, I was astonished at how much the old man had learned in seven years.
Mark Twain 1835–1910

Genius

Genius is only a greater aptitude for patience.
Comte de Buffon 1707–88

Everybody has talent at twenty-five. The difficult thing is to have it at fifty.
Edgar Degas 1834–1917

Mediocrity knows nothing higher than itself, but talent instantly recognizes genius.
Arthur Conan Doyle 1859–1930

Great wits are sure to madness near allied,
And thin partitions do their bounds divide.
John Dryden 1631–1700

Genius is one per cent inspiration, ninety-nine per cent perspiration.
Thomas Alva Edison 1847–1931

Little minds are interested in the extraordinary; great minds in the commonplace.
Elbert Hubbard 1859–1915

The true genius is a mind of large general powers, accidentally determined to some particular direction.
Samuel Johnson 1709–84

Genius does what it must, and Talent does what it can.
Owen Meredith 1831–91

Genius

Every positive value has its price in negative terms…The genius of Einstein leads to Hiroshima.
Pablo Picasso 1881–1973

When a true genius appears in the world, you may know him by this sign, that the dunces are all in confederacy against him.
Jonathan Swift 1667–1745

I have nothing to declare except my genius.
Oscar Wilde 1854–1900, *at the New York Custom House*

Gifts ····> Charity

Surprises are foolish things. The pleasure is not enhanced, and the inconvenience is often considerable.
Jane Austen 1775–1817

It is more blessed to give than to receive.
Bible

They gave it me,—for an un-birthday present.
Lewis Carroll 1832–98

One must be poor to know the luxury of giving.
George Eliot 1819–80

A gift though small is welcome.
Homer 8th century BC

I know it's not much, but it's the best I can do,
My gift is my song and this one's for you.
Elton John 1947– and **Bernie Taupin** 1950–

Presents, I often say, endear Absents.
Charles Lamb 1775–1834

Why is it no one ever sent me yet
One perfect limousine, do you suppose?
Ah no, it's always just my luck to get

One perfect rose.
Dorothy Parker 1893–1967

I am not in the giving vein to-day.
William Shakespeare 1564–1616

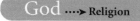

God ····▸ Religion

The nature of God is a circle of which the centre is everywhere and the circumference is nowhere.
Anonymous

In the beginning was the Word, and the Word was with God, and the Word was God.
Bible

He that loveth not knoweth not God; for God is love.
Bible

When men stop believing in God they don't believe in nothing; they believe in anything.
G. K. Chesterton 1874–1936

God moves in a mysterious way
His wonders to perform;
He plants his footsteps in the sea,
And rides upon the storm.
William Cowper 1731–1800

God is subtle but he is not malicious.
Albert Einstein 1879–1955

Operationally, God is beginning to resemble not a ruler but the last fading smile of a cosmic Cheshire cat.
Julian Huxley 1887–1975

An honest God is the noblest work of man.
Robert G. Ingersoll 1833–99

God

God seems to have left the receiver off the hook, and
time is running out.
Arthur Koestler 1905–83

Though the mills of God grind slowly, yet they grind
exceeding small;
Though with patience He stands waiting, with exactness
grinds He all.
Henry Wadsworth Longfellow 1807–82

Whatever your heart clings to and confides in, that is
really your God.
Martin Luther 1483–1546

If the triangles were to make a God they would give him
three sides.
Montesquieu 1689–1755

The Buddha, the Godhead, resides quite as comfortably in
the circuits of a digital computer or the gears of a cycle
transmission as he does at the top of a mountain or in
the petals of a flower.
Robert M. Pirsig 1928–

O Lord, to what a state dost Thou bring those who love
Thee!
St Teresa of Ávila 1512–82

For man proposes, but God disposes.
Thomas à Kempis c.1380–1471

If God did not exist, it would be necessary to invent him.
Voltaire 1694–1778

Our God, our help in ages past
Our hope for years to come,
Our shelter from the stormy blast,
And our eternal home.
Isaac Watts 1674–1748

Golf

If you watch a game, it's fun. If you play it, it's recreation. If you work at it, it's golf.
Bob Hope 1903–2003

Golf is a good walk spoiled.
Mark Twain 1835–1910

The least thing upset him on the links. He missed short putts because of the uproar of the butterflies in the adjoining meadows.
P. G. Wodehouse 1881–1975

Golf…is the infallible test. The man who can go into a patch of rough alone, with the knowledge that only God is watching him, and play his ball where it lies, is the man who will serve you faithfully and well.
P. G. Wodehouse 1881–1975

Good Looks

A pretty girl is like a melody
That haunts you night and day.
Irving Berlin 1888–1989

And she was fayr as is the rose in May.
Geoffrey Chaucer c.1343–1400

When a woman isn't beautiful, people always say, 'You have lovely eyes, you have lovely hair.'
Anton Chekhov 1860–1904

Beauty is the lover's gift.
William Congreve 1670–1729

Good Looks

Is it too much to ask that women be spared the daily struggle for superhuman beauty in order to offer it to the caresses of a subhumanly ugly mate?
Germaine Greer 1939–

I'm tired of all this nonsense about beauty being only skin-deep. That's deep enough. What do you want—an adorable pancreas?
Jean Kerr 1923–2003

The Lord prefers common-looking people. That is why he makes so many of them.
Abraham Lincoln 1809–65

Beauty is handed out as undemocratically as inherited peerages, and beautiful people have done nothing to deserve their astonishing reward.
John Mortimer 1923–

A beautiful face is a mute recommendation.
Publilius Syrus 1st century BC

Goodness ····▸ Evil

Every art and every investigation, and likewise every practical pursuit or undertaking, seems to aim at some good: hence it has been well said that the Good is That at which all things aim.
Aristotle 384–322 BC

He who would do good to another, must do it in minute particulars.
William Blake 1757–1827

Terrible is the temptation to be good.
Bertolt Brecht 1898–1956

Integrity has no need of rules.
Albert Camus 1913–60

No people do so much harm as those who go about doing good.
Bishop Mandell Creighton 1843–1901

What after all
Is a halo? It's only one more thing to keep clean.
Christopher Fry 1907–

Innocence always calls mutely for protection, when we would be so much wiser to guard ourselves against it: innocence is like a dumb leper who has lost his bell, wandering the world meaning no harm.
Graham Greene 1904–91

I expect to pass through this world but once; any good thing therefore that I can do, or any kindness that I can show to any fellow-creature, let me do it now; let me not defer or neglect it, for I shall not pass this way again.
Stephen Grellet 1773–1855

Be good, sweet maid, and let who will be clever.
Charles Kingsley 1819–75

Good and evil shall not be held equal. Turn away evil with that which is better; and behold the man between whom and thyself there was enmity, shall become, as it were, thy warmest friend.
The Koran

Virtue she finds too painful an endeavour,
Content to dwell in decencies for ever.
Alexander Pope 1688–1744

Dost thou think, because thou art virtuous, there shall be no more cakes and ale?
William Shakespeare 1564–1616

How far that little candle throws his beams!
So shines a good deed in a naughty world.
William Shakespeare 1564–1616

Goodness

What is virtue but the Trade Unionism of the married?
George Bernard Shaw 1856–1950

Our goodness derives not from our capacity to think but
to love.
St Teresa of Ávila 1512–82

Would that we had spent one whole day well in this
world!
Thomas à Kempis c.1380–1471

Virtue knows to a farthing what it has lost by not having
been vice.
Horace Walpole 1717–97

'Goodness, what beautiful diamonds!'
'Goodness had nothing to do with it.'
Mae West 1892–1980

That best portion of a good man's life,
His little, nameless, unremembered, acts
Of kindness and of love.
William Wordsworth 1770–1850

Gossip

There is so much good in the worst of us,
And so much bad in the best of us,
That it hardly becomes any of us
To talk about the rest of us.
Anonymous

Careless talk costs lives.
Anonymous *Second World War security slogan*

Every man is surrounded by a neighbourhood of
voluntary spies.
Jane Austen 1775–1817

They come together like the Coroner's Inquest, to sit
upon the murdered reputations of the week.
    William Congreve 1670–1729

Che ti fa ciò che quivi pispiglia?
Vien dietro a me, e lascia dir le genti.

What is it to thee what they whisper there? Come after
  me and let the people talk.
    Dante Alighieri 1265–1321

Gossip is a sort of smoke that comes from the dirty
tobacco-pipes of those who diffuse it: it proves nothing
but the bad taste of the smoker.
    George Eliot 1819–80

Love and scandal are the best sweeteners of tea.
    Henry Fielding 1707–54

Like all gossip—it's merely one of those half-alive things
that try to crowd out real life.
    E. M. Forster 1879–1970

It takes your enemy and your friend, working together, to
hurt you to the heart: the one to slander you and the
other to get the news to you.
    Mark Twain 1835–1910

There is only one thing in the world worse than being
talked about, and that is not being talked about.
    Oscar Wilde 1854–1900

Government ····▸ Politics

Let them hate, so long as they fear.
    Accius 170–c.86 BC

The happiness of society is the end of government.
    John Adams 1735–1826

Government

A monarchy is a merchantman which sails well, but will sometimes strike on a rock, and go to the bottom; whilst a republic is a raft which would never sink, but then your feet are always in the water.
   Fisher Ames 1758–1808

England is the mother of Parliaments.
   John Bright 1811–89

It is a 'beautiful maxim' that it is necessary to save five *sous* on unessential things, and to pour out millions when it is a question of your glory.
   Jean-Baptiste Colbert 1619–83

No Government can be long secure without a formidable Opposition.
   Benjamin Disraeli 1804–81

Though God hath raised me high, yet this I count the glory of my crown: that I have reigned with your loves.
   Elizabeth I 1533–1603

If the Government is big enough to give you everything you want, it is big enough to take away everything you have.
   Gerald Ford 1909–

The state is like the human body. Not all of its functions are dignified.
   Anatole France 1844–1924

My people and I have come to an agreement which satisfies us both. They are to say what they please, and I am to do what I please.
   Frederick the Great 1712–86

Your business is not to govern the country but it is, if you think fit, to call to account those who do govern it.
   W. E. Gladstone 1809–98, *to the House of Commons*

Many journalists have fallen for the conspiracy theory of government. I do assure you that they would produce more accurate work if they adhered to the cock-up theory.
Bernard Ingham 1932–

The important thing for Government is not to do things which individuals are doing already, and to do them a little better or a little worse; but to do those things which at present are not done at all.
John Maynard Keynes 1883–1946

Gouverner, c'est choisir.
To govern is to choose.
Duc de Lévis 1764–1830

We give the impression of being in office but not in power.
Norman Lamont 1942–

It is much safer for a prince to be feared than loved, if he is to fail in one of the two.
Niccolò Machiavelli 1469–1527

BIG BROTHER IS WATCHING YOU.
George Orwell 1903–50

The best government is that which governs least.
John L. O'Sullivan 1813–95

A parliament can do any thing but make a man a woman, and a woman a man.
Lord Pembroke c.1534–1601

For forms of government let fools contest;
Whate'er is best administered is best.
Alexander Pope 1688–1744

Wherever you have an efficient government you have a dictatorship.
Harry S. Truman 1884–1972

Government

Governments need both shepherds and butchers.
Voltaire 1694–1778

Greatness

The beauty of Israel is slain upon thy high places: how are the mighty fallen!
Bible

To be great is to be misunderstood.
Ralph Waldo Emerson 1803–82

A man does not attain the status of Galileo merely because he is persecuted; he must also be right.
Stephen Jay Gould 1941–2002

But be not afraid of greatness: some men are born great, some achieve greatness, and some have greatness thrust upon them.
William Shakespeare 1564–1616

All the world's great have been little boys who wanted the moon.
John Steinbeck 1902–68

Habit

Routine, in an intelligent man, is a sign of ambition.
W. H. Auden 1907–73

Habit is a great deadener.
Samuel Beckett 1906–89

Habit with him was all the test of truth,
'It must be right: I've done it from my youth.'
George Crabbe 1754–1832

Sow an act, and you reap a habit. Sow a habit and you reap a character. Sow a character, and you reap a destiny.
  Charles Reade 1814–84

Good habits: they are never good, because they are habits.
  Jean-Paul Sartre 1905–80

Happiness

Mirth is like a flash of lightning that breaks through a gloom of clouds, and glitters for a moment: cheerfulness keeps up a kind of day-light in the mind.
  Joseph Addison 1672–1719

A large income is the best recipe for happiness I ever heard of. It certainly may secure all the myrtle and turkey part of it.
  Jane Austen 1775–1817

Happiness washes away many things, just as suffering washes away many things.
  Heinrich Böll 1917–85

There may be Peace without Joy, and Joy without Peace, but the two combined make Happiness.
  John Buchan 1875–1940

For all the happiness mankind can gain
Is not in pleasure, but in rest from pain.
  John Dryden 1631–1700

Happiness makes up in height for what it lacks in length.
  Robert Frost 1874–1963

Point me out the happy man and I will point you out either egotism, selfishness, evil—or else an absolute ignorance.
  Graham Greene 1904–91

Happiness

I can sympathize with people's pains, but not with their pleasures. There is something curiously boring about somebody else's happiness.
Aldous Huxley 1894–1963

Happiness is not an ideal of reason but of imagination.
Immanuel Kant 1724–1804

A man enjoys the happiness he feels, a woman the happiness she gives.
Pierre Choderlos de Laclos 1741–1803

Happiness writes white.
Philip Larkin 1922–85

Happiness is a warm gun.
John Lennon 1940–80

Ask yourself whether you are happy, and you cease to be so.
John Stuart Mill 1806–73

Not to admire, is all the art I know,
To make men happy, and to keep them so.
Alexander Pope 1688–1744

I always say I don't think everyone has the right to happiness or to be loved. Even the Americans have written into their constitution that you have the right to the 'pursuit of happiness'. You have the right to try but that is all.
Claire Rayner 1931–

Freude, schöner Götterfunken,
Tochter aus Elysium.
Joy, beautiful radiance of the gods, daughter of Elysium.
Friedrich von Schiller 1759–1805

But a lifetime of happiness! No man alive could bear it: it would be hell on earth.
George Bernard Shaw 1856–1950

Call no man happy before he dies, he is at best but
fortunate.

Solon c.640–after 556 BC

Hatred

Better is a dinner of herbs where love is, than a stalled ox
and hatred therewith.

Bible

I do not love thee, Dr Fell.
The reason why I cannot tell;
But this I know, and know full well,
I do not love thee, Dr Fell.

Thomas Brown 1663–1704

Now hatred is by far the longest pleasure;
Men love in haste, but they detest at leisure.

Lord Byron 1788–1824

Love, friendship, respect do not unite people as much as
common hatred for something.

Anton Chekhov 1860–1904

I never hated a man enough to give him diamonds back.

Zsa Zsa Gabor 1919–

We can scarcely hate any one that we know.

William Hazlitt 1778–1830

If you hate a person, you hate something in him that is
part of yourself. What isn't part of ourselves doesn't
disturb us.

Hermann Hesse 1877–1962

No one is born hating another person because of the
colour of his skin, or his background, or his religion.
People must learn to hate, and if they can learn to hate,
they can be taught to love, for love comes more naturally

to the human heart than its opposite.
    Nelson Mandela 1918–

Always remember, others may hate you. Those who hate you don't win unless you hate them. And then you destroy yourself.
    Richard Nixon 1913–94

Health ····➤ Exercise, Sickness

The first law of dietetics seems to be: if it tastes good, it's bad for you.
    Isaac Asimov 1920–92

In the face of such overwhelming statistical possibilities, hypochondria has always seemed to me to be the only rational position to take on life.
    John Diamond 1953–2001

It was brilliant. You die of a heart attack but so what? You die thin.
    Bob Geldof 1954– , *on the Atkins diet*

Mens sana in corpore sano.
A sound mind in a sound body.
    Juvenal AD c.60–c.130

Life's not just being alive, but being well.
    Martial AD c.40–c.104

The best doctors are Dr Diet, Dr Quiet, and Dr Merryman.
    Proverb

Look to your health; and if you have it, praise God, and value it next to a good conscience; for health is the second blessing that we mortals are capable of; a blessing that money cannot buy.
    Izaak Walton 1593–1683

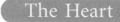
The Heart

The desires of the heart are as crooked as corkscrews
Not to be born is the best for man.
        W. H. Auden 1907–73

The human heart likes a little disorder in its geometry.
        Louis de Bernières 1954–

A man who has not passed through the inferno of his
passions has never overcome them.
        Carl Gustav Jung 1875–1961

I was never one who could put my hand on my heart
with tears dripping out of either eye, feeling the pain of
others.
        John Major 1943–

Calm of mind, all passion spent.
        John Milton 1608–74

The heart is an organ of fire.
        Michael Ondaatje 1943–

The heart has its reasons which reason knows nothing of.
        Blaise Pascal 1623–62

Unlearn'd, he knew no schoolman's subtle art,
No language, but the language of the heart.
        Alexander Pope 1688–1744

                A man whose blood
Is very snow-broth; one who never feels
The wanton stings and motions of the sense.
        William Shakespeare 1564–1616

Now that my ladder's gone
I must lie down where all ladders start
In the foul rag and bone shop of the heart.
        W. B. Yeats 1865–1939

Heaven

Heaven

And I saw a new heaven and a new earth: for the first heaven and the first earth were passed away; and there was no more sea.
Bible

The true paradises are the paradises that we have lost.
Marcel Proust 1871–1922

My idea of heaven is, eating *pâté de foie gras* to the sound of trumpets.
Sydney Smith 1771–1845

I will spend my heaven doing good on earth.
St Teresa of Lisieux 1873–97

Hell

Hell, madam, is to love no more.
Georges Bernanos 1888–1948

LASCIATE OGNI SPERANZA VOI CH'ENTRATE!
Abandon all hope, you who enter!
Dante Alighieri 1265–1321, *inscription at the entrance to Hell*

What is hell?
Hell is oneself,
Hell is alone, the other figures in it
Merely projections.
T. S. Eliot 1888–1965

Better to reign in hell, than serve in heaven.
John Milton 1608–74

Hell is other people.
Jean-Paul Sartre 1905–80

A perpetual holiday is a good working definition of hell.
George Bernard Shaw 1856–1950

Hell is a city much like London.
Percy Bysshe Shelley 1792–1822

Heroes

We can be heroes
Just for one day.
David Bowie 1947–

ANDREA: Unhappy the land that has no heroes!…
GALILEO: No. Unhappy the land that needs heroes.
Bertolt Brecht 1898–1956

No man is a hero to his valet.
Mme Cornuel 1605–94

I think that's just another word for a washed-up has-
been.
Bob Dylan 1941– , *on being an 'icon'*

Every hero becomes a bore at last.
Ralph Waldo Emerson 1803–82

Ultimately a hero is a man who would argue with the
Gods, and so awakens devils to contest his vision.
Norman Mailer 1923–

Heroing is one of the shortest-lived professions there is.
Will Rogers 1879–1935

In this world I would rather live two days like a tiger,
than two hundred years like a sheep.
Tipu Sultan c.1750–99

History

If history records good things of good men, the
thoughtful hearer is encouraged to imitate what is good.
The Venerable Bede AD 673–735

History

History repeats itself; historians repeat one another.
   Rupert Brooke 1887–1915

History is the essence of innumerable biographies.
   Thomas Carlyle 1795–1881

History is philosophy from examples.
   Dionysius of Halicarnassus fl. 30–7 BC

History is more or less bunk.
   Henry Ford 1863–1947

History is past politics, and politics is present history.
   E. A. Freeman 1823–92

History…is, indeed, little more than the register of the crimes, follies, and misfortunes of mankind.
   Edward Gibbon 1737–94

War makes rattling good history; but Peace is poor reading.
   Thomas Hardy 1840–1928

Hegel says somewhere that all great events and personalities in world history reappear in one fashion or another. He forgot to add: the first time as tragedy, the second as farce.
   Karl Marx 1818–83

Happy the people whose annals are blank in history-books!
   Montesquieu 1689–1755

History is not what you thought. *It is what you can remember.*
   W. C. Sellar 1898–1951 and **R. J. Yeatman** 1898–1968

Human history becomes more and more a race between education and catastrophe.
   H. G. Wells 1866–1946

Home ····> Houses, Housework

Home is home, though it be never so homely.
John Clarke d. 1658

'Home is the place where, when you have to go there,
They have to take you in.'
'I should have called it
Something you somehow haven't to deserve.'
Robert Frost 1874–1963

What's the good of a home if you are never in it?
George Grossmith 1847–1912 and **Weedon Grossmith** 1854–1919

Any old place I can hang my hat is home sweet home
to me.
William Jerome 1865–1932

The accent of one's birthplace lingers in the mind and in
the heart as it does in one's speech.
Duc de la Rochefoucauld 1613–80

E.T. phone home.
Melissa Mathison 1950–

Mid pleasures and palaces though we may roam,
Be it ever so humble, there's no place like home.
J. H. Payne 1791–1852

Home is where you come to when you have nothing
better to do.
Margaret Thatcher 1925–

Honour

The louder he talked of his honour, the faster we counted
our spoons.
Ralph Waldo Emerson 1803–82

Honour

GROUCHO MARX: Remember, you're fighting for this woman's honour...which is probably more than she ever did.
Bert Kalmar 1884–1947 et al.

I could not love thee, Dear, so much,
Loved I not honour more.
Richard Lovelace 1618–58

But he that filches from me my good name
Robs me of that which not enriches him,
And makes me poor indeed.
William Shakespeare 1564–1616

O! I have lost my reputation. I have lost the immortal part of myself, and what remains is bestial.
William Shakespeare 1564–1616

His honour rooted in dishonour stood,
And faith unfaithful kept him falsely true.
Alfred, Lord Tennyson 1809–92

Honours

Gongs and medals and ribbons really belong on a Christmas tree.
J. G. Ballard 1930–

Not a reluctant peer but a persistent commoner.
Tony Benn 1925– , *of his ultimately successful fight to disclaim his inherited title of Viscount Stansgate*

The rank is but the guinea's stamp,
The man's the gowd for a' that!
Robert Burns 1759–96

A medal glitters, but it also casts a shadow.
Winston Churchill 1874–1965, *on the envy caused by the award of honours*

What I like about the Order of the Garter is that there is no damned merit about it.
Lord Melbourne 1779–1848

When I want a peerage, I shall buy it like an honest man.
Lord Northcliffe 1865–1922

There is no stronger craving in the world than that of the rich for titles, except perhaps that of the titled for riches.
Hesketh Pearson 1887–1964

Titles distinguish the mediocre, embarrass the superior, and are disgraced by the inferior.
George Bernard Shaw 1856–1950

She needed no royal title to continue to generate her particular brand of magic.
Lord Spencer 1964– , *of his sister, Diana, Princess of Wales, at her funeral*

What harm have I ever done to the Labour Party?
R. H. Tawney 1880–1962, *on declining the offer of a peerage*

Kind hearts are more than coronets,
And simple faith than Norman blood.
Alfred, Lord Tennyson 1809–92

The cross of the Legion of Honour has been conferred on me. However, few escape that distinction.
Mark Twain 1835–1910

People fail you, children disappoint you, thieves break in, moths corrupt, but an OBE goes on for ever.
Fay Weldon 1931–

Hope ····▸ Despair, Optimism

Hope deferred maketh the heart sick: but when the desire cometh, it is a tree of life.
Bible

Hope

He that lives upon hope will die fasting.
Benjamin Franklin 1706–90

Walk on, walk on, with hope in your heart,
And you'll never walk alone.
Oscar Hammerstein II 1895–1960

Hope is definitely not the same thing as optimism. It is
not the conviction that something will turn out well, but
the certainty that something makes sense, regardless of
how it turns out.
Václav Havel 1936–

He that lives in hope danceth without music.
George Herbert 1593–1633

Nil desperandum.
Never despair.
Horace 65–8 BC

After all, tomorrow is another day.
Margaret Mitchell 1900–49

Hope springs eternal in the human breast:
Man never Is, but always To be blest.
Alexander Pope 1688–1744

    O, Wind,
If Winter comes, can Spring be far behind?
Percy Bysshe Shelley 1792–1822

Hospitality

The sooner every party breaks up the better.
Jane Austen 1775–1817

Be not forgetful to entertain strangers: for thereby some
have entertained angels unawares.
Bible

Hospitality

Like other parties of the kind, it was first silent, then talky, then argumentative, then disputatious, then unintelligible, then altogethery, then inarticulate, and then drunk.
Lord Byron 1788–1824

Come in the evening, or come in the morning,
Come when you're looked for, or come without warning.
Thomas Davis 1814–45

Hospitality consists in a little fire, a little food, and an immense quiet.
Ralph Waldo Emerson 1803–82

It's life's losers who really want to please—and wanting to please is a prerequisite of hospitality.
A. A. Gill 1954–

A host is like a general: misfortunes often reveal his genius.
Horace 65–8 BC

Some people can stay longer in an hour than others can in a week.
William Dean Howells 1837–1920

A successful party is a creative act, and creation is always painful.
Phyllis McGinley 1905–78

At a dinner party one should eat wisely but not too well, and talk well but not too wisely.
W. Somerset Maugham 1874–1965

May I join you in the doghouse, Rover?
I wish to retire till the party's over.
Ogden Nash 1902–71, *on a children's party*

For I, who hold sage Homer's rule the best,
Welcome the coming, speed the going guest.
Alexander Pope 1688–1744

Hospitality

Unbidden guests
Are often welcomest when they are gone.
William Shakespeare 1564–1616

He showed me his bill of fare to tempt me to dine with him; poh, said I, I value not your bill of fare, give me your bill of company.
Jonathan Swift 1667–1745

This door will open at a touch to welcome every friend.
Henry Van Dyke 1852–1933

If one plays good music, people don't listen and if one plays bad music people don't talk.
Oscar Wilde 1854–1900

Houses ····▶ Home

Houses are built to live in and not to look on; therefore let use be preferred before uniformity, except where both may be had.
Francis Bacon 1561–1626

For a man's house is his castle, *et domus sua cuique est tutissimum refugium* [and each man's home is his safest refuge].
Edward Coke 1552–1634

It takes a heap o' livin' in a house t' make it home.
Edgar A. Guest 1881–1959

A house is a machine for living in.
Le Corbusier 1887–1965

There is no such thing as a perfect house. (What one thinks of as perfection is merely what other people are living in.)
Phyllis McGinley 1905–78

Have nothing in your houses that you do not know to be useful, or believe to be beautiful.
William Morris 1834–96

Does anybody mind if I don't live in a house that is quaint?
Because, for one thing, quaint houses are generally houses where plumbing ain't.
Ogden Nash 1902–71

A comfortable house is a great source of happiness. It ranks immediately after health and a good conscience.
Sydney Smith 1771–1845

But every house where Love abides
And Friendship is a guest,
Is surely home, and home, sweet home,
For there the heart can rest.
Henry Van Dyke 1852–1933

Housework ····▸ Home

I am proud of my cake-making image but life is not that perfect. There are socks in my fruit bowl.
Jane Asher 1946–

Conran's Law of Housework—it expands to fill the time available plus half an hour.
Shirley Conran 1932–

There was no need to do any housework at all. After the first four years the dirt doesn't get any worse.
Quentin Crisp 1908–99

All the rudiments of success in life can be found in ironing a pair of trousers.
Chris Eubank 1966–

Housework

'I hate discussions of feminism that end up with who does the dishes,' she said. So do I. But at the end, there are always the damned dishes.
   Marilyn French 1929–

The labour of women in the house, certainly, enables men to produce more wealth than they otherwise could; and in this way women are economic factors in society. But so are horses.
   Charlotte Perkins Gilman 1860–1935

Dirt is only matter out of place.
   John Chipman Gray 1839–1915

The dust comes secretly day after day,
Lies on my ledge and dulls my shining things.
But O this dust that I shall drive away
Is flowers and Kings,
Is Solomon's temple, poets, Nineveh.
   Viola Meynell 1886–1956

There is scarcely any less bother in the running of a family than in that of an entire state. And domestic business is no less importunate for being less important.
   Montaigne 1533–92

God walks among the pots and pans.
   St Teresa of Ávila 1512–82

MR PRITCHARD: I must dust the blinds and then I must raise them.
MRS OGMORE-PRITCHARD: And before you let the sun in, mind it wipes its shoes.
   Dylan Thomas 1914–53

Hatred of domestic work is a natural and admirable result of civilization.
   Rebecca West 1892–1983

The Human Race

Drinking when we are not thirsty and making love all
year round, madam; that is all there is to distinguish us
from other animals.
Pierre-Augustin Caron de Beaumarchais 1732–99

There's a man all over for you, blaming on his boots the
faults of his feet.
Samuel Beckett 1906–89

We carry within us the wonders we seek without us: there
is all Africa and her prodigies in us.
Sir Thomas Browne 1605–82

I hate 'Humanity' and all such abstracts: but I love *people*.
Lovers of 'Humanity' generally hate *people and children*,
and keep parrots or puppy dogs.
Roy Campbell 1901–57

By nature men are alike. Through practice they have
become far apart.
Confucius 551–479 BC

What is man, when you come to think upon him, but a
minutely set, ingenious machine for turning, with infinite
artfulness, the red wine of Shiraz into urine?
Isak Dinesen 1885–1962

Is man an ape or an angel? Now I am on the side of the
angels.
Benjamin Disraeli 1804–81

Man is a tool-making animal.
Benjamin Franklin 1706–90

Out of the crooked timber of humanity no straight thing
can ever be made.
Immanuel Kant 1724–1804

The Human Race

To say, for example, that a man is made up of certain chemical elements is a satisfactory description only for those who intend to use him as a fertilizer.
H. J. Muller 1890–1967

I teach you the superman. Man is something to be surpassed.
Friedrich Nietzsche 1844–1900

Man is only a reed, the weakest thing in nature; but he is a thinking reed.
Blaise Pascal 1623–62

An honest man's the noblest work of God.
Alexander Pope 1688–1744

Man is the measure of all things.
Protagoras b. c.485 BC

How beauteous mankind is! O brave new world,
That has such people in't.
William Shakespeare 1564–1616

What a piece of work is a man! How noble in reason! how infinite in faculty! in form, in moving, how express and admirable! in action how like an angel! in apprehension how like a god! the beauty of the world! the paragon of animals!
William Shakespeare 1564–1616

There are many wonderful things, and nothing is more wonderful than man.
Sophocles c.496–406 BC

I am a man, I count nothing human foreign to me.
Terence c.190–159 BC

Man is the Only Animal that Blushes. Or needs to.
Mark Twain 1835–1910

We have to learn to be human alongside all sorts of others, the ones whose company we don't greatly like.
   Rowan Williams 1950–

We're all of us guinea pigs in the laboratory of God. Humanity is just a work in progress.
   Tennessee Williams 1911–83

Human Rights

We hold these truths to be self-evident, that all men are created equal, that they are endowed by their Creator with certain unalienable rights, that among these are life, liberty and the pursuit of happiness.
   American Declaration of Independence 1776

Liberté! Égalité! Fraternité!
Freedom! Equality! Brotherhood!
   Anonymous *motto of the French Revolution*

Natural rights is simple nonsense: natural and imprescriptible rights, rhetorical nonsense—nonsense upon stilts.
   Jeremy Bentham 1748–1832

Whatever each man can separately do, without trespassing upon others, he has a right to do for himself; and he has a right to a fair portion of all which society, with all its combinations of skill and force, can do in his favour.
   Edmund Burke 1729–97

No man can put a chain about the ankle of his fellow man without at last finding the other end fastened about his own neck.
   Frederick Douglass c.1818–95

To no man will we sell, or deny, or delay, right or justice.
   Magna Carta 1215

Human Rights

The poorest he that is in England hath a life to live as the greatest he.
Thomas Rainborowe d. 1648

Any law which violates the inalienable rights of man is essentially unjust and tyrannical; it is not a law at all.
Maximilien Robespierre 1758–94

We look forward to a world founded upon four essential human freedoms. The first is freedom of speech and expression—everywhere in the world. The second is freedom of every person to worship God in his own way—everywhere in the world. The third is freedom from want…The fourth is freedom from fear.
Franklin D. Roosevelt 1882–1945

That little man…he says women can't have as much rights as men, cause Christ wasn't a woman. Where did your Christ come from? From God and a woman. Man had nothing to do with Him.
Sojourner Truth c.1797–1883

All human beings are born free and equal in dignity and rights.
Universal Declaration of Human Rights 1948

Humour

Among those whom I like or admire, I can find no common denominator, but among those whom I love, I can: all of them make me laugh.
W. H. Auden 1907–73

For what do we live, but to make sport for our neighbours, and laugh at them in our turn?
Jane Austen 1775–1817

I make myself laugh at everything, for fear of having to weep at it.
Pierre-Augustin Caron de Beaumarchais 1732–99

Of all days, the one most surely wasted is the one on which one has not laughed.
Nicolas-Sébastien Chamfort 1741–94

A difference of taste in jokes is a great strain on the affections.
George Eliot 1819–80

The funniest thing about comedy is that you never know why people laugh. I know *what* makes them laugh but trying to get your hands on the *why* of it is like trying to pick an eel out of a tub of water.
W. C. Fields 1880–1946

What do you mean, funny? Funny-peculiar or funny ha-ha?
Ian Hay 1876–1952

[A pun] is a pistol let off at the ear; not a feather to tickle the intellect.
Charles Lamb 1775–1834

Wit is the epitaph of an emotion.
Friedrich Nietzsche 1844–1900

Laughter is pleasant, but the exertion is too much for me.
Thomas Love Peacock 1785–1866

Everything is funny as long as it is happening to Somebody Else.
Will Rogers 1879–1935

I am not only witty in myself, but the cause that wit is in other men.
William Shakespeare 1564–1616

Brevity is the soul of wit.
William Shakespeare 1564–1616

Humour

Delight hath a joy in it either permanent or present.
Laughter hath only a scornful tickling.
  Philip Sidney 1554–86

Humour is emotional chaos remembered in tranquillity.
  James Thurber 1894–1961

We are not amused.
  Queen Victoria 1819–1901

It's hard to be funny when you have to be clean.
  Mae West 1892–1980

Hypocrisy

Ye are like unto whited sepulchres, which indeed appear
beautiful outward, but are within full of dead men's
bones, and of all uncleanness.
  Bible

Compound for sins, they are inclined to,
By damning those they have no mind to.
  Samuel Butler 1612–80

The smylere with the knyf under the cloke.
  Geoffrey Chaucer c.1343–1400

Keep up appearances; there lies the test;
The world will give thee credit for the rest.
Outward be fair, however foul within;
Sin if thou wilt, but then in secret sin.
  Charles Churchill 1731–64

My tongue swore, but my mind's unsworn.
  Euripides c.485–c.406 BC, *lamenting the breaking of an oath*

Hypocrisy is a tribute which vice pays to virtue.
  Duc de la Rochefoucauld 1613–80

Hypocrisy, the only evil that walks
Invisible, except to God alone.
> **John Milton** 1608–74

>   I want that glib and oily art
To speak and purpose not.
> **William Shakespeare** 1564–1616

All Reformers, however strict their social conscience, live
in houses just as big as they can pay for.
> **Logan Pearsall Smith** 1865–1946

I sit on a man's back, choking him and making him carry
me, and yet assure myself and others that I am very sorry
for him and wish to ease his lot by all possible means—
except by getting off his back.
> **Leo Tolstoy** 1828–1910

Idealism

A cause may be inconvenient, but it's magnificent. It's like
champagne or high heels, and one must be prepared to
suffer for it.
> **Arnold Bennett** 1867–1931

Where there is no vision, the people perish.
> **Bible**

Oh, the vision thing.
> **George Bush** 1924– , *responding to the suggestion that he
> turn his attention from short-term campaign objectives and look
> to the longer term*

If a man hasn't discovered something he will die for, he
isn't fit to live.
> **Martin Luther King** 1929–68

We are all in the gutter, but some of us are looking at the
stars.
> **Oscar Wilde** 1854–1900

Idealism

I have spread my dreams under your feet;
Tread softly because you tread on my dreams.
W. B. Yeats 1865–1939

Ideas ····▸ Thinking

Nothing is more dangerous than an idea, when you have
only one idea.
Alain 1868–1951

There is one thing stronger than all the armies in the
world; and that is an idea whose time has come.
Anonymous

Probable impossibilities are to be preferred to improbable
possibilities.
Aristotle 384–322 BC

It isn't that they can't see the solution. It is that they
can't see the problem.
G. K. Chesterton 1874–1936

A stand can be made against invasion by an army; no
stand can be made against invasion by an idea.
Victor Hugo 1802–85

When you are a Bear of Very Little Brain, and you Think
of Things, you find sometimes that a Thing which
seemed very Thingish inside you is quite different when it
gets out into the open and has other people looking at it.
A. A. Milne 1882–1956

It could be said of me that in this book I have only made
up a bunch of other men's flowers, providing of my own
only the string that ties them together.
Montaigne 1533–92

You see things; and you say 'Why?' But I dream things that never were; and I say 'Why not?'
George Bernard Shaw 1856–1950

It is the nature of an hypothesis, when once a man has conceived it, that it assimilates every thing to itself, as proper nourishment; and, from the first moment of your begetting it, it generally grows the stronger by every thing you see, hear, read, or understand.
Laurence Sterne 1713–68

How seldom is it that theories stand the wear and tear of practice!
Anthony Trollope 1815–82

Ideas won't keep. Something must be done about them.
Alfred North Whitehead 1861–1947

Idleness

A man who has nothing to do with his own time has no conscience in his intrusion on that of others.
Jane Austen 1775–1817

Go to the ant thou sluggard; consider her ways, and be wise.
Bible

The foul sluggard's comfort: 'It will last my time.'
Thomas Carlyle 1795–1881

Idleness is only the refuge of weak minds.
Lord Chesterfield 1694–1773

I do nothing, granted. But I see the hours pass—which is better than trying to fill them.
E. M. Cioran 1911–95

It is better to wear out than to rust out.
Bishop Richard Cumberland 1631–1718

Idleness

Inertia can develop its own momentum.
Douglas Hurd 1930–

It is impossible to enjoy idling thoroughly unless one has plenty of work to do.
Jerome K. Jerome 1859–1927

I was raised to feel that doing nothing was a sin. I had to learn to do nothing.
Jenny Joseph 1932–

For Satan finds some mischief still
For idle hands to do.
Isaac Watts 1674–1748

Procrastination is the thief of time.
Edward Young 1683–1765

Ignorance

Ignorance is not innocence but sin.
Robert Browning 1812–89

Whatever Nature has in store for mankind, unpleasant as it may be, men must accept, for ignorance is never better than knowledge.
Enrico Fermi 1901–54

Where ignorance is bliss,
'Tis folly to be wise.
Thomas Gray 1716–71

Ignorance, madam, pure ignorance.
Samuel Johnson 1709–84, *on being asked why he had defined pastern as the 'knee' of a horse*

You know everybody is ignorant, only on different subjects.
Will Rogers 1879–1935

Learn to say, 'I don't know'. If used when appropriate, it will be often.
    Donald Rumsfeld 1932–

For most men, an ignorant enjoyment is better than an informed one; it is better to conceive the sky as a blue dome than a dark cavity; and the cloud as a golden throne than a sleety mist.
    John Ruskin 1819–1900

If one does not know to which port one is sailing, no wind is favourable.
    Seneca ('the Younger') c.4 BC–AD 65

As any fule kno.
    Geoffrey Willans 1911–58 and **Ronald Searle** 1920–

Imagination

All fantasy should have a solid base in reality.
    Max Beerbohm 1872–1956

To see a world in a grain of sand
And a heaven in a wild flower
Hold infinity in the palm of your hand
And eternity in an hour.
    William Blake 1757–1827

When the imagination sleeps, words are emptied of their meaning.
    Albert Camus 1913–60

Go, and catch a falling star,
Get with child a mandrake root,
Tell me, where all past years are,
Or who cleft the Devil's foot.
Teach me to hear mermaids singing.
    John Donne 1572–1631

Imagination

Where there is no imagination there is no horror.
Arthur Conan Doyle 1859–1930

Were it not for imagination, Sir, a man would be as
happy in the arms of a chambermaid as of a Duchess.
Samuel Johnson 1709–84

Heard melodies are sweet, but those unheard
Are sweeter.
John Keats 1795–1821

His imagination resembled the wings of an ostrich. It
enabled him to run, though not to soar.
Lord Macaulay 1800–59

The lunatic, the lover, and the poet,
Are of imagination all compact.
William Shakespeare 1564–1616

Must then a Christ perish in torment in every age to save
those that have no imagination?
George Bernard Shaw 1856–1950

The imagination is man's power over nature.
Wallace Stevens 1879–1955

Whither is fled the visionary gleam?
Where is it now, the glory and the dream?
William Wordsworth 1770–1850

Indifference

All colours will agree in the dark.
Francis Bacon 1561–1626

Because thou art lukewarm, and neither cold nor hot, I
will spew thee out of my mouth.
Bible

Catholics and Communists have committed great crimes, but at least they have not stood aside, like an established society, and been indifferent. I would rather have blood on my hands than water like Pilate.

Graham Greene 1904–91

Let them eat cake.

Marie-Antoinette 1755–93, *on being told that her people had no bread*

I wish I could care what you do or where you go but I can't…My dear, I don't give a damn.

Margaret Mitchell 1900–49, *'Frankly, my dear, I don't give a damn!' in Sidney Howard's screenplay*

Vacant heart and hand, and eye,—
Easy live and quiet die.

Sir Walter Scott 1771–1832

It is the disease of not listening, the malady of not marking, that I am troubled withal.

William Shakespeare 1564–1616

The worst sin towards our fellow creatures is not to hate them, but to be indifferent to them: that's the essence of inhumanity.

George Bernard Shaw 1856–1950

I was much further out than you thought
And not waving but drowning.

Stevie Smith 1902–71

The opposite of love is not hate, it's indifference. The opposite of art is not ugliness, it's indifference. The opposite of faith is not heresy, it's indifference. And the opposite of life is not death, it's indifference.

Elie Wiesel 1928–

Indifference

Cast a cold eye
On life, on death.
Horseman pass by!
  W. B. Yeats 1865–1939

Intelligence

See the happy moron,
He doesn't give a damn,
I wish I were a moron,
My God! perhaps I am!
  Anonymous

To the man-in-the-street, who, I'm sorry to say,
Is a keen observer of life,
The word 'Intellectual' suggests straight away
A man who's untrue to his wife.
  W. H. Auden 1907–73

A man is not necessarily intelligent because he has plenty
of ideas, any more than he is a good general because he
has plenty of soldiers.
  Nicolas-Sébastien Chamfort 1741–94

'Excellent,' I cried. 'Elementary,' said he.
  Arthur Conan Doyle 1859–1930, *commonly quoted as
  'Elementary, my dear Watson'*

As a human being, one has been endowed with just
enough intelligence to be able to see clearly how utterly
inadequate that intelligence is when confronted with what
exists.
  Albert Einstein 1879–1955

The test of a first-rate intelligence is the ability to hold
two opposed ideas in the mind at the same time, and still
retain the ability to function.
  F. Scott Fitzgerald 1896–1940

Invention and Discovery

So dumb he can't fart and chew gum at the same time.
Lyndon Baines Johnson 1908–73, *of Gerald Ford*

Sir, I have found you an argument; but I am not obliged
to find you an understanding.
Samuel Johnson 1709–84

I think, therefore I am is the statement of an intellectual
who underrates toothaches.
Milan Kundera 1929–

No one in this world, so far as I know—and I have
searched the records for years, and employed agents to
help me—has ever lost money by underestimating the
intelligence of the great masses of the plain people.
H. L. Mencken 1880–1956

You beat your pate, and fancy wit will come:
Knock as you please, there's nobody at home.
Alexander Pope 1688–1744

With stupidity the gods themselves struggle in vain.
Friedrich von Schiller 1759–1805

Intelligence is quickness to apprehend as distinct from
ability, which is capacity to act wisely on the thing
apprehended.
Alfred North Whitehead 1861–1947

Invention and Discovery

When man wanted to make a machine that would walk
he created the wheel, which does not resemble a leg.
Guillaume Apollinaire 1880–1918

Invention and Discovery

Eureka!
I've got it!
Archimedes c.287–212 BC

Printing, gunpowder, and the mariner's needle
[compass]…these three have changed the whole face and
state of things throughout the world.
Francis Bacon 1561–1626

Au fond de l'Inconnu pour trouver du nouveau!
Through the unknown, we'll find the new.
Charles Baudelaire 1821–67

Now who is responsible for this work of development on
which so much depends? To whom must the praise be
given? To the boys in the back rooms. They do not sit in
the limelight. But they are the men who do the work.
Lord Beaverbrook 1879–1964

The discovery of a new dish does more for human
happiness than the discovery of a star.
Anthelme Brillat-Savarin 1755–1826

LORD CARNARVON: Can you see anything?
CARTER: Yes, wonderful things.
Howard Carter 1874–1939, *on first looking into the tomb of
Tutankhamun*

Why sir, there is every possibility that you will soon be
able to tax it!
Michael Faraday 1791–1867, *to Gladstone, when asked about
the usefulness of electricity*

What is the use of a new-born child?
Benjamin Franklin 1706–90, *when asked what was the use of
a new invention*

Invention and Discovery

Then felt I like some watcher of the skies
When a new planet swims into his ken.
John Keats 1795–1821

praise without end the go-ahead zeal
of whoever it was invented the wheel;
but never a word for the poor soul's sake
that thought ahead, and invented the brake.
Howard Nemerov 1920–91

I don't know what I may seem to the world, but as to
myself, I seem to have been only like a boy playing on the
sea-shore and diverting myself in now and then finding a
smoother pebble or a prettier shell than ordinary, whilst
the great ocean of truth lay all undiscovered before me.
Isaac Newton 1642–1727

I remembered the line from the Hindu scripture, the
Bhagavad Gita…'I am become death, the destroyer of
worlds.'
J. Robert Oppenheimer 1904–67, *on the explosion of the first
atomic bomb near Alamogordo, New Mexico*

Semper aliquid novi Africam adferre.
Africa always brings [us] something new.
Pliny the Elder AD 23–79

If you wish to make an apple pie from scratch, you must
first invent the universe.
Carl Sagan 1934–96

Discovery consists of seeing what everybody has seen and
thinking what nobody has thought.
Albert von Szent-Györgyi 1893–1986

Name the greatest of all the inventors. Accident.
Mark Twain 1835–1910

Ireland

Ireland

Do you not feel that this island is moored only lightly to
the sea-bed, and might be off for the Americas at any
moment?
    Sebastian Barry 1955-

We've never been cool, we're hot. Irish people are Italians
who can't dress, Jamaicans who can't dance.
    Bono 1960-

For the great Gaels of Ireland
Are the men that God made mad,
For all their wars are merry,
And all their songs are sad.
    G. K. Chesterton 1874-1936

Ulster will fight; Ulster will be right.
    Lord Randolph Churchill 1849-94

            The famous
Northern reticence, the tight gag of place
And times.
    Seamus Heaney 1939-

Ireland is the old sow that eats her farrow.
    James Joyce 1882-1941

In Ireland the inevitable never happens and the
unexpected constantly occurs.
    John Pentland Mahaffy 1839-1919

Spenser's Ireland
has not altered;—
a place as kind as it is green,
the greenest place I've never seen.
    Marianne Moore 1887-1972

Romantic Ireland's dead and gone,
It's with O'Leary in the grave.
W. B. Yeats 1865–1939

Jealousy ····▶ Envy and Jealousy

Anyone here been raped and speaks English?
Anonymous *shouted by a British TV reporter in a crowd of Belgian civilians waiting to be airlifted out of the Belgian Congo, c.1960*

The Times has made many ministries.
Walter Bagehot 1826–77

I read the newspapers avidly. It is my one form of continuous fiction.
Aneurin Bevan 1897–1960

Tell it not in Gath, publish it not in the streets of Askelon.
Bible

As cold waters to a thirsty soul, so is good news from a far country.
Bible

When a dog bites a man, that is not news, because it happens so often. But if a man bites a dog, that is news.
John B. Bogart 1848–1921

When seagulls follow a trawler, it is because they think sardines will be thrown into the sea.
Eric Cantona 1966– , *at a press conference*

Small earthquake in Chile. Not many dead.
Claud Cockburn 1904–81, *winning entry for a dullest headline competition at* The Times

Journalism

Ill news hath wings, and with the wind doth go,
Comfort's a cripple and comes ever slow.
 Michael Drayton 1563–1631

When the legend becomes fact, print the legend.
 Willis Goldbeck and **James Warner Bellah**

You furnish the pictures and I'll furnish the war.
 William Randolph Hearst 1863–1951, *message to the artist Frederic Remington in Havana, Cuba, during the Spanish-American War of 1898*

Power without responsibility: the prerogative of the harlot throughout the ages.
 Rudyard Kipling 1865–1936, *summing up Lord Beaverbrook's political standpoint* vis-à-vis *the* Daily Express

The journalists have constructed for themselves a little wooden chapel, which they also call the Temple of Fame, in which they put up and take down portraits all day long and make such a hammering you can't hear yourself speak.
 Georg Christoph Lichtenberg 1742–99

A good newspaper, I suppose, is a nation talking to itself.
 Arthur Miller 1915–

All the news that's fit to print.
 Adolph S. Ochs 1858–1935, *motto of the* New York Times

A cynical, mercenary, demagogic, corrupt press will produce in time a people as base as itself.
 Joseph Pulitzer 1847–1911

The men with the muck-rakes are often indispensable to the well-being of society; but only if they know when to stop raking the muck.
 Theodore Roosevelt 1858–1919

Comment is free, but facts are sacred.
 C. P. Scott 1846–1932

The nature of bad news infects the teller.
William Shakespeare 1564–1616

Comment is free but facts are on expenses.
Tom Stoppard 1937–

We must try to find ways to starve the terrorist and the hijacker of the oxygen of publicity on which they depend.
Margaret Thatcher 1925–

The report of my death was an exaggeration.
Mark Twain 1835–1910, *usually quoted as 'Reports of my death have been greatly exaggerated'*

Rock journalism is people who can't write interviewing people who can't talk for people who can't read.
Frank Zappa 1940–93

Justice ⋯▶ The Law

Jedem das Seine.
To each his own.
Anonymous *inscription on the gate of Buchenwald concentration camp; often quoted as 'Everyone gets what he deserves'*

Audi partem alteram.
Hear the other side.
St Augustine of Hippo AD 354–430

Life for life,
Eye for eye, tooth for tooth.
Bible

It is better that ten guilty persons escape than one innocent suffer.
William Blackstone 1723–80

Justice

When I hear of an 'equity' in a case like this, I am reminded of a blind man in a dark room—looking for a black hat—which isn't there.
Lord Bowen 1835-94

No! No! Sentence first—verdict afterwards.
Lewis Carroll 1832-98

Justice is truth in action.
Benjamin Disraeli 1804-81

All sensible people are selfish, and nature is tugging at every contract to make the terms of it fair.
Ralph Waldo Emerson 1803-82

Fiat justitia et pereat mundus.
Let justice be done, though the world perish.
Emperor Ferdinand I 1503-64

Justice should not only be done, but should manifestly and undoubtedly be seen to be done.
Lord Hewart 1870-1943

A lawyer has no business with the justice or injustice of the cause which he undertakes, unless his client asks his opinion, and then he is bound to give it honestly. The justice or injustice of the cause is to be decided by the judge.
Samuel Johnson 1709-84

Injustice anywhere is a threat to justice everywhere.
Martin Luther King 1929-68

In England, justice is open to all—like the Ritz Hotel.
James Mathew 1830-1908

Here they hang a man first, and try him afterwards.
Molière 1622-73

What I say is that 'just' or 'right' means nothing but what is in the interest of the stronger party.
Plato 429-347 BC, *spoken by Thrasymachus*

The quality of mercy is not strained,
It droppeth as the gentle rain from heaven
Upon the place beneath: it is twice blessed;
It blesseth him that gives and him that takes.
William Shakespeare 1564–1616

Thrice is he armed that hath his quarrel just.
William Shakespeare 1564–1616

Two wrongs don't make a right, but they make a good excuse.
Thomas Szasz 1920–

Knowledge

Everyman, I will go with thee, and be thy guide,
In thy most need to go by thy side.
Anonymous Everyman (c.1509–19) *spoken by Knowledge*

The fox knows many things—the hedgehog one *big* one.
Archilochus 7th century BC

All men by nature desire knowledge.
Aristotle 384–322 BC

For also knowledge itself is power.
Francis Bacon 1561–1626

The price of wisdom is above rubies.
Bible

For now we see through a glass, darkly; but then face to face: now I know in part; but then shall I know even as also I am known.
Bible

It is better to know nothing than to know what ain't so.
Josh Billings 1818–85

Knowledge

If the doors of perception were cleansed everything would appear to man as it is, infinite.
William Blake 1757–1827

An expert is one who knows more and more about less and less.
Nicholas Murray Butler 1862–1947

Knowledge may give weight, but accomplishments give lustre, and many more people see than weigh.
Lord Chesterfield 1694–1773

There is no such thing on earth as an uninteresting subject; the only thing that can exist is an uninterested person.
G. K. Chesterton 1874–1936

MR GRADGRIND: Now, what I want is, Facts...Facts alone are wanted in life.
Charles Dickens 1812–70

Where is the wisdom we have lost in knowledge?
Where is the knowledge we have lost in information?
T. S. Eliot 1888–1965

Mere cleverness is not wisdom.
Euripides c.485–c.406 BC

For lust of knowing what should not be known,
We take the Golden Road to Samarkand.
James Elroy Flecker 1884–1915

Knowledge is of two kinds. We know a subject ourselves, or we know where we can find information upon it.
Samuel Johnson 1709–84

The motto of all the mongoose family is, 'Run and find out.'
Rudyard Kipling 1865–1936

A little learning is a dangerous thing;
Drink deep, or taste not the Pierian spring.
Alexander Pope 1688–1744

Knowledge without conscience is but the ruin of the soul.
François Rabelais c.1494–c.1553

There are known knowns; there are things we know we
know. We also know there are known unknowns; that is
to say we know there are some things we do not know.
But there are also unknown unknowns—the ones we
don't know we don't know.
Donald Rumsfeld 1932–

I know nothing except the fact of my ignorance.
Socrates 469–399 BC

Knowledge is good. It does not have to look good or
sound good or even do good. It is good just by being
knowledge. And the only thing that makes it knowledge is
that it is true. You can't have too much of it and there is
no little too little to be worth having.
Tom Stoppard 1937–

That was a little bit more information than I needed to
know.
Quentin Tarantino 1963–

Get your facts first, and then you can distort 'em as much
as you please.
Mark Twain 1835–1910

Our meddling intellect
Mis-shapes the beauteous forms of things:—
We murder to dissect.
William Wordsworth 1770–1850

Language

One picture is worth ten thousand words.
  Frederick R. Barnard

A word fitly spoken is like apples of gold in pictures of silver.
  Bible

A definition is the enclosing a wilderness of idea within a wall of words.
  Samuel Butler 1835–1902

Take care of the sense, and the sounds will take care of themselves.
  Lewis Carroll 1832–98

When I split an infinitive, God damn it, I split it so it will stay split.
  Raymond Chandler 1888–1959, *on a proof-reader's corrections to his work*

Colourless green ideas sleep furiously.
  Noam Chomsky 1928– , *illustrating that grammatical structure is independent of meaning*

This is the sort of English up with which I will not put.
  Winston Churchill 1874–1965, *on prepositions*

The man who first abused his fellows with swear-words instead of bashing their brains out with a club should be counted among those who laid the foundations of civilization.
  John Cohen 1911–

He who understands baboon would do more towards metaphysics than Locke.
  Charles Darwin 1809–82

Language is fossil poetry.
Ralph Waldo Emerson 1803–82

Merely corroborative detail, intended to give artistic
verisimilitude to an otherwise bald and unconvincing
narrative.
W. S. Gilbert 1836–1911

Language is the dress of thought.
Samuel Johnson 1709–84

The mystery of language was revealed to me. I knew then
that 'w-a-t-e-r' meant the wonderful cool something that
was flowing over my hand. That living word awakened
my soul, gave it light, joy, set it free!
Helen Keller 1880–1968

All that is not prose is verse; and all that is not verse is
prose.
Molière 1622–73

Good heavens! For more than forty years I have been
speaking prose without knowing it.
Molière 1622–73

Slang is a language that rolls up its sleeves, spits on its
hands and goes to work.
Carl Sandburg 1878–1967

You taught me language; and my profit on't
Is, I know how to curse.
William Shakespeare 1564–1616

A language is a dialect with an army and a navy.
Max Weinreich 1894–1969

The limits of my language mean the limits of my world.
Ludwig Wittgenstein 1889–1951

Languages

The great breeding people had gone out and multiplied;
colonies in every clime attest our success; French is the
patois of Europe; English is the language of the world.
Walter Bagehot 1826-77

It is a thing plainly repugnant to the Word of God, and
the custom of the Primitive Church, to have publick
Prayer in the Church, or to minister the Sacraments in a
tongue not understanded of the people.
Book of Common Prayer 1662

To God I speak Spanish, to women Italian, to men
French, and to my horse—German.
Emperor Charles V 1500-58

I like to be beholden to the great metropolitan English
speech, the sea which receives tributaries from every
region under heaven.
Ralph Waldo Emerson 1803-82

My English text is chaste, and all licentious passages are
left in the obscurity of a learned language.
Edward Gibbon 1737-94, *parodied as 'decent obscurity' in the*
Anti-Jacobin

I am always sorry when any language is lost, because
languages are the pedigree of nations.
Samuel Johnson 1709-84

We are walking lexicons. In a single sentence of idle
chatter we preserve Latin, Anglo-Saxon, Norse; we carry a
museum inside our heads, each day we commemorate
peoples of whom we have never heard.
Penelope Lively 1933-

It is impossible for an Englishman to open his mouth
without making some other Englishman hate or despise
him.
George Bernard Shaw 1856–1950

England and America are two countries divided by a
common language.
George Bernard Shaw 1856–1950

The Law ····▸ Crime, Justice

Written laws are like spider's webs; they will catch, it is
true, the weak and poor, but would be torn in pieces by
the rich and powerful.
Anacharsis 6th century BC

Law is a bottomless pit.
Dr Arbuthnot 1667–1735

Bad laws are the worst sort of tyranny.
Edmund Burke 1729–97

Salus populi suprema est lex.
The good of the people is the chief law.
Cicero 106–43 BC

Cui bono?
To whose profit?
Cicero 106–43 BC

If the law supposes that…the law is a ass—a idiot.
Charles Dickens 1812–70

'You must not tell us what the soldier, or any other man,
said, sir,' interposed the judge; 'it's not evidence.'
Charles Dickens 1812–70

No poet ever interpreted nature as freely as a lawyer
interprets the truth.
Jean Giraudoux 1882–1944

The Law

Laws grind the poor, and rich men rule the law.
Oliver Goldsmith 1728-74

A verbal contract isn't worth the paper it is written on.
Sam Goldwyn 1882-1974

I know no method to secure the repeal of bad or obnoxious laws so effective as their stringent execution.
Ulysses S. Grant 1822-85

The more laws and orders are made prominent,
The more thieves and bandits there will be.
Lao Tzu c.604-c.531 BC

I don't know as I want a lawyer to tell me what I cannot do. I hire him to tell me how to do what I want to do.
John Pierpont Morgan 1837-1913

Laws were made to be broken.
Christopher North 1785-1854

A lawyer with his briefcase can steal more than a hundred men with guns.
Mario Puzo 1920-99

Ignorance of the law excuses no man; not that all men know the law, but because 'tis an excuse every man will plead, and no man can tell how to confute him.
John Selden 1584-1654

The first thing we do, let's kill all the lawyers.
William Shakespeare 1564-1616

A precedent embalms a principle.
Lord Stowell 1745-1836

Everything not forbidden is compulsory.
T. H. White 1906-64

Asking the ignorant to use the incomprehensible to decide the unknowable.
Hiller B. Zobel 1932- , *on the jury system*

Leadership

Be neither saint nor sophist-led, but be a man.
Matthew Arnold 1822–88

By the structure of the world we often want, at the sudden occurrence of a grave tempest, to change the helmsman—to replace the pilot of the calm by the pilot of the storm.
Walter Bagehot 1826–77

If the blind lead the blind, both shall fall into the ditch.
Bible

The art of leadership is saying no, not yes. It is very easy to say yes.
Tony Blair 1953–

Leaders should never, ever try to look cool—that's for dictators.
Ben Elton 1959–

The art of leadership...consists in consolidating the attention of the people against a single adversary and taking care that nothing will split up that attention.
Adolf Hitler 1889–1945

The final test of a leader is that he leaves behind him in other men the conviction and the will to carry on.
Walter Lippmann 1889–1974

To grasp and hold a vision, that is the very essence of successful leadership—not only on the movie set where I learned it, but everywhere.
Ronald Reagan 1911–2004

Never be a pioneer. It's the Early Christian that gets the fattest lion.
Saki 1870–1916

Leadership

I don't mind how much my Ministers talk, so long as they do what I say.
   Margaret Thatcher 1925–

The buck stops here.
   Harry S. Truman 1884–1972

Leisure

To many people holidays are no voyage of discovery, but a ritual of reassurance.
   Phillip Adams 1939–

We are closer to the ants than to the butterflies. Very few people can endure much leisure.
   Gerald Brenan 1894–1987

There's sand in the porridge and sand in the bed,
And if this is pleasure we'd rather be dead.
   Noël Coward 1899–1973

What is this life if, full of care,
We have no time to stand and stare.
   W. H. Davies 1871–1940

Cannot avoid contrasting deliriously rapid flight of time when on a holiday with very much slower passage of days, and even hours, in other and more familiar surroundings.
   E. M. Delafield 1890–1943

How pleasant to sit on the beach,
On the beach, on the sand, in the sun,
With ocean galore within reach,
And nothing at all to be done!
   Ogden Nash 1902–71

To be able to fill leisure intelligently is the last product of civilization.
   Bertrand Russell 1872–1970

If all the year were playing holidays,
To sport would be as tedious as to work;
But when they seldom come, they wished for come.
   William Shakespeare 1564–1616

We're all going on a summer holiday,
No more worries for a week or two.
   Bruce Welch and **Brian Bennett**

The world is too much with us; late and soon,
Getting and spending, we lay waste our powers.
   William Wordsworth 1770–1850

Letters

You bid me burn your letters. But I must forget you first.
   John Adams 1735–1826, *to Abigail Adams*

Letters of thanks, letters from banks,
Letters of joy from girl and boy.
   W. H. Auden 1907–73

She'll vish there wos more, and that's the great art o' letter writin'.
   Charles Dickens 1812–70

Sir, more than kisses, letters mingle souls.
   John Donne 1572–1631

It is wonderful how much news there is when people write every other day; if they wait for a month, there is nothing that seems worth telling.
   O. Douglas 1877–1948

Letters

All letters, methinks, should be free and easy as one's discourse, not studied as an oration, nor made up of hard words like a charm.
   Dorothy Osborne 1627-95

Don't think that this is a letter. It is only a small eruption of a disease called friendship.
   Jean Renoir 1894-1979

A woman seldom writes her mind but in her postscript.
   Richard Steele 1672-1729

Liberty

Liberty is always unfinished business.
   Anonymous

Liberty is liberty, not equality or fairness or justice or human happiness or a quiet conscience.
   Isaiah Berlin 1909-97

The people never give up their liberties except under some delusion.
   Edmund Burke 1729-97

The condition upon which God hath given liberty to man is eternal vigilance.
   John Philpot Curran 1750-1817

I know not what course others may take; but as for me, give me liberty, or give me death!
   Patrick Henry 1736-99

It is better to die on your feet than to live on your knees.
   Dolores Ibarruri 1895-1989

The enemies of Freedom do not argue; they shout and they shoot.
   Dean Inge 1860-1954

The tree of liberty must be refreshed from time to time with the blood of patriots and tyrants. It is its natural manure.

Thomas Jefferson 1743–1826

They took away my liberty, not my freedom.

Brian Keenan 1950– , *of his captivity in Lebanon*

We shall pay any price, bear any burden, meet any hardship, support any friend, oppose any foe to assure the survival and the success of liberty.

John F. Kennedy 1917–63

Liberty is precious—so precious that it must be rationed.

Lenin 1870–1924

Stone walls do not a prison make,
Nor iron bars a cage.

Richard Lovelace 1618–58

Freedom is always and exclusively freedom for the one who thinks differently.

Rosa Luxemburg 1871–1919

If men are to wait for liberty till they become wise and good in slavery, they may indeed wait for ever.

Lord Macaulay 1800–59

The liberty of the individual must be thus far limited; he must not make himself a nuisance to other people.

John Stuart Mill 1806–73

Freedom is the freedom to say that two plus two make four. If that is granted, all else follows.

George Orwell 1903–50

Tyranny is always better organised than freedom.

Charles Péguy 1873–1914

O liberty! what crimes are committed in thy name!

Mme Roland 1754–93

Liberty

Man was born free, and everywhere he is in chains.
Jean-Jacques Rousseau 1712–78

What is freedom of expression? Without the freedom to offend, it ceases to exist.
Salman Rushdie 1947–

I am condemned to be free.
Jean-Paul Sartre 1905–80

Of course liberty is not licence. Liberty in my view is conforming to majority opinion.
Hugh Scanlon 1913–

Liberty means responsibility. That is why most men dread it.
George Bernard Shaw 1856–1950

A free society is a society where it is safe to be unpopular.
Adlai Stevenson 1900–65

Libraries ····▶ Books, Reading

The true University of these days is a collection of books.
Thomas Carlyle 1795–1881

A man should keep his little brain attic stocked with all the furniture that he is likely to use, and the rest he can put away in the lumber room of his library, where he can get it if he wants it.
Arthur Conan Doyle 1859–1930

No place affords a more striking conviction of the vanity of human hopes, than a public library.
Samuel Johnson 1709–84

Your *borrowers of books*—those mutilators of collections, spoilers of the symmetry of shelves, and creators of odd volumes.
Charles Lamb 1775–1834

A library is thought in cold storage.
Lord Samuel 1870–1963

Come, and take choice of all my library,
And so beguile thy sorrow.
William Shakespeare 1564–1616

Lies ····▸ Deceit, Truth

An abomination unto the Lord, but a very present help in time of trouble.
Anonymous *definition of a lie, an amalgamation of two biblical verses*

And, after all, what is a lie? 'Tis but
The truth in masquerade.
Lord Byron 1788–1824

One sometimes sees more clearly in the man who lies than in the man who tells the truth. Truth, like the light, blinds. Lying, on the other hand, is a beautiful twilight, which gives to each object its value.
Albert Camus 1913–60

That branch of the art of lying which consists in very nearly deceiving your friends without quite deceiving your enemies.
Francis M. Cornford 1874–1943, *on propaganda*

There are three kinds of lies: lies, damned lies and statistics.
Benjamin Disraeli 1804–81

Without lies humanity would perish of despair and boredom.
Anatole France 1844–1924

In human relations kindness and lies are worth a thousand truths.
Graham Greene 1904–91

Lies

Whoever would lie usefully should lie seldom.
Lord Hervey 1696–1743

The broad mass of a nation…will more easily fall victim
to a big lie than to a small one.
Adolf Hitler 1889–1945

There is no worse lie than a truth misunderstood by
those who hear it.
William James 1842–1910

Calumnies are answered best with silence.
Ben Jonson c.1573–1637

The lie in the soul is a true lie.
Benjamin Jowett 1817–93

He would, wouldn't he?
Mandy Rice-Davies 1944– , *on hearing that Lord Astor denied
her allegations*

It is well said in the old proverb, 'a lie will go round the
world while truth is pulling its boots on'.
C. H. Spurgeon 1834–92

The cruellest lies are often told in silence.
Robert Louis Stevenson 1850–94

He replied that I must needs be mistaken, or that I *said
the thing which was not.* (For they have no word in their
language to express lying or falsehood.)
Jonathan Swift 1667–1745

A deception that elevates us is dearer than a host of low
truths.
Marina Tsvetaeva 1892–1941

One of the most striking differences between a cat and a
lie is that a cat has only nine lives.
Mark Twain 1835–1910

He will lie even when it is inconvenient: the sign of the true artist.
Gore Vidal 1925–

Life ····▶ Life Sciences, Lifestyles

The Answer to the Great Question Of…Life, the Universe and Everything…[is] Forty-two.
Douglas Adams 1952–2001

It is in life as it is in ways, the shortest way is commonly the foulest, and surely the fairer way is not much about.
Francis Bacon 1561–1626

If it were possible to talk to the unborn, one could never explain to them how it feels to be alive, for life is washed in the speechless real.
Jacques Barzun 1907–

'Such,' he said, 'O King, seems to me the present life of men on earth, in comparison with that time which to us is uncertain, as if when on a winter's night you sit feasting with your ealdormen and thegns,—a single sparrow should fly swiftly into the hall, and coming in at one door, instantly fly out through another'.
The Venerable Bede AD 673–735

Man that is born of a woman is of few days, and full of trouble.
Bible

All that a man hath will he give for his life.
Bible

Life is just a bowl of cherries.
Lew Brown 1893–1958

Life

W. C. FIELDS: It's a funny old world—a man's lucky if he gets out of it alive.
Walter de Leon and **Paul M. Jones**

All that matters is love and work.
Sigmund Freud 1856–1939

Man wants but little here below,
Nor wants that little long.
Oliver Goldsmith 1728–74

No arts; no letters; no society; and which is worst of all, continual fear and danger of violent death; and the life of man, solitary, poor, nasty, brutish, and short.
Thomas Hobbes 1588–1679

Life is just one damned thing after another.
Elbert Hubbard 1859–1915

As far as we can discern, the sole purpose of human existence is to kindle a light in the darkness of mere being.
Carl Gustav Jung 1875–1961

Life must be understood backwards; but…it must be lived forwards.
Sören Kierkegaard 1813–1855

Man has but three events in his life: to be born, to live, and to die. He is not conscious of his birth, he suffers at his death and he forgets to live.
Jean de la Bruyère 1645–96

Ah! que la vie est quotidienne.
Oh, what a day-to-day business life is.
Jules Laforgue 1860–87

Life is first boredom, then fear.
Philip Larkin 1922–85

Life is like a sewer. What you get out of it depends on what you put into it.
　　Tom Lehrer 1928–

Life well spent is long.
　　Leonardo da Vinci 1452–1519

Life is real! Life is earnest!
And the grave is not its goal;
Dust thou art, to dust returnest,
Was not spoken of the soul.
　　Henry Wadsworth Longfellow 1807–82

There's a rule, I think. You get what you want in life, but not your second choice too.
　　Alison Lurie 1926–

What, knocked a tooth out? Never mind, dear, laugh it off, laugh it off; it's all part of life's rich pageant.
　　Arthur Marshall 1910–89

We live, not as we wish to, but as we can.
　　Menander 342–c.292 BC

I've looked at life from both sides now,
From win and lose and still somehow
It's life's illusions I recall;
I really don't know life at all.
　　Joni Mitchell 1945–

Man is born to live, not to prepare for life.
　　Boris Pasternak 1890–1960

TOM HANKS: My momma always said life was like a box of chocolates…you never know what you're gonna get.
　　Eric Ross

All the world's a stage,
And all the men and women merely players:
They have their exits and their entrances;

Life

And one man in his time plays many parts,
His acts being seven ages.
  William Shakespeare 1564–1616

Life is not meant to be easy, my child; but take courage:
it can be delightful.
  George Bernard Shaw 1856–1950

Not to be born is, past all prizing, best.
  Sophocles c.496–406 BC

Oh, isn't life a terrible thing, thank God?
  Dylan Thomas 1914–53

Our life is frittered away by detail…Simplify, simplify.
  Henry David Thoreau 1817–62

Expect nothing. Live frugally
on surprise.
  Alice Walker 1944–

This world is a comedy to those that think, a tragedy to
those that feel.
  Horace Walpole 1717–97

There seems to be a general overall pattern in most lives,
that nothing happens, and nothing happens, and then all
of a sudden everything happens.
  Fay Weldon 1931–

All the business of war, and indeed all the business of life,
is to endeavour to find out what you don't know by what
you do; that's what I called 'guessing what was at the
other side of the hill'.
  Duke of Wellington 1769–1852

Never to have lived is best, ancient writers say;
Never to have drawn the breath of life, never to have
  looked into the eye of day;
The second best's a gay goodnight and quickly turn away.
  W. B. Yeats 1865–1939

Life Sciences ····> Science

The Microbe is so very small
You cannot make him out at all.
>   **Hilaire Belloc** 1870–1953

Men will not be content to manufacture life: they will
want to improve on it.
>   **J. D. Bernal** 1901–71

It has, I believe, been often remarked that a hen is only
an egg's way of making another egg.
>   **Samuel Butler** 1835–1902

Today we are learning the language in which God created
life.
>   **Bill Clinton** 1946– , *announcing the deciphering of 90% of the
>   human genome*

We have discovered the secret of life!
>   **Francis Crick** 1916–2004, *on the discovery of the structure
>   of DNA*

Almost all aspects of life are engineered at the molecular
level, and without understanding molecules we can only
have a very sketchy understanding of life itself.
>   **Francis Crick** 1916–2004

I have called this principle, by which each slight variation,
if useful, is preserved, by the term of Natural Selection.
>   **Charles Darwin** 1809–82

The essence of life is statistical improbability on a colossal
scale.
>   **Richard Dawkins** 1941–

I'd lay down my life for two brothers or eight cousins.
>   **J. B. S. Haldane** 1892–1964

Life exists in the universe only because the carbon atom
possesses certain exceptional properties.
>   **James Jeans** 1877–1946

Life Sciences

The biologist passes, the frog remains.
> **Jean Rostand** 1894–1977, *sometimes quoted as 'Theories pass. The frog remains'*

Genes are not like engineering blueprints; they are more like recipes in a cookbook. They tell us what ingredients to use, in what quantities, and in what order—but they do not provide a complete, accurate plan of the final result.
> **Ian Stewart** 1945–

So, naturalists observe, a flea
Hath smaller fleas that on him prey;
And these have smaller fleas to bite 'em,
And so proceed *ad infinitum.*
> **Jonathan Swift** 1667–1745

Water is life's *mater* and *matrix*, mother and medium. There is no life without water.
> **Albert von Szent-Györgyi** 1893–1986

Was it through his grandfather or his grandmother that he claimed his descent from a monkey?
> **Bishop Samuel Wilberforce** 1805–73, *addressed to T. H. Huxley in a debate on Darwin's theory of evolution*

Biology is the search for the chemistry that works.
> **R. J. P. Williams** 1926–

Lifestyles ····▸ Life

Have fun. And go home when you're tired.
> **George Abbott** 1887–1995

I've lived a life that's full, I've travelled each and ev'ry highway
And more, much more than this. I did it my way.
> **Paul Anka** 1941–

Love and do what you will.
St Augustine of Hippo AD 354-430

A man hath no better thing under the sun, than to eat, and to drink, and to be merry.
Bible

Thou shalt love thy neighbour as thyself.
Bible

The hippies wanted peace and love. We wanted Ferraris, blondes and switchblades.
Alice Cooper 1948-

Do what thou wilt shall be the whole of the Law.
Aleister Crowley 1875-1947

Whatever you do, do cautiously, and look to the end.
Gesta Romanorum late 13th century

Just trust yourself and you'll learn the art of living.
Johann Wolfgang von Goethe 1749-1832

Live all you can; it's a mistake not to. It doesn't so much matter what you do in particular, so long as you have your life. If you haven't had that, what *have* you had?
Henry James 1843-1916

If I had no duties, and no reference to futurity, I would spend my life in driving briskly in a post-chaise with a pretty woman.
Samuel Johnson 1709-84

Turn on, tune in and drop out.
Timothy Leary 1920-96

Mon métier et mon art c'est vivre.
Living is my job and my art.
Montaigne 1533-92

Believe me! The secret of reaping the greatest fruitfulness and the greatest enjoyment from life is *to live dangerously*!
Friedrich Nietzsche 1844-1900

Lifestyles

To live at all is miracle enough.
Mervyn Peake 1911–68

Fais ce que voudras.
Do what you like.
François Rabelais c.1494–c.1553

You only live once, and the way I live, once is enough.
Frank Sinatra 1915–98

Take short views, hope for the best, and trust in God.
Sydney Smith 1771–1845

Keep your eyes open and your mouth shut.
John Steinbeck 1902–68

It's better to burn out
Than to fade away.
Neil Young 1945–

Literature ····▶ Writing

'Oh! it is only a novel!…only Cecilia, or Camilla, or
Belinda:' or, in short, only some work in which the most
thorough knowledge of human nature, the happiest
delineation of its varieties, the liveliest effusions of wit
and humour are conveyed to the world in the best chosen
language.
Jane Austen 1775–1817

A losing trade, I assure you, sir: literature is a drug.
George Borrow 1803–81

All tragedies are finished by a death,
All comedies are ended by a marriage;
The future states of both are left to faith.
Lord Byron 1788–1824

Literature is a luxury; fiction is a necessity.
G. K. Chesterton 1874–1936

The central function of imaginative literature is to make you realize that other people act on moral convictions different from your own.
William Empson 1906–84

Yes—oh dear yes—the novel tells a story.
E. M. Forster 1879–1970

Works of serious purpose and grand promises often have a purple patch or two stitched on, to shine far and wide.
Horace 65–8 BC

It takes a great deal of history to produce a little literature.
Henry James 1843–1916

Literature is my Utopia.
Helen Keller 1880–1968

Never trust the artist. Trust the tale.
D. H. Lawrence 1885–1930

Our American professors like their literature clear and cold and pure and very dead.
Sinclair Lewis 1885–1951

Literature is news that STAYS news.
Ezra Pound 1885–1972

Remarks are not literature.
Gertrude Stein 1874–1946

A novel is a mirror which passes over a highway. Sometimes it reflects to your eyes the blue of the skies, at others the churned-up mud of the road.
Stendhal 1783–1842

The good ended happily, and the bad unhappily. That is what fiction means.
Oscar Wilde 1854–1900

London

Was für Plunder!
What rubbish!
> **Gebhard Lebrecht Blücher** 1742–1819, *often misquoted as
> 'Was für plündern [What a place to plunder]!'*

The great wen of all.
> **William Cobbett** 1762–1835

Crowds without company, and dissipation without
pleasure.
> **Edward Gibbon** 1737–94

Maybe it's because I'm a Londoner
That I love London so.
> **Hubert Gregg** 1914–2004

When a man is tired of London, he is tired of life.
> **Samuel Johnson** 1709–84

I thought of London spread out in the sun,
Its postal districts packed like squares of wheat.
> **Philip Larkin** 1922–85

Earth has not anything to show more fair:
Dull would he be of soul who could pass by
A sight so touching in its majesty.
> **William Wordsworth** 1770–1850

Love ····▶ Lovers, Marriage, Sex

You know very well that love is, above all, the gift of
oneself!
> **Jean Anouilh** 1910–87

If you want to get to know someone better, you shouldn't take them out for a candlelit dinner, you should watch them at work. When they're full of concentration, only not concentrating on you.
    Julian Barnes 1946-

A man chases a girl (until she catches him).
    Irving Berlin 1888–1989

Many waters cannot quench love, neither can the floods drown it.
    Bible

Greater love hath no man than this, that a man lay down his life for his friends.
    Bible

Though I speak with the tongues of men and of angels, and have not charity, I am become as sounding brass, or a tinkling cymbal...
And though I have all faith; so that I could remove mountains; and have not charity, I am nothing.
    Bible

And now abideth faith, hope, charity, these three; but the greatest of these is charity.
    Bible

There is no fear in love; but perfect love casteth out fear.
    Bible

Love seeketh not itself to please,
Nor for itself hath any care;
But for another gives its ease,
And builds a Heaven in Hell's despair.
    William Blake 1757–1827

O, my Luve's like a red, red rose
That's newly sprung in June;
O my Luve's like the melodie

Love

That's sweetly play'd in tune.
Robert Burns 1759–96

In love, everything is true, everything is false; and it is the one subject on which one cannot express an absurdity.
Nicolas-Sébastien Chamfort 1741–94

Love and a cottage! Eh, Fanny! Ah, give me indifference and a coach and six!
George Colman, the Elder 1732–94 and **David Garrick** 1717–79

Say what you will, 'tis better to be left than never to have been loved.
William Congreve 1670–1729

L'amor che muove il sole e l'altre stelle.
The love that moves the sun and the other stars.
Dante Alighieri 1265–1321

Love itself is what is left over when being in love has burned away.
Louis de Bernières 1954–

If you could see my legs when I take my boots off, you'd form some idea of what unrequited affection is.
Charles Dickens 1812–70

Love is a growing or full constant light;
And his first minute, after noon, is night.
John Donne 1572–1631

Love built on beauty, soon as beauty, dies.
John Donne 1572–1631

I am the Love that dare not speak its name.
Lord Alfred Douglas 1870–1945

And love's the noblest frailty of the mind.
John Dryden 1631–1700

Love's pleasure lasts but a moment; love's sorrow lasts all
  through life.
  Jean-Pierre Claris de Florian 1755-94

Oh, if only we could lean over the soul we love and see
as in a mirror the image we cast there!
  André Gide 1869-1951

If I love you, what does that matter to you!
  Johann Wolfgang von Goethe 1749-1832

Love in a hut, with water and a crust,
Is—Love, forgive us!—cinders, ashes, dust.
  John Keats 1795-1821

There is no disguise which can hide love for long where it
exists, or feign it where it does not.
  Duc de la Rochefoucauld 1613-80

How alike are the groans of love to those of the dying.
  Malcolm Lowry 1909-57

Where both deliberate, the love is slight;
Who ever loved that loved not at first sight?
  Christopher Marlowe 1564-93

Had we but world enough, and time,
This coyness, lady, were no crime.
  Andrew Marvell 1621-78

The love that lasts longest is the love that is never
returned.
  W. Somerset Maugham 1874-1965

If I am pressed to say why I loved him, I feel it can only
be explained by replying: 'Because it was he; because it
was me.'
  Montaigne 1533-92

No, there's nothing half so sweet in life
As love's young dream.
  Thomas Moore 1779-1852

Love

If I can't love Hitler, I can't love at all.
Rev. A. J. Muste 1885–1967

Love is so short, forgetting is so long.
Pablo Neruda 1904–73

Pace non trovo et non ò da far guerra,
e temo et spero, et ardo et son un ghiaccio.
I find no peace, and I am not at war,
I fear and hope, and burn and I am ice.
Petrarch 1304–74

Birds do it, bees do it,
Even educated fleas do it.
Let's do it, let's fall in love.
Cole Porter 1891–1964

Love consists in this, that two solitudes protect and touch
and greet each other.
Rainer Maria Rilke 1875–1926

Life has taught us that love does not consist in gazing at
each other but in looking together in the same direction.
Antoine de Saint-Exupéry 1900–44

Love means not ever having to say you're sorry.
Erich Segal 1937–

The course of true love never did run smooth.
William Shakespeare 1564–1616

                    Then, must you speak
Of one that loved not wisely but too well.
William Shakespeare 1564–1616

For stony limits cannot hold love out,
And what love can do that dares love attempt.
William Shakespeare 1564–1616

To be wise, and love,
Exceeds man's might.
  William Shakespeare 1564–1616

Let me not to the marriage of true minds
Admit impediments. Love is not love
Which alters when it alteration finds.
  William Shakespeare 1564–1616

The fickleness of the women I love is only equalled by the
infernal constancy of the women who love me.
  George Bernard Shaw 1856–1950

Why so pale and wan, fond lover?
Prithee, why so pale?
Will, when looking well can't move her,
Looking ill prevail?
  John Suckling 1609–42

'Tis better to have loved and lost
Than never to have loved at all.
  Alfred, Lord Tennyson 1809–92

Omnia vincit Amor: et nos cedamus Amori.
Love conquers all things: let us too give in to Love.
  Virgil 70–19 BC

Yet each man kills the thing he loves,
By each let this be heard,
Some do it with a bitter look,
Some with a flattering word.
The coward does it with a kiss,
The brave man with a sword!
  Oscar Wilde 1854–1900

A pity beyond all telling,
Is hid in the heart of love.
  W. B. Yeats 1865–1939

Lovers

One is never too old for romance.
   Ingrid Bergman 1915–82

As the apple tree among the trees of the wood, so is my beloved among the sons.
   Bible

Right worshipful and well-beloved Valentine, I commend myself to you with all my heart, wishing to hear that all is well with you: I beseech Almighty God to keep you well according to his pleasure and your heart's desire.
   Margery Brews *letter to John Paston, 1477*

He's more myself than I am. Whatever our souls are made of his and mine are the same.
   Emily Brontë 1818–48

If thou must love me, let it be for nought
Except for love's sake only.
   Elizabeth Barrett Browning 1806–61

How do I love thee? Let me count the ways.
   Elizabeth Barrett Browning 1806–61

To see her is to love her,
And love but her for ever;
For Nature made her what she is
And never made anither!
   Robert Burns 1759–96

My heart has made its mind up
And I'm afraid it's you.
   Wendy Cope 1945–

My soul is so knit to yours that it is but a divided life I live without you.
   George Eliot 1819–80

Lovers

HUMPHREY BOGART: Here's looking at you, kid.
   Julius J. Epstein 1909–2001 et al.

I'd like to be your preference
And hence
I'd like to be around when you unhook.
I'd like to be your only audience,
The final name in your appointment book,
Your future tense.
   John Fuller 1937–

The ones we choose to love become our anchor
when the hawser of the blood-tie's hacked, or frays.
   Tony Harrison 1953–

Stay, little Valentine, stay,
Each day is Valentine's day.
   Lorenz Hart 1895–1943

I was more pleased with possessing your heart than with
any other happiness.
   Héloïse c.1098–1164

All you need is love.
   John Lennon 1940–80 and **Paul McCartney** 1942–

So many contradictions, so many contrary movements are
true, and can be explained in three words: *I love you.*
   Julie de Lespinasse 1732–76

The life that I have
Is all that I have
And the life that I have
Is yours.
The love that I have
Of the life that I have
Is yours and yours and yours.
   Leo Marks 1920–2001, *given to the British secret agent Violette
   Szabo (1921–45), for use with the Special Operations Executive*

Lovers

Difficult or easy, pleasant or bitter, you are the same you:
I cannot live with you—or without you.
   Martial AD C.40–C.104

          It were all one
That I should love a bright particular star
And think to wed it, he is so above me.
   William Shakespeare 1564–1616

Why is it that the most unoriginal thing we can say to
one another is still the thing we long to hear? 'I love you'
is always a quotation.
   Jeanette Winterson 1959–

Luck

What we call luck is the inner man externalized. We make
things happen to us.
   Robertson Davies 1913–95

The best mascot is a good mechanic.
   Amelia Earhart 1898–1937

There is much good luck in the world, but it is luck. We
are none of us safe. We are children, playing or
quarrelling on the line.
   E. M. Forster 1879–1970

Care and diligence bring luck.
   Thomas Fuller 1654–1734

Some folk want their luck buttered.
   Thomas Hardy 1840–1928

Watch out w'en you'er gittin all you want. Fattenin' hogs
ain't in luck.
   Joel Chandler Harris 1848–1908

All you know about it [luck] for certain is that it's bound
to change.
   Bret Harte 1836–1902

Miracles do happen, but one has to work very hard for
them.
   Chaim Weizmann 1874–1952

Madness

Whenever God prepares evil for a man, He first damages
his mind, with which he deliberates.
   Anonymous

Babylon in all its desolation is a sight not so awful as that
of the human mind in ruins.
   Scrope Davies c.1783–1852

Quem Jupiter vult perdere, dementat prius.
Whom God would destroy He first sends mad.
   James Duport 1606–79

Mad, is he? Then I hope he will *bite* some of my other
generals.
   George II 1683–1760, *replying to the Duke of Newcastle, who
   had complained that General Wolfe was a madman*

There was only one catch and that was Catch-22…Orr
would be crazy to fly more missions and sane if he
didn't, but if he was sane he had to fly them. If he flew
them he was crazy and didn't have to; but if he didn't
want to he was sane and had to.
   Joseph Heller 1923–99

Every one is more or less mad on one point.
   Rudyard Kipling 1865–1936

Madness

Madness need not be all breakdown. It may also be break-through.
R. D. Laing 1927–89

They called me mad, and I called them mad, and damn them, they outvoted me.
Nathaniel Lee c.1653–92

Is there no way out of the mind?
Sylvia Plath 1932–63

The psychopath is the furnace that gives no heat.
Derek Raymond 1931–94

Though this be madness, yet there is method in't.
William Shakespeare 1564–1616

O! let me not be mad, not mad, sweet heaven;
Keep me in temper; I would not be mad!
William Shakespeare 1564–1616

Management ····▸ Careers, Planning

Committee—a group of men who individually can do nothing but as a group decide that nothing can be done.
Fred Allen 1894–1956

A place for everything and everything in its place.
Mrs Beeton 1836–65

An industrial worker would sooner have a £5 note but a countryman must have praise.
Ronald Blythe 1922–

Oh, the Germans classify, but the French arrange!
Willa Cather 1873–1947

You're either part of the solution or you're part of the problem.
Eldridge Cleaver 1935–98

Some great men owe most of their greatness to the ability of detecting in those they destine for their tools the exact quality of strength that matters for their work.

Joseph Conrad 1857–1924

If management are using a word you don't understand, nine times out of ten they are making you redundant.

John Edwards

When people ask me whether I'd rather be thought of as a funny man or a great boss, my answer is always the same: they are not mutually exclusive.

Ricky Gervais and **Stephen Merchant** David Brent as manager

A camel is a horse designed by a committee.

Alec Issigonis 1906–88

There cannot be a crisis next week. My schedule is already full.

Henry Kissinger 1923–

If it ain't broke, don't fix it.

Bert Lance 1931–

Every time I create an appointment, I create a hundred malcontents and one ingrate.

Louis XIV 1638–1715

There is always a well-known solution to every human problem—neat, plausible, and wrong.

H. L. Mencken 1880–1956

Time spent on any item of the agenda will be in inverse proportion to the sum involved.

C. Northcote Parkinson 1909–93

In a hierarchy every employee tends to rise to his level of incompetence.

Laurence Peter 1919–

Management

Surround yourself with the best people you can find, delegate authority, and don't interfere.
Ronald Reagan 1911–2004

There is nothing in the world which does not have its decisive moment, and the masterpiece of good management is to recognize and grasp this moment.
Cardinal de Retz 1613–79

A problem left to itself dries up or goes rotten. But fertilize a problem with a solution—you'll hatch out dozens.
N. F. Simpson 1919–

The shortest way to do many things is to do only one thing at once.
Samuel Smiles 1812–1904

Management that wants to change an institution must first show it loves that institution.
John Tusa 1936–

Dans ce pays-ci il est bon de tuer de temps en temps un amiral pour encourager les autres.
In this country [England] it is thought well to kill an admiral from time to time to encourage the others.
Voltaire 1694–1778

Manners ····> Behaviour

Evil communications corrupt good manners.
Bible

Most vices may be committed very genteelly: a man may debauch his friend's wife genteelly: he may cheat at cards genteelly.
James Boswell 1740–95

The tribute which intelligence pays to humbug.
St John Brodrick 1856–1942, *definition of tact*

Curtsey while you're thinking what to say. It saves time.
Lewis Carroll 1832–98

Take the tone of the company that you are in.
Lord Chesterfield 1694–1773

Very notable was his distinction between coarseness and vulgarity (coarseness, revealing something; vulgarity, concealing something).
E. M. Forster 1879–1970

The art of pleasing consists in being pleased.
William Hazlitt 1778–1830

An insolent reply from a polite person is a bad sign.
Hippocrates c.460–c.370 BC

There are few who would not rather be taken in adultery than in provincialism.
Aldous Huxley 1894–1963

To Americans, English manners are far more frightening than none at all.
Randall Jarrell 1914–65

Punctuality is the politeness of kings.
Louis XVIII 1755–1824

Stand not upon the order of your going.
William Shakespeare 1564–1616

He is the very pineapple of politeness!
Richard Brinsley Sheridan 1751–1816

The Japanese have perfected good manners and made them indistinguishable from rudeness.
Paul Theroux 1941–

This is the only country in the world where you step on somebody's foot and he apologises.
Keith Waterhouse 1929–

Manners

Manners are especially the need of the plain. The pretty
can get away with anything.
    Evelyn Waugh 1903–66

Marriage ····▶ Love, Weddings

It is a truth universally acknowledged, that a single man
in possession of a good fortune, must be in want of a
wife.
    Jane Austen 1775–1817

Wives are young men's mistresses, companions for middle
age, and old men's nurses.
    Francis Bacon 1561–1626

Being a husband is a whole-time job. That is why so
many husbands fail. They cannot give their entire
attention to it.
    Arnold Bennett 1867–1931

What therefore God hath joined together, let not man put
asunder.
    Bible

To have and to hold from this day forward, for better for
worse, for richer for poorer, in sickness and in health, to
love, cherish, and to obey, till death us do part.
    Book of Common Prayer 1662

Think you, if Laura had been Petrarch's wife,
He would have written sonnets all his life?
    Lord Byron 1788–1824

Still I can't contradict, what so oft has been said,
'Though women are angels, yet wedlock's the devil.'
    Lord Byron 1788–1824

The deep, deep peace of the double-bed after the hurly-burly of the chaise-longue.
Mrs Patrick Campbell 1865–1940, *on her recent marriage*

Oh! how many torments lie in the small circle of a wedding-ring!
Colley Cibber 1671–1757

I learnt a long time ago that the only people who count in any marriage are the two that are in it.
Hillary Rodham Clinton 1947–

Marriage is a wonderful invention; but, then again, so is a bicycle repair kit.
Billy Connolly 1942–

The heart of marriage is memories.
Bill Cosby 1937–

I would be married, but I'd have no wife,
I would be married to a single life.
Richard Crashaw c.1612–49

The chains of marriage are so heavy that it takes two to bear them, and sometimes three.
Alexandre Dumas 1824–95

Man's best possession is a sympathetic wife.
Euripides c.485–c.406 BC

Do you think your mother and I should have lived comfortably so long together, if ever we had been married?
John Gay 1685–1732

You shall be together when the white wings of death
  scatter your days.
Ay, you shall be together even in the silent memory of
  God.
But let there be spaces in your togetherness,

Marriage

And let the winds of the heavens dance between you.
Kahlil Gibran 1883–1931

I…chose my wife, as she did her wedding gown, not for a
fine glossy surface, but such qualities as would wear well.
Oliver Goldsmith 1728–74

The critical period in matrimony is breakfast-time.
A. P. Herbert 1890–1971

Then be not coy, but use your time;
And while ye may, go marry:
For having lost but once your prime,
You may for ever tarry.
Robert Herrick 1591–1674

The triumph of hope over experience.
Samuel Johnson 1709–84, *of a man who remarried
immediately after the death of a wife with whom he had been
unhappy*

I am your clay.
You are my clay.
In life we share a single quilt.
In death we will share one coffin.
Kuan Tao-sheng 1262–1319

So they were married—to be the more together—
And found they were never again so much together,
Divided by the morning tea,
By the evening paper,
By children and tradesmen's bills.
Louis MacNeice 1907–63

One doesn't have to get anywhere in a marriage. It's not
a public conveyance.
Iris Murdoch 1919–99

The great secret of a successful marriage is to treat all disasters as incidents and none of the incidents as disasters.

Harold Nicolson 1886–1968

Marriage may often be a stormy lake, but celibacy is almost always a muddy horsepond.

Thomas Love Peacock 1785–1866

Tolerance is the one essential ingredient.

Prince Philip 1921– , *his recipe for a successful marriage*

It doesn't much signify whom one marries, for one is sure to find next morning that it was someone else.

Samuel Rogers 1763–1855

A young man married is a man that's marred.

William Shakespeare 1564–1616

Kiss me Kate, we will be married o' Sunday.

William Shakespeare 1564–1616

Marriage is popular because it combines the maximum of temptation with the maximum of opportunity.

George Bernard Shaw 1856–1950

Chains do not hold a marriage together. It is threads, hundreds of tiny threads which sew people together through the years. That is what makes a marriage last— more than passion or even sex!

Simone Signoret 1921–85

My definition of marriage…it resembles a pair of shears, so joined that they cannot be separated; often moving in opposite directions, yet always punishing anyone who comes between them.

Sydney Smith 1771–1845

Marriage

Marriage is like life in this—that it is a field of battle, and not a bed of roses.

Robert Louis Stevenson 1850–94

Marriage isn't a word...it's a *sentence*!

King Vidor 1895–1982

In married life three is company and two none.

Oscar Wilde 1854–1900

Mathematics

Let no one enter who does not know geometry [mathematics].

Anonymous *inscription on Plato's door, probably at the Academy at Athens*

If in other sciences we should arrive at certainty without doubt and truth without error, it behoves us to place the foundations of knowledge in mathematics.

Roger Bacon c.1220–c.1292

They are neither finite quantities, or quantities infinitely small, nor yet nothing. May we not call them the ghosts of departed quantities?

Bishop George Berkeley 1685–1753, *on Newton's infinitesimals*

I never could make out what those damned dots meant.

Lord Randolph Churchill 1849–94, *on decimal points*

Equations are more important to me, because politics is for the present, but an equation is something for eternity.

Albert Einstein 1879–1955

There is no 'royal road' to geometry.

Euclid fl. c.300 BC

This book is written in mathematical language and its characters are triangles, circles and other geometrical figures, without whose help…one wanders in vain through a dark labyrinth.

Galileo Galilei 1564–1642, *often quoted as 'The book of nature is written…'*

Mathematics are a species of Frenchman; if you say something to them, they translate it into their own language and presto! it is something entirely different.

Johann Wolfgang von Goethe 1749–1832

Prime numbers are what is left when you have taken all the patterns away. I think prime numbers are like life.

Mark Haddon 1962–

No-one could study mathematics intensively for more than five hours a day and remain sane.

J. B. S. Haldane 1892–1964

Beauty is the first test: there is no permanent place in the world for ugly mathematics.

Godfrey Harold Hardy 1877–1947

Someone told me that each equation I included in the book would halve the sales.

Stephen Hawking 1942–

God made the integers, all the rest is the work of man.

Leopold Kronecker 1823–91

In mathematics you don't understand things. You just get used to them.

John von Neumann 1903–57

God is always doing geometry.

Plato 429–347 BC

Mathematics may be defined as the subject in which we never know what we are talking about, nor whether what we are saying is true.

Bertrand Russell 1872–1970

Mathematics

What would life be like without arithmetic, but a scene of horrors?
Sydney Smith 1771–1845

Meaning ····▸ Words

No one means all he says, and yet very few say all they mean, for words are slippery and thought is viscous.
Henry Brooks Adams 1838–1918

'Then you should say what you mean,' the March Hare went on. 'I do,' Alice hastily replied; 'at least—at least I mean what I say—that's the same thing, you know.' 'Not the same thing a bit!' said the Hatter. 'Why, you might just as well say that "I see what I eat" is the same thing as "I eat what I see!" '
Lewis Carroll 1832–98

It depends on what the meaning of 'is' is.
Bill Clinton 1946–

The meaning doesn't matter if it's only idle chatter of a transcendental kind.
W. S. Gilbert 1836–1911

It all depends what you mean by...
C. E. M. Joad 1891–1953, *characteristic response to questions*

God and I both knew what it meant once; now God alone knows.
Friedrich Klopstock 1724–1803

I pray thee, understand a plain man in his plain meaning.
William Shakespeare 1564–1616

The little girl had the making of a poet in her who, being told to be sure of her meaning before she spoke, said, 'How can I know what I think till I see what I say?'
Graham Wallas 1858–1932

Medicine ····▸ Health, Sickness

Medicinal discovery,
It moves in mighty leaps,
It leapt straight past the common cold
And gave it us for keeps.
Pam Ayres 1947–

Cure the disease and kill the patient.
Francis Bacon 1561–1626

The remedy is worse than the disease.
Francis Bacon 1561–1626

Physician, heal thyself.
Bible

He that sinneth before his Maker, let him fall into the
hand of the physician.
Bible (Apocrypha)

We all labour against our own cure, for death is the cure
of all diseases.
Sir Thomas Browne 1605–82

I don't believe in vitamin pills. I swear by men, darling—
and as many as possible.
Joan Collins 1933–

Every day, in every way, I am getting better and better.
Émile Coué 1857–1926, *to be said 15 to 20 times, morning and
evening*

We shall have to learn to refrain from doing things
merely because we know how to do them.
Theodore Fox 1899–1989

When our organs have been transplanted
And the new ones made happy to lodge in us,
Let us pray one wish be granted—

Medicine

We retain our zones erogenous.
E. Y. Harburg 1898–1981

Life is short, the art long.
Hippocrates c.460–357 BC, *often quoted as* 'Ars longa, vita brevis'

As to diseases, make a habit of two things—to help, or at least to do no harm.
Hippocrates c.460–c.370 BC

It is a most extraordinary thing, but I never read a patent medicine advertisement without being impelled to the conclusion that I am suffering from the particular disease therein dealt with in its most virulent form.
Jerome K. Jerome 1859–1927

GÉRONTE: It seems to me you are locating them wrongly: the heart is on the left and the liver is on the right.
SGANARELLE: Yes, in the old days that was so, but we have changed all that.
Molière 1622–73

It may seem a strange principle to enunciate as the very first requirement in a Hospital that it should do the sick no harm.
Florence Nightingale 1820–1910

One finger in the throat and one in the rectum makes a good diagnostician.
William Osler 1849–1919

The irony is that the healthier Western society becomes, the more medicine it craves.
Roy Porter 1946–2002

Throw physic to the dogs; I'll none of it.
William Shakespeare 1564–1616

Formerly, when religion was strong and science weak,
men mistook magic for medicine; now, when science is
strong and religion weak, men mistake medicine for
magic.
Thomas Szasz 1920–

Meeting ····> Parting

Gin a body meet a body
Comin thro' the rye,
Gin a body kiss a body
Need a body cry?
Robert Burns 1759–96

'Is there anybody there?' said the Traveller,
Knocking on the moonlit door.
Walter de la Mare 1873–1956

HUMPHREY BOGART: Of all the gin joints in all the towns
in all the world, she walks into mine.
Julius J. Epstein 1909–2001 et al.

Some enchanted evening,
You may see a stranger,
You may see a stranger,
Across a crowded room.
Oscar Hammerstein II 1895–1960

Not many sounds in life, and I include all urban and all
rural sounds, exceed in interest a knock at the door.
Charles Lamb 1775–1834

How d'ye do, and how is the old complaint?
Lord Palmerston 1784–1865, *reputed to be his greeting to all
those he did not know*

Meeting

We'll meet again, don't know where,
Don't know when,
But I know we'll meet again some sunny day.
  Ross Parker 1914-74 and **Hugh Charles** 1907-

When shall we three meet again
In thunder, lightning, or in rain?
  William Shakespeare 1564-1616

Ill met by moonlight, proud Titania.
  William Shakespeare 1564-1616

Dr Livingstone, I presume?
  Henry Morton Stanley 1841-1904

Why don't you come up sometime, and see me?
  Mae West 1892-1980

Memory

And we forget because we must
And not because we will.
  Matthew Arnold 1822-88

Someone said that God gave us memory so that we might
have roses in December.
  J. M. Barrie 1860-1937

Nobody can remember more than seven of anything.
  Cardinal Robert Bellarmine 1542-1621, *reason for omitting
  the eight beatitudes from his catechism*

Memories are not shackles, Franklin, they are garlands.
  Alan Bennett 1934-

We'll tak a cup o' kindness yet,
For auld lang syne.
  Robert Burns 1759-96

Memory

Our memories are card-indexes consulted, and then put
back in disorder by authorities whom we do not control.
Cyril Connolly 1903–74

I have forgot much, Cynara! gone with the wind.
Ernest Dowson 1867–1900

Everyone seems to remember with great clarity what they
were doing on November 22nd, 1963, at the precise
moment they heard President Kennedy was dead.
Frederick Forsyth 1938–

Your memory is a monster; *you* forget—*it* doesn't. It
simply files things away. It keeps things for you, or hides
things from you—and summons them to your recall with
a will of its own. You think you have a memory; but it
has you!
John Irving 1942–

A cigarette that bears a lipstick's traces,
An airline ticket to romantic places;
And still my heart has wings
These foolish things
Remind me of you.
Holt Marvell 1901–69

You may break, you may shatter the vase, if you will,
But the scent of the roses will hang round it still.
Thomas Moore 1779–1852

And suddenly the memory revealed itself. The taste was
that of the little piece of madeleine which…my aunt
Léonie used to give me, dipping it first in her own cup of
tea or tisane.
Marcel Proust 1871–1922

Better by far you should forget and smile
Than that you should remember and be sad.
Christina Rossetti 1830–94

Memory

When to the sessions of sweet silent thought
I summon up remembrance of things past.
William Shakespeare 1564–1616

There's rosemary, that's for remembrance; pray, love,
remember.
William Shakespeare 1564–1616

Men

Are all men in disguise except those crying?
Dannie Abse 1923–

Men have had every advantage of us in telling their own
story. Education has been theirs in so much higher a
degree; the pen has been in their hands.
Jane Austen 1775–1817

Why would I talk about the men in my life? For me, life
is not about men.
Catherine Deneuve 1943–

Men are but children of a larger growth;
Our appetites as apt to change as theirs,
And full as craving too, and full as vain.
John Dryden 1631–1700

A man…is *so* in the way in the house!
Elizabeth Gaskell 1810–65

Man is Nature's sole mistake!
W. S. Gilbert 1836–1911

Years ago, manhood was an opportunity for achievement,
and now it is a problem to be overcome.
Garrison Keillor 1942–

Men and Women

Why can't a woman be more like a man?
Men are so honest, so thoroughly square;
Eternally noble, historically fair.
   Alan Jay Lerner 1918–86

Give me macho, or give me death.
   Madonna 1958–

Somehow a bachelor never quite gets over the idea that
he is a thing of beauty and a boy forever.
   Helen Rowland 1875–1950

Sigh no more, ladies, sigh no more,
Men were deceivers ever.
   William Shakespeare 1564–1616

It's not the men in my life that counts—it's the life in my
men.
   Mae West 1892–1980

Men and Women ····▶ Woman's Role

Women are really much nicer than men:
No wonder we like them.
   Kingsley Amis 1922–95

In societies where men are truly confident of their own
worth, women are not merely tolerated but valued.
   Aung San Suu Kyi 1945–

Man's love is of man's life a thing apart,
'Tis woman's whole existence.
   Lord Byron 1788–1824

The man's desire is for the woman; but the woman's
desire is rarely other than for the desire of the man.
   Samuel Taylor Coleridge 1772–1834

Men and Women

There is more difference within the sexes than between them.
Ivy Compton-Burnett 1884–1969

In the sex-war thoughtlessness is the weapon of the male, vindictiveness of the female.
Cyril Connolly 1903–74

Women have very little idea of how much men hate them.
Germaine Greer 1939–

The female of the species is more deadly than the male.
Rudyard Kipling 1865–1936

A woman can forgive a man for the harm he does her, but she can never forgive him for the sacrifices he makes on her account.
W. Somerset Maugham 1874–1965

Men have a much better time of it than women. For one thing, they marry later. For another thing, they die earlier.
H. L. Mencken 1880–1956

He for God only, she for God in him.
John Milton 1608–74

I admit it is better fun to punt than to be punted, and that a desire to have all the fun is nine-tenths of the law of chivalry.
Dorothy L. Sayers 1893–1957

Of all human struggles there is none so treacherous and remorseless as the struggle between the artist man and the mother woman.
George Bernard Shaw 1856–1950

A woman without a man is like a fish without a bicycle.
Gloria Steinem 1934–

Whereas nature turns girls into women, society has to make boys into men.
Anthony Stevens

'Tis strange what a man may do, and a woman yet think him an angel.
William Makepeace Thackeray 1811–63

Me Tarzan, you Jane.
Johnny Weissmuller 1904–84

Whatever women do they must do twice as well as men to be thought half as good.
Charlotte Whitton 1896–1975

All women become like their mothers. That is their tragedy. No man does. That's his.
Oscar Wilde 1854–1900

Middle Age

Years ago we discovered the exact point, the dead centre of middle age. It occurs when you are too young to take up golf and too old to rush up to the net.
Franklin P. Adams 1881–1960

You are living in a land you no longer recognize. You don't know the language.
Martin Amis 1949–

I am past thirty, and three parts iced over.
Matthew Arnold 1822–88

Mr Salteena was an elderly man of 42.
Daisy Ashford 1881–1972

Nel mezzo del cammin di nostra vita.
Midway along the path of our life.
Dante Alighieri 1265–1321

Middle Age

At eighteen our convictions are hills from which we look;
at forty-five they are caves in which we hide.
 F. Scott Fitzgerald 1896–1940

The afternoon of human life must also have a significance
of its own and cannot be merely a pitiful appendage to
life's morning.
 Carl Gustav Jung 1875–1961

Men at forty
Learn to close softly
The doors to rooms they will not be
Coming back to.
 Donald Justice 1925–

At forty-five,
What next, what next?
At every corner,
I meet my Father,
my age, still alive.
 Robert Lowell 1917–77

The lovely thing about being forty is that you can
appreciate twenty-five-year-old men more.
 Colleen McCullough 1937–

Do you think my mind is maturing late,
Or simply rotted early?
 Ogden Nash 1902–71, *on facing forty*

One of the pleasures of middle age is to *find out* that one
WAS right, and that one was much righter than one knew
at say 17 or 23.
 Ezra Pound 1885–1972

One's prime is elusive. You little girls, when you grow up,
must be on the alert to recognise your prime at whatever
time of your life it may occur.
 Muriel Spark 1918–

By the time you hit 50, I reckon you've earned your wrinkles, so why not be proud of them?
Twiggy 1949–

The Mind

It is not enough to have a good mind; the main thing is to use it well.
René Descartes 1596–1650

On earth there is nothing great but man; in man there is nothing great but mind.
William Hamilton 1788–1856

O the mind, mind has mountains; cliffs of fall
Frightful, sheer, no-man-fathomed.
Gerard Manley Hopkins 1844–89

Everyone complains of his memory, and no one complains of his judgement.
Duc de la Rochefoucauld 1613–80

The mind loves the unknown. It loves images whose meaning is unknown, since the meaning of the mind itself is unknown.
René Magritte 1898–1967

The mind is its own place, and in itself
Can make a heaven of hell, a hell of heaven.
John Milton 1608–74

Those who are caught in mental cages can often picture freedom, it just has no attractive power.
Iris Murdoch 1919–99

That's the classical mind at work, runs fine inside but looks dingy on the surface.
Robert M. Pirsig 1928–

The Mind

Why waste money on psychotherapy when you can listen to the B Minor Mass?
Michael Torke 1961-

Every human brain is born not as a blank tablet (a *tabula rasa*) waiting to be filled in by experience but as 'an exposed negative waiting to be slipped into developer fluid'.
Edward O. Wilson 1929- , *on the nature v. nurture debate*

To give a sex to mind was not very consistent with the principles of a man [Rousseau] who argued so warmly, and so well, for the immortality of the soul.
Mary Wollstonecraft 1759-97, *often quoted as 'Mind has no sex'*

Misfortune

Prosperity doth best discover vice, but adversity doth best discover virtue.
Francis Bacon 1561-1626

And always keep a-hold of Nurse
For fear of finding something worse.
Hilaire Belloc 1870-1953

Man is born unto trouble, as the sparks fly upward.
Bible

For in every ill-turn of fortune the most unhappy sort of unfortunate man is the one who has been happy.
Boethius AD C.476-524

...Nessun maggior dolore,
Che ricordarsi del tempo felice
Nella miseria.

Misfortune

There is no greater pain than to remember a happy time
   when one is in misery.
    Dante Alighieri 1265–1321

And all my endeavours are unlucky explorers
come back, abandoning the expedition.
    Keith Douglas 1920–44

In the words of one of my more sympathetic
correspondents, it has turned out to be an 'annus
horribilis'.
    Elizabeth II 1926–

I left the room with silent dignity, but caught my foot in
the mat.
    George Grossmith 1847–1912 and **Weedon Grossmith**
    1854–1919

In the misfortune of our best friends, we always find
something which is not displeasing to us.
    Duc de la Rochefoucauld 1613–80

When fortune empties her chamberpot on your head,
smile—and say 'we are going to have a summer shower'.
    John A. Macdonald 1815–91

now and then
there is a person born
who is so unlucky
that he runs into accidents
which started to happen
to somebody else.
    Don Marquis 1878–1937

I had never had a piece of toast
Particularly long and wide,
But fell upon the sanded floor,
And always on the buttered side.
    James Payn 1830–98

Misfortune

Sweet are the uses of adversity,
Which like the toad, ugly and venomous,
Wears yet a precious jewel in his head.
William Shakespeare 1564-1616

The fatal law of gravity: when you are down everything
falls on you.
Sylvia Townsend Warner 1893-1978

One likes people much better when they're battered down
by a prodigious siege of misfortune than when they
triumph.
Virginia Woolf 1882-1941

Mistakes

The weak have one weapon: the errors of those who
think they are strong.
Georges Bidault 1899-1983

Truth lies within a little and certain compass, but error is
immense.
Henry St John, 1st Viscount Bolingbroke 1678-1751

It is worse than a crime, it is a blunder.
Antoine Boulay de la Meurthe 1761-1840, *on hearing of the execution of the Duc d'Enghien*

I would rather be wrong, by God, with Plato...than be
correct with those men.
Cicero 106-43 BC, *of Pythagoreans*

I beseech you, in the bowels of Christ, think it possible
you may be mistaken.
Oliver Cromwell 1599-1658

Errors, like straws, upon the surface flow;
He who would search for pearls must dive below.
John Dryden 1631-1700

If all else fails, immortality can always be assured by a spectacular error.
> **J. K. Galbraith** 1908–

Mistakes are a fact of life
It is the response to error that counts.
> **Nikki Giovanni** 1943–

An expert is someone who knows some of the worst mistakes that can be made in his subject and who manages to avoid them.
> **Werner Heisenberg** 1901–76

I'm aggrieved when sometimes even excellent Homer nods.
> **Horace** 65–8 BC

Crooked things may be as stiff and unflexible as straight: and men may be as positive in error as in truth.
> **John Locke** 1632–1704

The man who makes no mistakes does not usually make anything.
> **Edward John Phelps** 1822–1900

One Galileo in two thousand years is enough.
> **Pope Pius XII** 1876–1958, *on being asked to proscribe the works of Teilhard de Chardin*

A man should never be ashamed to own he has been in the wrong, which is but saying, in other words, that he is wiser to-day than he was yesterday.
> **Alexander Pope** 1688–1744

'Forward, the Light Brigade!'
Was there a man dismayed?
Not though the soldier knew
Some one had blundered.
> **Alfred, Lord Tennyson** 1809–92

Mistakes

To lose one parent, Mr Worthing, may be regarded as a misfortune; to lose both looks like carelessness.
Oscar Wilde 1854–1900

Moderation

Nothing in excess.
Anonymous *inscribed on the temple of Apollo at Delphi*

To many, total abstinence is easier than perfect moderation.
St Augustine of Hippo AD 354–430

We know what happens to people who stay in the middle of the road. They get run down.
Aneurin Bevan 1897–1960

I would remind you that extremism in the defence of liberty is no vice! And let me remind you also that moderation in the pursuit of justice is no virtue!
Barry Goldwater 1909–98

There's nothing in the middle of the road but yellow stripes and dead armadillos.
Jim Hightower

There is moderation in everything.
Horace 65–8 BC

You will go most safely by the middle way.
Ovid 43 BC–AD c.17

To gild refinèd gold, to paint the lily…
Is wasteful and ridiculous excess.
William Shakespeare 1564–1616

Above all, gentlemen, not the slightest zeal.
Charles-Maurice de Talleyrand 1754–1838

Money ····➤ Poverty, Wealth

Nothing that costs only a dollar is worth having.
Elizabeth Arden 1876–1966

Money is like muck, not good except it be spread.
Francis Bacon 1561–1626

Money, it turned out, was exactly like sex, you thought of nothing else if you didn't have it and thought of other things if you did.
James Baldwin 1924–87

Money speaks sense in a language all nations understand.
Aphra Behn 1640–89

The love of money is the root of all evil.
Bible

Nothing to be done without a bribe I find, in love as well as law.
Susannah Centlivre c.1669–1723

The sinews of war, unlimited money.
Cicero 106–43 BC

MR MICAWBER: Annual income twenty pounds, annual expenditure nineteen nineteen six, result happiness. Annual income twenty pounds, annual expenditure twenty pounds ought and six, result misery.
Charles Dickens 1812–70

Money doesn't talk, it swears.
Bob Dylan 1941–

A bank is a place that will lend you money if you can prove that you don't need it.
Bob Hope 1903–2003

Money

If possible honestly, if not, somehow, make money.
   Horace 65–8 BC

For I don't care too much for money,
For money can't buy me love.
   John Lennon 1940–80 and **Paul McCartney** 1942–

Take care of the pence, and the pounds will take care of themselves.
   William Lowndes 1652–1724

Money is like a sixth sense without which you cannot make a complete use of the other five.
   W. Somerset Maugham 1874–1965

Money couldn't buy friends but you got a better class of enemy.
   Spike Milligan 1918–2002

I want to spend, and spend, and spend.
   Vivian Nicholson 1936– , *said to reporters on arriving to collect football pools winnings of £152,000*

Expenditure rises to meet income.
   C. Northcote Parkinson 1909–93

'My boy,' he says, 'always try to rub up against money, for if you rub up against money long enough, some of it may rub off on you.'
   Damon Runyon 1884–1946

I can get no remedy against this consumption of the purse: borrowing only lingers and lingers it out, but the disease is incurable.
   William Shakespeare 1564–1616

Pennies don't fall from heaven. They have to be earned on earth.
   Margaret Thatcher 1925–

Morality

> *Quid non mortalia pectora cogis,*
> *Auri sacra fames!*
> To what do you not drive human hearts, cursed craving
> for gold!
> **Virgil** 70–19 BC

Morality

Morality is a private and costly luxury.
Henry Brooks Adams 1838–1918

Standards are always out of date. That is what makes
them standards.
Alan Bennett 1934–

Food comes first, then morals.
Bertolt Brecht 1898–1956

Cum finis est licitus, etiam media sunt licita.
The end justifies the means.
Hermann Busenbaum 1600–68

What I know most surely about morality and the duty of
man I owe to sport.
Albert Camus 1913–60, *often quoted as '…I owe to football'*

I think I did something for the worst possible reason—
just because I could.
Bill Clinton 1946– , *on his relationship with Monica Lewinsky*

The last temptation is the greatest treason:
To do the right deed for the wrong reason.
T. S. Eliot 1888–1965

State a moral case to a ploughman and a professor. The
former will decide it as well, and often better than the
latter, because he has not been led astray by artificial
rules.
Thomas Jefferson 1743–1826

Morality

Two things fill the mind with ever new and increasing wonder and awe, the more often and the more seriously reflection concentrates upon them: the starry heaven above me and the moral law within me.
Immanuel Kant 1724–1804

We know no spectacle so ridiculous as the British public in one of its periodical fits of morality.
Lord Macaulay 1800–59

If people want a sense of purpose, they should get it from their archbishops. They should not hope to receive it from their politicians.
Harold Macmillan 1894–1986

The most useful thing about a principle is that it can always be sacrificed to expediency.
W. Somerset Maugham 1874–1965

Morality is the herd-instinct in the individual.
Friedrich Nietzsche 1844–1900

There is no good or evil, there is only power, and those too weak to seek it.
J. K. Rowling 1965–

There is nothing either good or bad, but thinking makes it so.
William Shakespeare 1564–1616

We know that a man can read Goethe or Rilke in the evening, that he can play Bach and Schubert, and go to his day's work at Auschwitz in the morning.
George Steiner 1926–

Moral indignation is jealousy with a halo.
H. G. Wells 1866–1946

Mothers

What *do* girls do who haven't any mothers to help them
through their troubles?
   Louisa May Alcott 1832–88

I have reached the age when a woman begins to perceive
that she is growing into the person she least plans to
resemble: her mother.
   Anita Brookner 1928–

The mother's yearning, that completest type of the life in
another life which is the essence of real human love, feels
the presence of the cherished child even in the debased,
degraded man.
   George Eliot 1819–80

If I were damned of body and soul,
I know whose prayers would make me whole,
Mother o' mine, O mother o' mine.
   Rudyard Kipling 1865–1936

Here's to the happiest years of our lives
Spent in the arms of other men's wives.
Gentlemen!—Our mothers!
   Edwin Lutyens 1869–1944, *proposing a toast*

Few misfortunes can befall a boy which bring worse
consequences than to have a really affectionate mother.
   W. Somerset Maugham 1874–1965

It is a dead-end job. You've no sooner learned the skills
than you are redundant.
   Claire Rayner 1931– , *on motherhood*

The hand that rocks the cradle
Is the hand that rules the world.
   William Ross Wallace d. 1881

275

Mothers

Mothers go on getting blamed until they're eighty, but
shouldn't take it personally.
Katharine Whitehorn 1928–

Mountains

The Alps, the Rockies and all other mountains are related
to the earth, the Himalayas to the heavens.
J. K. Galbraith 1908–

Well, we knocked the bastard off!
Edmund Hillary 1919– , *on conquering Mount Everest, 1953*

It is a fine thing to be out on the hills alone. A man can
hardly be a beast or a fool alone on a great mountain.
Francis Kilvert 1840–79

Because it's there.
George Leigh Mallory 1886–1924, *on being asked why he*
wanted to climb Mount Everest

My mountain did not seem to me a lifeless thing of rock
and ice, but warm and friendly and living. She was a
mother hen, and the other mountains were chicks under
her wings.
Tenzing Norgay 1914–86, *on Everest*

Murder

Thou shalt not kill.
Bible

Mordre wol out; that se we day by day.
Geoffrey Chaucer c.1343–1400

Thou shalt not kill; but need'st not strive
Officiously to keep alive.
Arthur Hugh Clough 1819–61

Murder considered as one of the fine arts.
Thomas De Quincey 1785–1859

Kill a man, and you are an assassin. Kill millions of men, and you are a conqueror. Kill everyone, and you are a god.
Jean Rostand 1894–1977

Murder most foul, as in the best it is;
But this most foul, strange, and unnatural.
William Shakespeare 1564–1616

I don't think a man who has watched the sun going down could walk away and commit a murder.
Laurens van der Post 1906–96

Music ····▸ Singing

Beethoven tells you what it's like to be Beethoven and Mozart tells you what it's like to be human. Bach tells you what it's like be the universe.
Douglas Adams 1952–2001

Please do not shoot the pianist. He is doing his best.
Anonymous *printed notice in a dancing saloon, c.1882*

If you still have to ask…shame on you.
Louis Armstrong 1901–71, *when asked what jazz is; sometimes quoted as 'Man, if you gotta ask you'll never know'*

All music is folk music, I ain't never heard no horse sing a song.
Louis Armstrong 1901–71

There are two golden rules for an orchestra: start together and finish together. The public doesn't give a damn what goes on in between.
Thomas Beecham 1879–1961

Music

Music has charms to sooth a savage breast.
   William Congreve 1670–1729

Extraordinary how potent cheap music is.
   Noël Coward 1899–1973

It is only that which cannot be expressed otherwise that is worth expressing in music.
   Frederick Delius 1862–1934

There is music in the air.
   Edward Elgar 1857–1934

The hills are alive with the sound of music,
With songs they have sung for a thousand years.
   Oscar Hammerstein II 1895–1960

Difficult do you call it, Sir? I wish it were impossible.
   Samuel Johnson 1709–84, *on the performance of a celebrated violinist*

Down the road someone is practising scales,
The notes like little fishes vanish with a wink of tails.
   Louis MacNeice 1907–63

Fortissimo at last!
   Gustav Mahler 1860–1911, *on seeing Niagara Falls*

The symphony must be like the world. It must embrace everything.
   Gustav Mahler 1860–1911

Art is not national. It is international. Music is not written in red, white and blue; it is written with the heart's blood of the composer.
   Nellie Melba 1861–1931

Such sweet compulsion doth in music lie.
   John Milton 1608–74

Music is spiritual. The music business is not.
   Van Morrison 1945–

Melody is the essence of music. I compare a good melodist to a fine racer, and counterpoints to hack post-horses.
Wolfgang Amadeus Mozart 1756–91

If I don't practise for one day, I know it; if I don't practise for two days, the critics know it; if I don't practise for three days, the audience knows it.
Ignacy Jan Paderewski 1860–1941

Music is your own experience, your thoughts, your wisdom. If you don't live it, it won't come out of your horn.
Charlie Parker 1920–55

Music begins to atrophy when it departs too far from the dance...poetry begins to atrophy when it gets too far from music.
Ezra Pound 1885–1972

Applause is a receipt, not a note of demand.
Artur Schnabel 1882–1951

If music be the food of love, play on;
Give me excess of it, that, surfeiting,
The appetite may sicken, and so die.
William Shakespeare 1564–1616

Hell is full of musical amateurs: music is the brandy of the damned.
George Bernard Shaw 1856–1950

Music is feeling, then, not sound.
Wallace Stevens 1879–1955

A good composer does not imitate; he steals.
Igor Stravinsky 1882–1971

You just pick a chord, go twang, and you've got music.
Sid Vicious 1957–79

Names

Names

Proper names are poetry in the raw. Like all poetry they are untranslatable.
W. H. Auden 1907–73

With a name like yours, you might be any shape, almost.
Lewis Carroll 1832–98, *Humpty Dumpty to Alice*

Colin is the sort of name you give your goldfish for a joke.
Colin Firth 1960–

A self-made man may prefer a self-made name.
Learned Hand 1872–1961, *on Samuel Goldfish changing his name to Samuel Goldwyn*

A nickname is the heaviest stone that the devil can throw at a man.
William Hazlitt 1778–1830

If you should have a boy do not christen him John…'Tis a bad name and goes against a man. If my name had been Edmund I should have been more fortunate.
John Keats 1795–1821

Just as crystallization of surnames was one of the steps in human civilization, their relinquishment gradually increases as we revert to savagery.
Anthony Powell 1905–2000

What's in a name? that which we call a rose
By any other name would smell as sweet.
William Shakespeare 1564–1616

JAQUES: I do not like her name.
ORLANDO: There was no thought of pleasing you when she was christened.
William Shakespeare 1564–1616

KATHARINE HEPBURN: Nature, Mr Allnutt, is what we are put into this world to rise above.
    James Agee 1909–55

Nature does nothing without purpose or uselessly.
    Aristotle 384–322 BC

The subtlety of nature is greater many times over than the subtlety of the senses and understanding.
    Francis Bacon 1561–1626

All things are artificial, for nature is the art of God.
    Sir Thomas Browne 1605–82

There is a pleasure in the pathless woods,
There is a rapture on the lonely shore,
There is society, where none intrudes,
By the deep sea, and music in its roar:
I love not man the less, but nature more.
    Lord Byron 1788–1824

What a book a devil's chaplain might write on the clumsy, wasteful, blundering, low, and horridly cruel works of nature!
    Charles Darwin 1809–82

People thought they could explain and conquer nature—yet the outcome is that they destroyed it and disinherited themselves from it.
    Václav Havel 1936–

You may drive out nature with a pitchfork, yet she'll be constantly running back.
    Horace 65–8 BC

For nature, heartless, witless nature,
Will neither care nor know
What stranger's feet may find the meadow

Nature

And trespass there and go.
A. E. Housman 1859–1936

In her [Nature's] inventions nothing is lacking, and
nothing is superfluous.
Leonardo da Vinci 1452–1519

It is far from easy to judge whether she [Nature] has
proved a kind parent to man or a harsh step-mother.
Pliny the Elder AD 23–79

And this our life, exempt from public haunt,
Finds tongues in trees, books in the running brooks,
Sermons in stones, and good in everything.
William Shakespeare 1564–1616

Nature, red in tooth and claw.
Alfred, Lord Tennyson 1809–92

Nature is not a temple, but a workshop, and man's the
workman in it.
Ivan Turgenev 1818–83

One impulse from a vernal wood
May teach you more of man,
Of moral evil and of good,
Than all the sages can.
William Wordsworth 1770–1850

Night ····▸ Day

Lighten our darkness, we beseech thee, O Lord; and by
thy great mercy defend us from all perils and dangers of
this night.
Book of Common Prayer 1662

Old Age

I cannot walk through the suburbs in the solitude of the night without thinking that the night pleases us because it suppresses idle details, just as our memory does.
Jorge Luis Borges 1899–1986

The Sun's rim dips; the stars rush out;
At one stride comes the dark.
Samuel Taylor Coleridge 1772–1834

The curfew tolls the knell of parting day,
The lowing herd wind slowly o'er the lea,
The ploughman homeward plods his weary way,
And leaves the world to darkness and to me.
Thomas Gray 1716–71

The cares that infest the day
Shall fold their tents, like the Arabs,
And as silently steal away.
Henry Wadsworth Longfellow 1807–82

Night came down, and enfolded the earth in her dusky wings.
Virgil 70–19 BC

Old Age

Age will not be defied.
Francis Bacon 1561–1626

To me old age is always fifteen years older than I am.
Bernard Baruch 1870–1965

The days of our age are threescore years and ten; and though men be so strong that they come to fourscore years: yet is their strength then but labour and sorrow; so soon passeth it away, and we are gone.
Bible

Old Age

If I'd known I was gonna live this long, I'd have taken better care of myself.
Eubie Blake 1883–1983, *on reaching the age of 100*

What is called the serenity of age is only perhaps a euphemism for the fading power to feel the sudden shock of joy or sorrow.
Arthur Bliss 1891–1975

The man who works and is not bored is never old.
Pablo Casals 1876–1973

Considering the alternative, it's not too bad at all.
Maurice Chevalier 1888–1972, *when asked what he felt about the advancing years on his 72nd birthday*

Oh, to be seventy again!
Georges Clemenceau 1841–1929, *on seeing a pretty girl on his eightieth birthday*

While there's snow on the roof, it doesn't mean the fire has gone out in the furnace.
John G. Diefenbaker 1895–1979, *approaching his 80th birthday*

I grow old...I grow old...
I shall wear the bottoms of my trousers rolled.
T. S. Eliot 1888–1965

Age does not make us childish, as men tell,
It merely finds us children still at heart.
Johann Wolfgang von Goethe 1749–1832

You will recognize, my boy, the first sign of old age: it is when you go out into the streets of London and realize for the first time how young the policemen look.
Seymour Hicks 1871–1949

Nothing really wrong with him—only anno domini, but that's the most fatal complaint of all, in the end.
James Hilton 1900–54

When I am an old woman I shall wear purple
With a red hat which doesn't go, and doesn't suit me.
   Jenny Joseph 1932–

Perhaps being old is having lighted rooms
Inside your head, and people in them, acting.
People you know, yet can't quite name.
   Philip Larkin 1922–85

Will you still need me, will you still feed me,
When I'm sixty four?
   John Lennon 1940–80 and **Paul McCartney** 1942–

Old people have one advantage compared with young
ones. They have been young themselves, and young
people haven't been old.
   Lord Longford 1905–2001

Growing old is no more than a bad habit which a busy
man has no time to form.
   André Maurois 1885–1967

The unending problem of growing old was not how he
changed, but how things did.
   Toni Morrison 1931–

Growing old is like being increasingly penalized for a
crime you haven't committed.
   Anthony Powell 1905–2000

In a dream you are never eighty.
   Anne Sexton 1928–74

How ill white hairs become a fool and jester!
   William Shakespeare 1564–1616

Second childishness, and mere oblivion,
Sans teeth, sans eyes, sans taste, sans everything.
   William Shakespeare 1564–1616

Every man desires to live long; but no man would be old.
   Jonathan Swift 1667–1745

Old Age

Do not go gentle into that good night,
Old age should burn and rave at close of day;
Rage, rage against the dying of the light.
Dylan Thomas 1914-53

Old age is the most unexpected of all things that happen
to a man.
Leon Trotsky 1879-1940

Time has shaken me by the hand and death is not far
behind.
John Wesley 1703-91

When you are old and grey and full of sleep,
And nodding by the fire, take down this book
And slowly read and dream of the soft look
Your eyes had once, and of their shadows deep.
W. B. Yeats 1865-1939

Opinion

Why should you mind being wrong if someone can show
you that you are?
A. J. Ayer 1910-89

I've never had a humble opinion. If you've got an
opinion, why be humble about it?
Joan Baez 1941-

He that complies against his will,
Is of his own opinion still.
Samuel Butler 1612-80

They that approve a private opinion, call it opinion; but
they that mislike it, heresy: and yet heresy signifies no
more than private opinion.
Thomas Hobbes 1588-1679

Every man has a right to utter what he thinks truth, and
every other man has a right to knock him down for it.
Martyrdom is the test.
   Samuel Johnson 1709–84

There are nine and sixty ways of constructing tribal lays,
And—every—single—one—of—them—is—right!
   Rudyard Kipling 1865–1936

Thank God, in these days of enlightenment and
establishment, everyone has a right to his own opinions,
and chiefly to the opinion that nobody else has a right to
theirs.
   Ronald Knox 1888–1957

New opinions are always suspected, and usually opposed,
without any other reason but because they are not already
common.
   John Locke 1632–1704

Opinion in good men is but knowledge in the making.
   John Milton 1608–74

Some praise at morning what they blame at night;
But always think the last opinion right.
   Alexander Pope 1688–1744

The opinions that are held with passion are always those
for which no good ground exists; indeed the passion is
the measure of the holder's lack of rational conviction.
   Bertrand Russell 1872–1970

Optimism ·····▸ Hope, Pessimism

The lark's on the wing;
The snail's on the thorn:
God's in his heaven—

Optimism

All's right with the world!
Robert Browning 1812–89

I have known him come home to supper with a flood of tears, and a declaration that nothing was now left but a jail; and go to bed making a calculation of the expense of putting bow-windows to the house, 'in case anything turned up,' which was his favourite expression.
Charles Dickens 1812–70, *of Mr Micawber*

Grab your coat, and get your hat,
Leave your worry on the doorstep,
Just direct your feet
To the sunny side of the street.
Dorothy Fields 1905–74

Cheer up! the worst is yet to come!
Philander Chase Johnson 1866–1939

Sin is behovely, but all shall be well and all shall be well and all manner of thing shall be well.
Julian of Norwich 1343–after 1416

an optimist is a guy
that has never had
much experience.
Don Marquis 1878–1937

You've got to ac-cent-tchu-ate the positive
Elim-my-nate the negative
Latch on to the affirmative
Don't mess with Mister In-between.
Johnny Mercer 1909–76

In this best of possible worlds…all is for the best.
Voltaire 1694–1778

Good painters imitate nature, bad ones spew it up.
Cervantes 1547–1616

The sound of water escaping from mill-dams, etc.,
willows, old rotten planks, slimy posts, and
brickwork…those scenes made me a painter and I am
grateful.
John Constable 1776–1837

Remark all these roughnesses, pimples, warts, and
everything as you see me; otherwise I will never pay a
farthing for it.
Oliver Cromwell 1599–1658, *to Lely, on the painting of his
portrait; commonly quoted as 'warts and all'*

All painting, no matter what you're painting, is abstract
in that it's got to be organized.
David Hockney 1937–

Mostly painting is like putting a message in a bottle and
flinging it into the sea.
Howard Hodgkin 1932–

Art does not reproduce the visible; rather, it makes
visible.
Paul Klee 1879–1940

You should not paint the chair, but only what someone
has felt about it.
Edvard Munch 1863–1944

I paint objects as I think them, not as I see them.
Pablo Picasso 1881–1973

No, painting is not made to decorate apartments. It's an
offensive and defensive weapon against the enemy.
Pablo Picasso 1881–1973

Painting

An imitation in lines and colours on any surface of all that is to be found under the sun.
   Nicolas Poussin 1594–1665

I have seen, and heard, much of Cockney impudence before now; but never expected to hear a coxcomb ask two hundred guineas for flinging a pot of paint in the public's face.
   John Ruskin 1819–1900, *on Whistler's* Nocturne in Black and Gold

Every time I paint a portrait I lose a friend.
   John Singer Sargent 1856–1925

I am a painter and I nail my pictures together.
   Kurt Schwitters 1887–1948

Painting is saying "Ta" to God.
   Stanley Spencer 1891–1959

No, I ask it for the knowledge of a lifetime.
   James McNeill Whistler 1834–1903, *in his case against Ruskin, replying to the question: 'For two days' labour, you ask two hundred guineas?'*

Parents ····➤ Children, The Family

The joys of parents are secret, and so are their griefs and fears.
   Francis Bacon 1561–1626

Honour thy father and thy mother.
   Bible

A wise son maketh a glad father: but a foolish son is the heaviness of his mother.
   Bible

Having one child makes you a parent; having two you are a referee.
   David Frost 1939–

Parents

Your children are not your children.
They are the sons and daughters of Life's longing for
  itself.
They came through you but not from you
And though they are with you yet they belong not to you.
  Kahlil Gibran 1883–1931

They fuck you up, your mum and dad.
They may not mean to, but they do.
They fill you with the faults they had
And add some extra, just for you.
  Philip Larkin 1922–85

Children aren't happy with nothing to ignore,
And that's what parents were created for.
  Ogden Nash 1902–71

If you bungle raising your children I don't think whatever
else you do well matters very much.
  Jacqueline Kennedy Onassis 1929–94

A Jewish man with parents alive is a fifteen-year-old boy,
and will remain a fifteen-year-old boy until *they die*!
  Philip Roth 1933–

No matter how old a mother is she watches her middle-
aged children for signs of improvement.
  Florida Scott-Maxwell

Parentage is a very important profession, but no test of
fitness for it is ever imposed in the interest of the
children.
  George Bernard Shaw 1856–1950

The natural term of the affection of the human animal
for its offspring is six years.
  George Bernard Shaw 1856–1950

You shouldn't sit in judgment of your parents. We did the
best we could while being people too.
  John Updike 1932–

Parents

Parents are the bones on which children sharpen their teeth.

Peter Ustinov 1921–2004

My children are ungrateful: they don't care. That is my great reward. They are free.

Fay Weldon 1931–

Children begin by loving their parents; after a time they judge them; rarely, if ever, do they forgive them.

Oscar Wilde 1854–1900

A slavish bondage to parents cramps every faculty of the mind.

Mary Wollstonecraft 1759–97

Parting ····▶ Meeting

Once I leave, I leave. I am not going to speak to the man on the bridge, and I am not going to spit on the deck.

Stanley Baldwin 1867–1947, *on resigning*

ARNOLD SCHWARZENEGGER: I'll be back.

James Cameron 1954–

Atque in perpetuum, frater, ave atque vale.
And so, my brother, hail, and farewell evermore!

Catullus c.84–c.54 BC

You have sat too long here for any good you have been doing. Depart, I say, and let us have done with you. In the name of God, go!

Oliver Cromwell 1599–1658, *addressing the Rump Parliament*

Parting is all we know of heaven,
And all we need of hell.

Emily Dickinson 1830–86

Since there's no help, come let us kiss and part,
Nay, I have done: you get no more of me.
Michael Drayton 1563–1631

Neither could find anything to say. There comes a
moment during leave-taking when the loved one is no
longer with us.
Gustave Flaubert 1821–80

GROUCHO MARX: If you can't leave in a taxi you can leave
in a huff. If that's too soon, you can leave in a minute
and a huff.
Bert Kalmar 1884–1947 et al.

Leave them while you're looking good.
Anita Loos 1893–1981

Fare well my dear child and pray for me, and I shall for
you and all your friends that we may merrily meet in
heaven.
Sir Thomas More 1478–1535

Good-night, good-night! parting is such sweet sorrow
That I shall say good-night till it be morrow.
William Shakespeare 1564–1616

The Past

Even a god cannot change the past.
Agathon b. c.445 BC

Nostalgia isn't what it used to be.
Anonymous

In every age 'the good old days' were a myth. No one
ever thought they were good at the time. For every age
has consisted of crises that seemed intolerable to the
people who lived through them.
Brooks Atkinson 1894–1984

The Past

Stands the Church clock at ten to three?
And is there honey still for tea?
  Rupert Brooke 1887–1915

The moving finger writes; and, having writ,
Moves on: nor all thy piety nor wit
Shall lure it back to cancel half a line,
Nor all thy tears wash out a word of it.
  Edward Fitzgerald 1809–83

The past is a foreign country: they do things differently
there.
  L. P. Hartley 1895–1972

What are those blue remembered hills,
What spires, what farms are those?
That is the land of lost content,
I see it shining plain,
The happy highways where I went
And cannot come again.
  A. E. Housman 1859–1936

O God! Put back Thy universe and give me yesterday.
  Henry Arthur Jones 1851–1929 and **Henry Herman** 1832–94

Yesterday, all my troubles seemed so far away,
Now it looks as though they're here to stay.
Oh I believe in yesterday.
  John Lennon 1940–80 and **Paul McCartney** 1942–

The past is like a collection of photographs: some are
familiar and on constant display, others need searching
for in dusty drawers.
  John Mortimer 1923–

Think of it, soldiers; from the summit of these pyramids,
forty centuries look down upon you.
  Napoleon I 1769–1821

Things ain't what they used to be.
Ted Persons

I tell you the past is a bucket of ashes.
Carl Sandburg 1878–1967

Those who cannot remember the past are condemned to repeat it.
George Santayana 1863–1952

What's gone and what's past help
Should be past grief.
William Shakespeare 1564–1616

O! call back yesterday, bid time return.
William Shakespeare 1564–1616

People who are always praising the past
And especially the times of faith as best
Ought to go and live in the Middle Ages
And be burnt at the stake as witches and sages.
Stevie Smith 1902–71

I think that today's youth have a tendency to live in the present and work for the future—and to be totally ignorant of the past.
Steven Spielberg 1947–

The past is the only dead thing that smells sweet.
Edward Thomas 1878–1917

Mais où sont les neiges d'antan?
But where are the snows of yesteryear?
François Villon b. 1431

Patriotism

What pity is it
That we can die but once to serve our country!
Joseph Addison 1672–1719

Patriotism

Patriotism is a lively sense of collective responsibility.
Nationalism is a silly cock crowing on its own dunghill.
   Richard Aldington 1892–1962

A steady patriot of the world alone,
The friend of every country but his own.
   George Canning 1770–1827

Patriotism is not enough. I must have no hatred or
bitterness towards anyone.
   Edith Cavell 1865–1915, *on the eve of her execution*

            Be England what she will,
With all her faults, she is my country still.
   Charles Churchill 1731–64

Our country! In her intercourse with foreign nations, may
she always be in the right; but our country, right or
wrong.
   Stephen Decatur 1779–1820

If I had to choose between betraying my country and
betraying my friend, I hope I should have the guts to
betray my country.
   E. M. Forster 1879–1970

I may be uninspiring, but I'll be damned if I'm an alien!
   George V 1865–1936, *on H. G. Wells's comment on 'an alien
   and uninspiring court'*

That this House will in no circumstances fight for its
King and Country.
   D. M. Graham 1911–99, *motion worded by Graham for a
   debate at the Oxford Union, 1933*

I only regret that I have but one life to lose for my
country.
   Nathan Hale 1755–76, *prior to his execution by the British for
   spying*

Patriotism

Dulce et decorum est pro patria mori.
Lovely and honourable it is to die for one's country.
Horace 65–8 BC

We don't want to fight, yet by jingo! if we do,
We've got the ships, we've got the men, and got the
money too.
G. W. Hunt 1829?–1904

Patriotism is the last refuge of a scoundrel.
Samuel Johnson 1709–84

And so, my fellow Americans: ask not what your country
can do for you—ask what you can do for your country.
John F. Kennedy 1917–63

I would die for my country but I would never let my
country die for me.
Neil Kinnock 1942–

These are the times that try men's souls. The summer
soldier and the sunshine patriot will, in this crisis, shrink
from the service of their country; but he that stands it
now, deserves the love and thanks of men and women.
Thomas Paine 1737–1809

My country, right or wrong; if right, to be kept right; and
if wrong, to be set right!
Carl Schurz 1829–1906

Breathes there the man, with soul so dead,
Who never to himself hath said,
This is my own, my native land!
Sir Walter Scott 1771–1832

You'll never have a quiet world till you knock the
patriotism out of the human race.
George Bernard Shaw 1856–1950

Patriotism

I vow to thee, my country—all earthly things above—
Entire and whole and perfect, the service of my love.
Cecil Spring-Rice 1859–1918

The cricket test—which side do they cheer for?…Are you
still looking back to where you came from or where you
are?
Norman Tebbit 1931– , *on the loyalties of Britain's immigrant population*

Peace

They shall beat their swords into plowshares, and their
spears into pruninghooks: nation shall not lift up sword
against nation, neither shall they learn war any more.
Bible

The peace of God, which passeth all understanding, shall
keep your hearts and minds through Christ Jesus.
Bible

Give peace in our time, O Lord.
Book of Common Prayer 1662

This is the second time in our history that there has
come back from Germany to Downing Street peace with
honour. I believe it is peace for our time.
Neville Chamberlain 1869–1940

E'n la sua volontade è nostra pace.
In His will is our peace.
Dante Alighieri 1265–1321

Lord Salisbury and myself have brought you back peace—
but a peace I hope with honour.
Benjamin Disraeli 1804–81

Go placidly amid the noise and the haste, and remember
what peace there may be in silence.

    Max Ehrmann 1872–1945

I think that people want peace so much that one of these
days governments had better get out of the way and let
them have it.

    Dwight D. Eisenhower 1890–1969

Kissinger brought peace to Vietnam the same way
Napoleon brought peace to Europe: by losing.

    Joseph Heller 1923–99

Give peace a chance.

    John Lennon 1940–80 and **Paul McCartney** 1942–

A war can perhaps be won single-handedly. But peace—
lasting peace—cannot be secured without the support of
all.

    Luiz Inácio Lula da Silva 1945–

You can't separate peace from freedom because no one
can be at peace unless he has his freedom.

    Malcolm X 1925–65

…Peace hath her victories
No less renowned than war.

    John Milton 1608–74

You can't switch on peace like a light.

    Mo Mowlam 1949–

Enough of blood and tears. Enough.

    Yitzhak Rabin 1922–95

…The naked, poor, and manglèd Peace,
Dear nurse of arts, plenties, and joyful births.

    William Shakespeare 1564–1616

They make a wilderness and call it peace.

    Tacitus AD c.56–after 117

Peace

Qui desiderat pacem, praeparet bellum.
Let him who desires peace, prepare for war.
Vegetius fourth century AD

Perfection

The pursuit of perfection, then, is the pursuit of
sweetness and light.
Matthew Arnold 1822–88

Pictures of perfection as you know make me sick and
wicked.
Jane Austen 1775–1817

Faultless to a fault.
Robert Browning 1812–89

Trifles make perfection, and perfection is no trifle.
Michelangelo 1475–1564

Perfection is terrible, it cannot have children.
Sylvia Plath 1932–63

The best is the best, though a hundred judges have
declared it so.
Arthur Quiller-Couch 1863–1944

Perfection is finally attained not when there is no longer
anything to add but when there is no longer anything to
take away, when a body has been stripped down to its
nakedness.
Antoine de Saint-Exupéry 1900–44

How many things by season seasoned are
To their right praise and true perfection!
William Shakespeare 1564–1616

No one can be perfectly free till all are free; no one can
be perfectly moral till all are moral; no one can be
perfectly happy till all are happy.
   Herbert Spencer 1820–1903

Finality is death. Perfection is finality.
Nothing is perfect. There are lumps in it.
   James Stephens 1882–1950

He is all fault who hath no fault at all:
For who loves me must have a touch of earth.
   Alfred, Lord Tennyson 1809–92

The best is the enemy of the good.
   Voltaire 1694–1778

The intellect of man is forced to choose
Perfection of the life, or of the work.
   W. B. Yeats 1865–1939

Pessimism ····▸ Despair, Optimism

The optimist proclaims that we live in the best of all
possible worlds; and the pessimist fears this is true.
   James Branch Cabell 1879–1958

I don't consider myself a pessimist. I think of a pessimist
as someone who is waiting for it to rain. And I feel
soaked to the skin.
   Leonard Cohen 1934–

If way to the Better there be, it exacts a full look at the
   worst.
   Thomas Hardy 1840–1928

Nothing to do but work,
Nothing to eat but food,
Nothing to wear but clothes

Pessimism

To keep one from going nude.
Benjamin Franklin King 1857–94

Man hands on misery to man.
It deepens like a coastal shelf.
Get out as early as you can,
And don't have any kids yourself.
Philip Larkin 1922–85

If we see light at the end of the tunnel,
It's the light of the oncoming train.
Robert Lowell 1917–77

'Twixt the optimist and pessimist
The difference is droll:
The optimist sees the doughnut
But the pessimist sees the hole.
McLandburgh Wilson 1892–

Philosophy

The Socratic manner is not a game at which two can play.
Max Beerbohm 1872–1956

Metaphysics is the finding of bad reasons for what we believe upon instinct.
F. H. Bradley 1846–1924

If it was so, it might be; and if it were so, it would be: but as it isn't, it ain't. That's logic.
Lewis Carroll 1832–98

There is nothing so absurd but some philosopher has said it.
Cicero 106–43 BC

When philosophy paints its grey on grey, then has a shape of life grown old. By philosophy's grey on grey it cannot be rejuvenated but only understood. The owl of Minerva spreads its wings only with the falling of the dusk.

G. W. F. Hegel 1770–1831

I refute it *thus*.

Samuel Johnson 1709–84, *kicking a large stone by way of refuting Bishop Berkeley's theory of the non-existence of matter*

Philosophy will clip an Angel's wings.

John Keats 1795–1821

The philosophers have only interpreted the world in various ways; the point is to change it.

Karl Marx 1818–83

How charming is divine philosophy!
Not harsh and crabbèd, as dull fools suppose,
But musical as is Apollo's lute,

John Milton 1608–74

No more things should be presumed to exist than are absolutely necessary.

William of Occam c.1285–1349, *not found in this form in his writings, although he frequently used similar expressions, e.g. 'Plurality should not be assumed unnecessarily'*

The unexamined life is not worth living.

Socrates 469–399 BC

The safest general characterization of the European philosophical tradition is that it consists of a series of footnotes to Plato.

Alfred North Whitehead 1861–1947

Philosophy is a battle against the bewitchment of our intelligence by means of language.

Ludwig Wittgenstein 1889–1951

Photography

A photograph is a secret about a secret. The more it tells you the less you know.
> **Diane Arbus** 1923-71

The camera's eye
Does not lie,
But it cannot show
The life within.
> **W. H. Auden** 1907-73

I never cared for fashion much. Amusing little seams and witty little pleats. It was the girls I liked.
> **David Bailey** 1938- , *of his career as a photographer*

Most things in life are moments of pleasure and a lifetime of embarrassment; photography is a moment of embarrassment and a lifetime of pleasure.
> **Tony Benn** 1925-

If your pictures aren't good enough, you aren't close enough.
> **Robert Capa** 1913-54

To me, photography is the simultaneous recognition, in a fraction of a second, of the significance of an event as well as of a precise organization of forms which give that event its proper expression.
> **Henri Cartier-Bresson** 1908-

The paparazzi are nothing but dogs of war.
> **Catherine Deneuve** 1943-

You press the button, we do the rest.
> **George Eastman** 1854-1932, *advertising slogan to launch the Kodak camera, 1888*

The important thing is not the camera but the eye.
> **Alfred Eisenstaedt** 1898-1995

The photographer is like the cod which produces a million eggs in order that one may reach maturity.
George Bernard Shaw 1856–1950

Planning

Be prepared.
Lord Baden-Powell 1857–1941, *motto of the Scout Association*

We are ready for any unforeseen event which may or may not happen.
George W. Bush 1946–

First things first, second things never.
Shirley Conran 1932–

In preparing for battle I have always found that plans are useless, but planning is indispensable.
Dwight D. Eisenhower 1890–1969

I think the necessity of being *ready* increases. Look to it.
Abraham Lincoln 1809–65

No plan of operations reaches with any certainty beyond the first encounter with the enemy's main force.
Helmuth von Moltke 1800–91, *often quoted as 'no plan survives first contact with the enemy'*

A good plan violently executed *Now* is better than a perfect plan next week.
George S. Patton 1885–1945

If we had had more time for discussion we should probably have made a great many more mistakes.
Leon Trotsky 1879–1940

Pleasure

One half of the world cannot understand the pleasures of the other.
> **Jane Austen** 1775–1817

The great pleasure in life is doing what people say you cannot do.
> **Walter Bagehot** 1826–77

I'm tired of Love: I'm still more tired of Rhyme.
But Money gives me pleasure all the time.
> **Hilaire Belloc** 1870–1953

Let us have wine and women, mirth and laughter,
Sermons and soda-water the day after.
> **Lord Byron** 1788–1824

Life is a matter of passing the time enjoyably. There may be other things in life, but I've been too busy passing my time enjoyably to think very deeply about them.
> **Peter Cook** 1937–95

Remorse, the fatal egg by pleasure laid.
> **William Cowper** 1731–1800

The less we indulge our pleasures the more we enjoy them.
> **Juvenal** AD c.60–c.130

Ever let the fancy roam,
Pleasure never is at home.
> **John Keats** 1795–1821

The greatest pleasure I know, is to do a good action by stealth, and to have it found out by accident.
> **Charles Lamb** 1775–1834

Who loves not woman, wine, and song
Remains a fool his whole life long.
> **Martin Luther** 1483–1546

The Puritan hated bear-baiting, not because it gave pain to the bear, but because it gave pleasure to the spectators.
Lord Macaulay 1800–59

It is a curious thing that people only ask if you are enjoying yourself when you aren't.
Edith Nesbit 1858–1924

Pleasure is nothing else but the intermission of pain.
John Selden 1584–1654

Life would be very pleasant if it were not for its enjoyments.
R. S. Surtees 1805–64

All the things I really like to do are either illegal, immoral, or fattening.
Alexander Woollcott 1887–1943

Poetry

It is barbarous to write a poem after Auschwitz.
Theodor Adorno 1903–69

The difference between genuine poetry and the poetry of Dryden, Pope, and all their school, is briefly this: their poetry is conceived and composed in their wits, genuine poetry is conceived and composed in the soul.
Matthew Arnold 1822–88

A poet's hope: to be,
like some valley cheese,
local, but prized elsewhere.
W. H. Auden 1907–73

Prose is when all the lines except the last go on to the end. Poetry is when some of them fall short of it.
Jeremy Bentham 1748–1832

Poetry

The reason Milton wrote in fetters when he wrote of
Angels and God, and at liberty when of Devils and Hell,
is because he was a true Poet, and of the Devil's party
without knowing it.
      William Blake 1757–1827

All poets are mad.
      Robert Burton 1577–1640

There's nothing in the world for which a poet will give
up writing, not even when he is a Jew and the language
of his poems is German.
      Paul Celan 1920–70

That willing suspension of disbelief for the moment,
which constitutes poetic faith.
      Samuel Taylor Coleridge 1772–1834

Prose = words in their best order;—poetry = the *best*
words in the best order.
      Samuel Taylor Coleridge 1772–1834

I used to think all poets were Byronic.
They're mostly wicked as a ginless tonic
And wild as pension plans.
      Wendy Cope 1945–

Immature poets imitate; mature poets steal.
      T. S. Eliot 1888–1965

Poetry is a subject as precise as geometry.
      Gustave Flaubert 1821–80

I'd as soon write free verse as play tennis with the net
down.
      Robert Frost 1874–1963

Like a piece of ice on a hot stove the poem must ride on
its own melting. A poem may be worked over once it is
in being, but may not be worried into being.
      Robert Frost 1874–1963

As soon as war is declared it will be impossible to hold
the poets back. Rhyme is still the most effective drum.
   Jean Giraudoux 1882–1944

Skilled or unskilled, we all scribble poems.
   Horace 65-8 BC

[BOSWELL:] Sir, what is poetry?
[JOHNSON:] Why Sir, it is much easier to say what it is
   not. We all *know* what light is; but it is not easy to *tell*
   what it is.
   Samuel Johnson 1709–84

If poetry comes not as naturally as the leaves to a tree it
had better not come at all.
   John Keats 1795–1821

A poem should not mean
But be.
   Archibald MacLeish 1892–1982

Writing a book of poetry is like dropping a rose petal
down the Grand Canyon and waiting for the echo.
   Don Marquis 1878–1937

The poet is always indebted to the universe, paying
interest and fines on sorrow.
   Vladimir Mayakovsky 1893–1930

Rhyme being…but the invention of a barbarous age, to
set off wretched matter and lame metre.
   John Milton 1608-74

Most people ignore most poetry
because
most poetry ignores most people.
   Adrian Mitchell 1932-

All a poet can do today is warn.
   Wilfred Owen 1893–1918

Poetry

Poets are the unacknowledged legislators of the world.
Percy Bysshe Shelley 1792–1822

[The poet] cometh unto you, with a tale which holdeth children from play, and old men from the chimney corner.
Philip Sidney 1554–86

Poetry is the spontaneous overflow of powerful feelings: it takes its origin from emotion recollected in tranquillity.
William Wordsworth 1770–1850

We make out of the quarrel with others, rhetoric, but of the quarrel with ourselves, poetry.
W. B. Yeats 1865–1939

Politicians ····▶ Politics

A constitutional statesman is in general a man of common opinion and uncommon abilities.
Walter Bagehot 1826–77

I am not going to spend any time whatsoever in attacking the Foreign Secretary…If we complain about the tune, there is no reason to attack the monkey when the organ grinder is present.
Aneurin Bevan 1897–1960

Your representative owes you, not his industry only, but his judgement; and he betrays, instead of serving you, if he sacrifices it to your opinion.
Edmund Burke 1729–97

An honest politician is one who when he's bought stays bought.
Simon Cameron 1799–1889

A minister who moves about in society is in a position to read the signs of the times even in a festive gathering, but one who remains shut up in his office learns nothing.

Duc de Choiseul 1719–85

It is the ability to foretell what is going to happen tomorrow, next week, next month, and next year. And to have the ability afterwards to explain why it didn't happen.

Winston Churchill 1874–1965, *on the qualifications for becoming a politician*

There are no true friends in politics. We are all sharks circling, and waiting, for traces of blood to appear in the water.

Alan Clark 1928–99

'Do you pray for the senators, Dr Hale?' 'No, I look at the senators and I pray for the country.'

Edward Everett Hale 1822–1909

Politicians are entitled to change their minds. But when they adjust their principles some explanation is necessary.

Roy Hattersley 1932–

If a due participation of office is a matter of right, how are vacancies to be obtained? Those by death are few; by resignation none.

Thomas Jefferson 1743–1826, *usually quoted as 'Few die and none resign'*

Forever poised between a cliché and an indiscretion.

Harold Macmillan 1894–1986, *on the life of a Foreign Secretary*

What I want is men who will support me when I am in the wrong.

Lord Melbourne 1779–1848, *replying to a politician who said 'I will support you as long as you are in the right'*

Politicians

A statesman is a politician who places himself at the service of the nation. A politician is a statesman who places the nation at his service.
Georges Pompidou 1911–74

All political lives, unless they are cut off in midstream at a happy juncture, end in failure, because that is the nature of politics and of human affairs.
Enoch Powell 1912–98

We all know that Prime Ministers are wedded to the truth, but like other married couples they sometimes live apart.
Saki 1870–1916

A statesman is a politician who's been dead 10 or 15 years.
Harry S. Truman 1884–1972

All those men have their price.
Robert Walpole 1676–1745, *of fellow parliamentarians*

Politics ····▶ Democracy, Government

In politics the middle way is none at all.
John Adams 1735–1826

Man is by nature a political animal.
Aristotle 384–322 BC

[Russian Communism is] the illegitimate child of Karl Marx and Catherine the Great.
Clement Attlee 1883–1967

Politics is the art of the possible.
Otto von Bismarck 1815–98

A statesman…must wait until he hears the steps of God sounding through events; then leap up and grasp the hem of his garment.
Otto von Bismarck 1815–98

Magnanimity in politics is not seldom the truest wisdom;
and a great empire and little minds go ill together.
Edmund Burke 1729-97

In politics, there is no use looking beyond the next
fortnight.
Joseph Chamberlain 1836-1914

Safe is spelled D-U-L-L. Politics has got to be a fun
activity, otherwise people turn their back on it.
Alan Clark 1928-99

In politics, what begins in fear usually ends in folly.
Samuel Taylor Coleridge 1772-1834

You campaign in poetry. You govern in prose.
Mario Cuomo 1932-

International life is right-wing, like nature. The social
contract is left-wing, like humanity.
Régis Debray 1940-

'Two nations; between whom there is no intercourse and
no sympathy; who are as ignorant of each other's habits,
thoughts, and feelings, as if they were dwellers in different
zones, or inhabitants of different planets...' 'You speak
of—' said Egremont, hesitatingly, 'THE RICH AND THE
POOR.'
Benjamin Disraeli 1804-81

Damn your principles! Stick to your party.
Benjamin Disraeli 1804-81

I never dared be radical when young
For fear it would make me conservative when old.
Robert Frost 1874-1963

Politics is not the art of the possible. It consists in
choosing between the disastrous and the unpalatable.
J. K. Galbraith 1908-

Politics

If I could not go to Heaven but with a party, I would not go there at all.
Thomas Jefferson 1743–1826

The great nations have always acted like gangsters, and the small nations like prostitutes.
Stanley Kubrick 1928–99

Who? Whom?
Lenin 1870–1924, *definition of political science, meaning 'Who will outstrip whom?'*

Politics is a marathon, not a sprint.
Ken Livingstone 1945–

If you want to succeed in politics, you must keep your conscience well under control.
David Lloyd George 1863–1945

The opposition of events.
Harold Macmillan 1894–1986, *on his biggest problem; popularly quoted as 'Events, dear boy. Events'*

Politics is war without bloodshed while war is politics with bloodshed.
Mao Tse-tung 1893–1976

Political language…is designed to make lies sound truthful and murder respectable, and to give an appearance of solidity to pure wind.
George Orwell 1903–50

Politics is the art of preventing people from taking part in affairs which properly concern them.
Paul Valéry 1871–1945

Socialism can only arrive by bicycle.
José Antonio Viera Gallo 1943–

A week is a long time in politics.
Harold Wilson 1916–95

A liberal is a conservative who's been arrested.
    Tom Wolfe 1931–

Pollution ····➤ Environment

Woe to her that is filthy and polluted, to the oppressing city!
    Bible

NOISE, *n.* A stench in the ear…The chief product and authenticating sign of civilization.
    Ambrose Bierce 1842–c.1914

Over increasingly large areas of the United States, spring now comes unheralded by the return of the birds, and the early mornings are strangely silent where once they were filled with the beauty of bird song.
    Rachel Carson 1907–64

Man has been endowed with reason, with the power to create, so that he can add to what he's been given. But up to now he hasn't been a creator, only a destroyer. Forests keep disappearing, rivers dry up, wild life's become extinct, the climate's ruined and the land grows poorer and uglier every day.
    Anton Chekhov 1860–1904

The river Rhine, it is well known,
Doth wash your city of Cologne;
But tell me, Nymphs, what power divine
Shall henceforth wash the river Rhine?
    Samuel Taylor Coleridge 1772–1834

The sea is the universal sewer.
    Jacques Cousteau 1910–97

Pollution knows no boundaries any more than do money or information.
    Peter F. Drucker 1909–

Pollution

Clear the air! clean the sky! wash the wind!
   T. S. Eliot 1888–1965

The sanitary and mechanical age we are now entering
makes up for the mercy it grants to our sense of smell by
the ferocity with which it assails our sense of hearing. As
usual, what we call 'progress' is the exchange of one
nuisance for another nuisance.
   Havelock Ellis 1859–1939

And all is seared with trade; bleared, smeared with toil;
And wears man's smudge and shares man's smell.
   Gerard Manley Hopkins 1844–89

It goes so heavily with my disposition that this goodly
frame, the earth, seems to me a sterile promontory; this
most excellent canopy, the air, look you, this brave
o'erhanging firmament, this majestical roof fretted with
golden fire, why, it appears no other thing to me but a
foul and pestilent congregation of vapours.
   William Shakespeare 1564–1616

By avarice and selfishness, and a grovelling habit, from
which none of us is free, of regarding the soil as
property…the landscape is deformed.
   Henry David Thoreau 1817–62

Poverty

Anyone who has ever struggled with poverty knows how
extremely expensive it is to be poor.
   James Baldwin 1924–87

Come away; poverty's catching.
   Aphra Behn 1640–89

What mean ye that ye beat my people to pieces, and
grind the faces of the poor?
   Bible

When I give food to the poor they call me a saint. When I ask why the poor have no food they call me a communist.

Helder Camara 1909-99

The poor are Europe's blacks.

Nicolas-Sébastien Chamfort 1741-94

People don't resent having nothing nearly as much as too little.

Ivy Compton-Burnett 1884-1969

The murmuring poor, who will not fast in peace.

George Crabbe 1754-1832

Give me not poverty lest I steal.

Daniel Defoe 1660-1731

There is no scandal like rags, nor any crime so shameful as poverty.

George Farquhar 1678-1707

I want there to be no peasant in my kingdom so poor that he is unable to have a chicken in his pot every Sunday.

Henri IV 1553-1610

Oh! God! that bread should be so dear,
And flesh and blood so cheap!

Thomas Hood 1799-1845

It's easy to be independent when you've got money. But to be independent when you haven't got a thing—that's the Lord's test.

Mahalia Jackson 1911-72

Resolve not to be poor: whatever you have, spend less. Poverty is a great enemy to human happiness; it certainly destroys liberty, and it makes some virtues impracticable, and others extremely difficult.

Samuel Johnson 1709-84

Poverty

The misfortunes of poverty carry with them nothing harder to bear than that it makes men ridiculous.

Juvenal AD c.60–c.130

Battles and sex are the only free diversions in slum life. Couple them with drink, which costs money, and you have the three principal outlets for that escape complex which is for ever working in the tenement dweller's subconscious mind.

Alexander McArthur and **H. Kingsley Long**

I never saw a beggar yet who would recognise guilt if it bit him on his unwashed ass.

Tony Parsons 1953–

Poverty is a lot like childbirth—you know it is going to hurt before it happens, but you'll never know how much until you experience it.

J. K. Rowling 1965–

The greatest of evils and the worst of crimes is poverty.

George Bernard Shaw 1856–1950

Poverty is no disgrace to a man, but it is confoundedly inconvenient.

Sydney Smith 1771–1845

Sixteen tons, what do you get?
Another day older and deeper in debt.
Say brother, don't you call me 'cause I can't go
I owe my soul to the company store.

Merle Travis 1917–83

Power

Power tends to corrupt and absolute power corrupts absolutely.

Lord Acton 1834–1902

All rising to great place is by a winding stair.
Francis Bacon 1561–1626

Every dictator uses religion as a prop to keep himself in power.
Benazir Bhutto 1953–

The most potent weapon in the hands of the oppressor is the mind of the oppressed.
Steve Biko 1946–77

A man may build himself a throne of bayonets, but he cannot sit on it.
Dean Inge 1860–1954, *quoted by Boris Yeltsin at the time of the failed military coup in Russia, 1991*

Power is the great aphrodisiac.
Henry Kissinger 1923–

Power? It's like a Dead Sea fruit. When you achieve it, there is nothing there.
Harold Macmillan 1894–1986

Political power grows out of the barrel of a gun.
Mao Tse-tung 1893–1976

Who controls the past controls the future: who controls the present controls the past.
George Orwell 1903–50

You only have power over people as long as you don't take *everything* away from them. But when you've robbed a man of *everything* he's no longer in your power—he's free again.
Alexander Solzhenitsyn 1918–

The Pope! How many divisions has *he* got?
Joseph Stalin 1879–1953, *on being asked to encourage Catholicism in Russia by way of conciliating the Pope*

The hand that signed the paper felled a city.
Dylan Thomas 1914–53

Practicality

It's grand, and you canna expect to be baith grand and comfortable.
J. M. Barrie 1860–1937

Put your trust in God, my boys, and keep your powder dry.
Valentine Blacker 1728–1823, 'Oliver's Advice', often attributed to Oliver Cromwell himself

Whenever our neighbour's house is on fire, it cannot be amiss for the engines to play a little on our own.
Edmund Burke 1729–97

The colour of the cat doesn't matter as long as it catches the mice.
Deng Xiaoping 1904–97

Common sense is the best distributed commodity in the world, for every man is convinced that he is well supplied with it.
René Descartes 1596–1650

Common sense is nothing more than a deposit of prejudices laid down in the mind before you reach eighteen.
Albert Einstein 1879–1955

Praise the Lord and pass the ammunition.
Howell Forgy 1908–83, at Pearl Harbor, while sailors passed ammunition by hand to the deck

So I really think that American gentlemen are the best after all, because kissing your hand may make you feel very very good but a diamond and safire bracelet lasts forever.
Anita Loos 1893–1981

Be nice to people on your way up because you'll meet
'em on your way down.
Wilson Mizner 1876–1933

Common sense is not so common.
Voltaire 1694–1778

Praise

He who discommendeth others obliquely commendeth
himself.
Sir Thomas Browne 1605–82

The advantage of doing one's praising for oneself is that
one can lay it on so thick and exactly in the right places.
Samuel Butler 1835–1902

Imitation is the sincerest of flattery.
Charles Caleb Colton c.1780–1832

All censure of a man's self is oblique praise. It is in order
to shew how much he can spare.
Samuel Johnson 1709–84

And even the ranks of Tuscany
Could scarce forbear to cheer.
Lord Macaulay 1800–59

Damn with faint praise, assent with civil leer,
And without sneering, teach the rest to sneer.
Alexander Pope 1688–1744

But when I tell him he hates flatterers,
He says he does, being then most flattered.
William Shakespeare 1564–1616

Praise

I suppose flattery hurts no one, that is, if he doesn't inhale.

Adlai Stevenson 1900–65

Prayer

Pray to the gods only when you're making some effort on your own behalf, otherwise your prayers are wasted.

Aesop

O Lord! thou knowest how busy I must be this day: if I forget thee, do not thou forget me.

Jacob Astley 1579–1652, *before the Battle of Edgehill*

Surely the form of a prayer does not matter, and the only distinction God makes is between good will and ill; or so I have come to believe.

Margaret Atwood 1939–

The wish for prayer is a prayer in itself.

Georges Bernanos 1888–1948

Ask, and it shall be given you; seek, and ye shall find; knock, and it shall be opened unto you.

Bible

And lips say, 'God be pitiful,'
Who ne'er said, 'God be praised.'

Elizabeth Barrett Browning 1806–61

He prayeth best, who loveth best
All things both great and small.

Samuel Taylor Coleridge 1772–1834

I throw myself down in my Chamber, and I call in, and invite God, and his Angels thither, and when they are there, I neglect God and his Angels, for the noise of a fly, for the rattling of a coach, for the whining of a door.

John Donne 1572–1631

To lift up the hands in prayer gives God glory, but a man with a dungfork in his hand, a woman with a slop-pail, give him glory too.

Gerard Manley Hopkins 1844–89

The prayers of the dying are especially precious to God, because they will soon be in His presence.

Basil Hume 1923–99

One single grateful thought raised to heaven is the most perfect prayer.

G. E. Lessing 1729–81

Often when I pray I wonder if I am not posting letters to a non-existent address.

C. S. Lewis 1898–1963

The family that prays together stays together.

Al Scalpone

My words fly up, my thoughts remain below:
Words without thoughts never to heaven go.

William Shakespeare 1564–1616

I am just going to pray for you at St Paul's, but with no very lively hope of success.

Sydney Smith 1771–1845

If thou shouldst never see my face again,
Pray for my soul. More things are wrought by prayer
Than this world dreams of.

Alfred, Lord Tennyson 1809–92

Whatever a man prays for, he prays for a miracle. Every prayer reduces itself to this: Great God, grant that twice two be not four.

Ivan Turgenev 1818–83

You can't pray a lie.

Mark Twain 1835–1910

Prejudice

Prejudice ....➤ Race

Bigotry may be roughly defined as the anger of men who have no opinions.
G. K. Chesterton 1874–1936

Being a star has made it possible for me to get insulted in places where the average Negro could never *hope* to go and get insulted.
Sammy Davis Jnr. 1925–90

Minds are like parachutes. They only function when they are open.
James Dewar 1842–1923

Human diversity makes tolerance more than a virtue, it makes it a requirement for survival.
René Dubos 1901–82

If my theory of relativity is proven correct, Germany will claim me as a German and France will declare that I am a citizen of the world. Should my theory prove untrue, France will say that I am a German and Germany will declare that I am a Jew.
Albert Einstein 1879–1955

Make hatred hated!
Anatole France 1844–1924

Drive out prejudices through the door, and they will return through the window.
Frederick the Great 1712–86

Without the aid of prejudice and custom, I should not be able to find my way across the room.
William Hazlitt 1778–1830

When prejudice commands, reason is silent.
    Helvétius 1715–71

And wherefore is he wearing such a conscience-stricken
    air?
Oh they're taking him to prison for the colour of his
    hair.
    A. E. Housman 1859–1936

Four legs good, two legs bad.
    George Orwell 1903–50

We should therefore claim, in the name of tolerance, the
right not to tolerate the intolerant.
    Karl Popper 1902–94

When people feel deeply, impartiality is bias.
    Lord Reith 1889–1971

The only good Indian is a dead Indian.
    Philip Henry Sheridan 1831–88

Bigotry tries to keep truth safe in its hand
With a grip that kills it.
    Rabindranath Tagore 1861–1941

The Present

Can ye not discern the signs of the times?
    Bible

Take therefore no thought for the morrow: for the
morrow shall take thought for the things of itself.
Sufficient unto the day is the evil thereof.
    Bible

The Present

Exhaust the little moment. Soon it dies.
And be it gash or gold it will not come
Again in this identical disguise.
  Gwendolyn Brooks 1917–2000

The rule is, jam to-morrow and jam yesterday—but never
jam today.
  Lewis Carroll 1832–98

The present is the funeral of the past,
And man the living sepulchre of life.
  John Clare 1793–1864

Unborn TO-MORROW, and dead YESTERDAY,
Why fret about them if TO-DAY be sweet!
  Edward Fitzgerald 1809–83

Carpe diem, quam minimum credula postero.
Seize the day, put no trust in the future.
  Horace 65–8 BC

Things are both more trivial than they ever were, and
more important than they ever were, and the difference
between the trivial and the important doesn't seem to
matter. But the nowness of everything is absolutely
wondrous.
  Dennis Potter 1935–94, *on his approaching death*

What is love? 'tis not hereafter;
Present mirth hath present laughter;
What's to come is still unsure.
  William Shakespeare 1564–1616

The Presidency

My country has in its wisdom contrived for me the most
insignificant office that ever the invention of man
contrived or his imagination conceived.
  John Adams 1735–1826, *of the vice-presidency*

The Presidency

The US presidency is a Tudor monarchy plus telephones.
    Anthony Burgess 1917–93

Somewhere out in this audience may even be someone
who will one day follow in my footsteps, and preside over
the White House as the President's spouse. I wish him
well!
    Barbara Bush 1925–

When I was a boy I was told that anybody could become
President. I'm beginning to believe it.
    Clarence Darrow 1857–1938

No easy problems ever come to the President of the
United States. If they are easy to solve, somebody else has
solved them.
    Dwight D. Eisenhower 1890–1969

All the security around the American president is just to
make sure the man who shoots him gets caught.
    Norman Mailer 1923–

When the President does it, that means that it is not
illegal.
    Richard Nixon 1913–94

I trust Bush with my daughter, but I trust Clinton with
my job.
    Craig Paterson

I have got such a bully pulpit!
    Theodore Roosevelt 1858–1919

The answer to the runaway Presidency is not the
messenger-boy Presidency. The American democracy must
discover a middle way between making the President a
tsar and making him a puppet.
    Arthur M. Schlesinger Jr. 1917–

Pride

Pride

Pride goeth before destruction, and an haughty spirit before a fall.
Bible

For whosoever exalteth himself shall be abased; and he that humbleth himself shall be exalted.
Bible

He that is down needs fear no fall,
He that is low no pride.
He that is humble ever shall
Have God to be his guide.
John Bunyan 1628–88

URIAH HEEP: We are so very 'umble.
Charles Dickens 1812–70

Pride helps us; and pride is not a bad thing when it only urges us to hide our own hurts, not to hurt others.
George Eliot 1819–80

I can trace my ancestry back to a protoplasmal primordial atomic globule. Consequently, my family pride is something in-conceivable. I can't help it. I was born sneering.
W. S. Gilbert 1836–1911

In 1969 I published a small book on Humility. It was a pioneering work which has not, to my knowledge, been superseded.
Lord Longford 1905–2001

PLEASE ACCEPT MY RESIGNATION. I DON'T WANT TO BELONG TO ANY CLUB THAT WILL ACCEPT ME AS A MEMBER.
Groucho Marx 1890–1977

No one can make you feel inferior without your consent.
    Eleanor Roosevelt 1884–1962

Arrogance is a highly under-appreciated character trait.
    Sting 1951–

As for conceit, what man will do any good who is not conceited? Nobody holds a good opinion of a man who has a low opinion of himself.
    Anthony Trollope 1815–82

Progress

Belief in progress is a doctrine of idlers and Belgians. It is the individual relying upon his neighbours to do his work.
    Charles Baudelaire 1821–67

Want is one only of five giants on the road of reconstruction...the others are Disease, Ignorance, Squalor and Idleness.
    William Henry Beveridge 1879–1963

The thing that hath been, it is that which shall be; and that which is done is that which shall be done: and there is no new thing under the sun.
    Bible

Man aspires to the stars. But if he can get his sewage and refuse distributed and utilised in orderly fashion he will be doing very well.
    Roy Bridger

What have the Romans ever done for us?
    Graham Chapman 1941–89 et al.

pity this busy monster, manunkind,
not. Progress is a comfortable disease.
    e. e. cummings 1894–1962

Progress

The European talks of progress because by an ingenious application of some scientific acquirements he has established a society which has mistaken comfort for civilization.
Benjamin Disraeli 1804–81

Is it progress if a cannibal uses knife and fork?
Stanislaw Lec 1909–66

One step forward two steps back.
Lenin 1870–1924

If I have seen further it is by standing on the shoulders of giants.
Isaac Newton 1642–1727

'Change' is scientific, 'progress' is ethical; change is indubitable, whereas progress is a matter of controversy.
Bertrand Russell 1872–1970

The reasonable man adapts himself to the world: the unreasonable one persists in trying to adapt the world to himself. Therefore all progress depends on the unreasonable man.
George Bernard Shaw 1856–1950

And he gave it for his opinion, that whoever could make two ears of corn or two blades of grass to grow upon a spot of ground where only one grew before, would deserve better of mankind, and do more essential service to his country than the whole race of politicians put together.
Jonathan Swift 1667–1745

Without deviation from the norm, progress is not possible.
Frank Zappa 1940–93

Protest

'It's always best on these occasions to do what the mob do.' 'But suppose there are two mobs?' suggested Mr Snodgrass. 'Shout with the largest,' replied Mr Pickwick.
Charles Dickens 1812-70

I hope to have chiselled on my gravestone: 'He incited them to disaffect'.
George Galloway 1954-

Making noise is an effective means of opposition.
Joseph Goebbels 1897-1945

The citizen's first duty is unrest.
Günter Grass 1927-

Even a purely moral act that has no hope of any immediate and visible political effect can gradually and indirectly, over time, gain in political significance.
Václav Havel 1936-

Ev'rywhere I hear the sound of marching, charging feet, boy,
'Cause summer's here and the time is right for fighting in the street, boy.
Mick Jagger 1943-   and **Keith Richards** 1943-

One-fifth of the people are against everything all the time.
Robert Kennedy 1925-68

A riot is at bottom the language of the unheard.
Martin Luther King 1929-68

Never forget that only dead fish swim with the stream.
Malcolm Muggeridge 1903-90

Minorities...are almost always in the right.
Sydney Smith 1771-1845

Protest

I've always had the impression that real militants are like cleaning women, doing a thankless, daily but necessary job.

François Truffaut 1932–84

Punishment ····▶ see also Crime

All punishment is mischief: all punishment in itself is evil.

Jeremy Bentham 1748–1832

He that spareth his rod hateth his son.

Bible

He that is without sin among you, let him first cast a stone at her.

Bible

Hanging is too good for him, said Mr Cruelty.

John Bunyan 1628–88

Excessive bail shall not be required, nor excessive fines imposed, nor cruel and unusual punishment inflicted.

Constitution of the United States 1787

Punishment is not for revenge, but to lessen crime and reform the criminal.

Elizabeth Fry 1780–1845

Whenever the offence inspires less horror than the punishment, the rigour of penal law is obliged to give way to the common feelings of mankind.

Edward Gibbon 1737–94

My object all sublime
I shall achieve in time—
To let the punishment fit the crime—
The punishment fit the crime.

W. S. Gilbert 1836–1911

Awaiting the sensation of a short, sharp shock,
From a cheap and chippy chopper on a big black block.

W. S. Gilbert 1836–1911

Men are not hanged for stealing horses, but that horses
may not be stolen.

George Savile, Marquess of Halifax 1633–95

This is the first of punishments, that no guilty man is
acquitted if judged by himself.

Juvenal AD c.60–c.130

In that case, if we are to abolish the death penalty, let the
murderers take the first step.

Alphonse Karr 1808–90

The boy learns not to fear sin, but the *punishment* for it,
and thus he learns to lie.

Charles Kingsley 1819–75

Society needs to condemn a little more and understand a
little less.

John Major 1943–

I went out to Charing Cross, to see Major-general
Harrison hanged, drawn, and quartered; which was done
there, he looking as cheerful as any man could do in that
condition.

Samuel Pepys 1633–1703

Quotations

The surest way to make a monkey of a man is to quote
him.

Robert Benchley 1889–1945

It is a good thing for an uneducated man to read books
of quotations.

Winston Churchill 1874–1965

Quotations

I know heaps of quotations, so I can always make quite a fair show of knowledge.
O. Douglas 1877–1948

I hate quotation. Tell me what you know.
Ralph Waldo Emerson 1803–82

Windbags can be right. Aphorists can be wrong. It is a tough world.
James Fenton 1949–

An anthology is like all the plums and orange peel picked out of a cake.
Walter Raleigh 1861–1922

I always have a quotation for everything—it saves original thinking.
Dorothy L. Sayers 1893–1957

Famous remarks are very seldom quoted correctly.
Simeon Strunsky 1879–1948

What a good thing Adam had. When he said a good thing he knew nobody had said it before.
Mark Twain 1835–1910

OSCAR WILDE: How I wish I had said that.
WHISTLER: You will, Oscar, you will.
James McNeill Whistler 1834–1903

Some for renown on scraps of learning dote,
And think they grow immortal as they quote.
Edward Young 1683–1765

Race ····▸ Equality, Prejudice

Black is beautiful.
Anonymous *slogan of American civil rights campaigners, mid-1960s*

You have seen how a man was made a slave; you shall see how a slave was made a man.
>   **Frederick Douglass** c.1818–95

Irish Americans are about as Irish as black Americans are African.
>   **Bob Geldof** 1954–

I herewith commission you to carry out all preparations with regard to…a *total solution* of the Jewish question in those territories of Europe which are under German influence.
>   **Hermann Goering** 1893–1946

Though it be a thrilling and marvellous thing to be merely young and gifted in such times, it is doubly so, doubly dynamic—to be young, gifted and *black*.
>   **Lorraine Hansberry** 1930–65

And if the white man thought that Asians were a low, filthy nation, Asians could still smile with relief—at least, they were not Africans. And if the white man thought that Africans were a low, filthy nation, Africans in southern Africa could still smile—at least, they were not bushmen. They all have their monsters.
>   **Bessie Head** 1937–86

When I look out at this convention, I see the face of America, red, yellow, brown, black, and white. We are all precious in God's sight—the real rainbow coalition.
>   **Jesse Jackson** 1941–

There are no 'white' or 'coloured' signs on the foxholes or graveyards of battle.
>   **John F. Kennedy** 1917–63

I have a dream that my four little children will one day live in a nation where they will not be judged by the colour of their skin but by the content of their character.
>   **Martin Luther King** 1929–68

Race

There are very few Eskimos, but millions of Whites, just like mosquitoes. It is something very special and wonderful to be an Eskimo—they are like the snow geese. If an Eskimo forgets his language and Eskimo ways, he will be nothing but just another mosquito.

Abraham Okpik d. 1997

Our mistreatment was just not right, and I was tired of it.

Rosa Parks 1913– , *of her refusal to surrender her seat on a segregated bus in Alabama to a white man*

Where today are the Pequot? Where are the Narragansett, the Mohican, the Pokanoket, and many other once powerful tribes of our people? They have vanished before the avarice and oppression of the white man, as snow before the summer sun.

Tecumseh 1768–1813

Am I not a man and a brother.

Josiah Wedgwood 1730–95, *legend on Wedgwood cameo, depicting a kneeling Negro slave in chains*

Growing up, I came up with this name: I'm a Cablinasian.

Tiger Woods 1975– , *explaining his rejection of 'African-American' as the term to describe his Caucasian, Afro-American, Native American, Thai, and Chinese ancestry*

Railways

This is the Night Mail crossing the Border,
Bringing the cheque and the postal order,
Letters for the rich, letters for the poor,
The shop at the corner, the girl next door.

W. H. Auden 1907–73

Railways and the Church have their critics, but both are the best ways of getting a man to his ultimate destination.
Revd W. Awdry 1911–97

The only way of catching a train I have ever discovered is to miss the train before.
G. K. Chesterton 1874–1936

Railway termini. They are our gates to the glorious and the unknown. Through them we pass out into adventure and sunshine, to them, alas! we return.
E. M. Forster 1879–1970

Sir, Saturday morning, although recurring at regular and well-foreseen intervals, always seems to take this railway by surprise.
W. S. Gilbert 1836–1911, *letter to the station-master at Baker Street, on the Metropolitan line*

That life-quickening atmosphere of a big railway station where everything is something trembling on the brink of something else.
Vladimir Nabokov 1899–1977

Reading ····➤ Books

[Thomas Hobbes] was wont to say that if he had read as much as other men, he should have known no more than other men.
John Aubrey 1626–97

In science, read, by preference, the newest works; in literature, the oldest.
Edward Bulwer-Lytton 1803–73

Choose an author as you choose a friend.
Wentworth Dillon, Earl of Roscommon c.1633–1685

Reading

What do we ever get nowadays from reading to equal the excitement and the revelation in those first fourteen years?
Graham Greene 1904-91

A man ought to read just as inclination leads him; for what he reads as a task will do him little good.
Samuel Johnson 1709-84

Curiously enough, one cannot *read* a book: one can only reread it. A good reader, a major reader, an active and creative reader is a rereader.
Vladimir Nabokov 1899-1977

The bookful blockhead, ignorantly read,
With loads of learned lumber in his head.
Alexander Pope 1688-1744

POLONIUS: What do you read, my lord?
HAMLET: Words, words, words.
William Shakespeare 1564-1616

People say that life is the thing, but I prefer reading.
Logan Pearsall Smith 1865-1946

Reading is to the mind what exercise is to the body.
Richard Steele 1672-1729

Reality

It's as large as life, and twice as natural!
Lewis Carroll 1832-98

Reality goes bounding past the satirist like a cheetah laughing as it lopes ahead of the greyhound.
Claud Cockburn 1904-81

> Human kind
Cannot bear very much reality.
T. S. Eliot 1888-1965

All theory, dear friend, is grey, but the golden tree of
actual life springs ever green.
    Johann Wolfgang von Goethe 1749–1832

What is rational is actual and what is actual is rational.
    G. W. F. Hegel 1770–1831

Each person experiences his own reality, and no one else
can be the judge of what that reality really is.
    Shirley Maclaine 1934–

The camera makes everyone a tourist in other people's
reality, and eventually in one's own.
    Susan Sontag 1933–

They said, 'You have a blue guitar,
You do not play things as they are.'
The man replied, 'Things as they are
Are changed upon the blue guitar.'
    Wallace Stevens 1879–1955

The nineteenth century dislike of Realism is the rage of
Caliban seeing his own face in the glass.
    Oscar Wilde 1854–1900

BLANCHE: I don't want realism.
MITCH: Naw, I guess not.
BLANCHE: I'll tell you what I want. Magic!
    Tennessee Williams 1911–83

Religion ····▸ The Church, God, Prayer

Render therefore unto Caesar the things which are
Caesar's; and unto God the things that are God's.
    Bible

It is time the West confronted its ignorance of Islam.
Jews, Muslims and Christians are all children of Abraham.
    Tony Blair 1953–

Religion

One religion is as true as another.
Robert Burton 1577–1640

Christians have burnt each other, quite persuaded
That all the Apostles would have done as they did.
Lord Byron 1788–1824

Putting moral virtues at the highest, and religion at the
lowest, religion must still be allowed to be a collateral
security, at least, to virtue; and every prudent man will
sooner trust to two securities than to one.
Lord Chesterfield 1694–1773

Science without religion is lame, religion without science
is blind.
Albert Einstein 1879–1955

The various modes of worship, which prevailed in the
Roman world, were all considered by the people as
equally true; by the philosopher, as equally false; and by
the magistrate, as equally useful. And thus toleration
produced not only mutual indulgence, but even religious
concord.
Edward Gibbon 1737–94

In all ages of the world, priests have been enemies of
liberty.
David Hume 1711–76

I go into the Muslim mosque and the Jewish synagogue
and the Christian church and I see one altar.
Jalal ad-Din ar-Rumi 1207–73

'Twas only fear first in the world made gods.
Ben Jonson c.1573–1637

Better authentic mammon than a bogus god.
Louis MacNeice 1907–63

I count religion but a childish toy,
And hold there is no sin but ignorance.
Christopher Marlowe 1564–93

Religion…is the opium of the people.
Karl Marx 1818–83

Things have come to a pretty pass when religion is
allowed to invade the sphere of private life.
Lord Melbourne 1779–1848, *on hearing an evangelical sermon*

It is convenient that there be gods, and, as it is
convenient, let us believe that there are.
Ovid 43 BC–AD C.17

My country is the world, and my religion is to do good.
Thomas Paine 1737–1809

Is that which is holy loved by the gods because it is holy,
or is it holy because it is loved by the gods?
Plato 429–347 BC

Religion to me has always been the wound, not the
bandage.
Dennis Potter 1935–94

A sense of the sacred without a sense of humour becomes
leaden.
Robert Runcie 1921–2000

'Men of sense are really but of one religion.'…'Pray, my
lord, what religion is that which men of sense agree in?'
'Madam,' says the earl immediately, 'men of sense never
tell it.'
Lord Shaftesbury 1621–83

We have just enough religion to make us hate, but not
enough to make us love one another.
Jonathan Swift 1667–1745

Orthodoxy is my doxy; heterodoxy is another man's doxy.
Bishop William Warburton 1698–1779

Religion

I went to America to convert the Indians; but oh, who shall convert me?
  John Wesley 1703-91

So many gods, so many creeds,
So many paths that wind and wind,
While just the art of being kind
Is all the sad world needs.
  Ella Wheeler Wilcox 1855-1919

Retirement

I go to Bournemouth in lieu of Paradise.
  Lord Hugh Cecil 1869-1956, *on retiring from Eton*

The transition from Who's Who to Who's He.
  Eddie George 1938-

Retirement from the concert hall is like giving up smoking. You have got to finish completely.
  Beniamino Gigli 1890-1957

That [retirement] kind of says giving up to me. It's like going to bed lying down. I can't.
  Rolf Harris 1930-

When you get done, you get done.
  Stephen King 1947- , *announcing his retirement from writing*

Learn to live well, or fairly make your will;
You've played, and loved, and ate, and drunk your fill:
Walk sober off; before a sprightlier age
Comes tittering on, and shoves you from the stage.
  Alexander Pope 1688-1744

As to that leisure evening of life, I must say that I do not want it. I can conceive of no contentment of which toil is not to be the immediate parent.
  Anthony Trollope 1815-82

I contemplate retirement every evening, and then I forget about it in the morning.
Peter Ustinov 1921–2004

Revenge is a kind of wild justice, which the more man's nature runs to, the more ought law to weed it out.
Francis Bacon 1561–1626

Vengeance is mine; I will repay, saith the Lord.
Bible

Sweet is revenge—especially to women.
Lord Byron 1788–1824

It may be that vengeance is sweet, and that the gods forbade vengeance to men because they reserved for themselves so delicious and intoxicating a drink. But no one should drain the cup to the bottom. The dregs are often filthy-tasting.
Winston Churchill 1874–1965

Heaven has no rage, like love to hatred turned,
Nor Hell a fury, like a woman scorned.
William Congreve 1670–1729

The Germans…are going to be squeezed as a lemon is squeezed—until the pips squeak.
Eric Geddes 1875–1937

Nobody ever forgets where he buried a hatchet.
Frank McKinney ('Kin') Hubbard 1868–1930

Get your retaliation in first.
Carwyn James 1929–83

Revenge

Men should be either treated generously or destroyed,
because they take revenge for slight injuries—for heavy
ones they cannot.
　　Niccolò Machiavelli 1469–1527

Don't get mad, get everything.
　　Ivana Trump 1949– , *advice to wronged wives*

Revolution

Better to abolish serfdom from above than to wait till it
begins to abolish itself from below.
　　Tsar Alexander II 1818–81

The most radical revolutionary will become a
conservative on the day after the revolution.
　　Hannah Arendt 1906–75

Those who have served the cause of the revolution have
ploughed the sea.
　　Simón Bolívar 1783–1830

Revolutions are celebrated when they are no longer
dangerous.
　　Pierre Boulez 1925–

Rebellion to tyrants is obedience to God.
　　John Bradshaw 1602–59

Would it not be easier
In that case for the government
To dissolve the people
And elect another?
　　Bertolt Brecht 1898–1956, *on the 1953 uprising in East
　　Germany*

All modern revolutions have ended in a reinforcement of
the State.
　　Albert Camus 1913–60

A desperate disease requires a dangerous remedy.
    Guy Fawkes 1570–1606

How much the greatest event it is that ever happened in the world! and how much the best!
    Charles James Fox 1749–1806, *on the fall of the Bastille*

I will die like a true-blue rebel. Don't waste any time in mourning—organize.
    Joe Hill 1879–1915, *farewell telegram prior to his death by firing squad*

The generation which commences a revolution can rarely complete it.
    Thomas Jefferson 1743–1826

Après nous le déluge.
After us the deluge.
    Madame de Pompadour 1721–64

J'ai vécu.
I survived.
    Abbé Emmanuel Joseph Sieyès 1748–1836, *when asked what he had done during the French Revolution*

I have seen the future; and it works.
    Lincoln Steffens 1866–1936, *following a visit to the Soviet Union in 1919*

Bliss was it in that dawn to be alive,
But to be young was very heaven!
    William Wordsworth 1770–1850, *on the French revolution*

Royalty

[A king] is the fountain of honour.
    Francis Bacon 1561–1626

We must not let in daylight upon magic.
    Walter Bagehot 1826–77

Royalty

The Sovereign has, under a constitutional monarchy such as ours, three rights—the right to be consulted, the right to encourage, the right to warn.
   Walter Bagehot 1826-77

To be Prince of Wales is not a position. It is a predicament.
   Alan Bennett 1934-

A subject and a sovereign are clean different things.
   Charles I 1600-49

I'd like to be a queen in people's hearts but I don't see myself being Queen of this country.
   Diana, Princess of Wales 1961-97

Everyone likes flattery; and when you come to Royalty you should lay it on with a trowel.
   Benjamin Disraeli 1804-81

I have found it impossible to carry the heavy burden of responsibility and to discharge my duties as King as I would wish to do without the help and support of the woman I love.
   Edward VIII 1894-1972, *radio broadcast following his abdication*

I know I have the body of a weak and feeble woman, but I have the heart and stomach of a king, and of a king of England too.
   Elizabeth I 1533-1603

It is a very curious thing that no matter where I go, in whatever country, the children always think I should be wearing a silver dress and a golden crown. They must all be bitterly disappointed. Maybe I should.
   Elizabeth II 1926-

We could not go anywhere without sending word ahead so that life might be put on parade for us.
   Infanta Eulalia of Spain 1864-1958

L'État c'est moi.
I am the State.
> **Louis XIV** 1638–1715

Royalty is the gold filling in a mouthful of decay.
> **John Osborne** 1929-

Uneasy lies the head that wears a crown.
> **William Shakespeare** 1564–1616

Monarchy is only the string that ties the robber's bundle.
> **Percy Bysshe Shelley** 1792–1822

I will be good.
> **Queen Victoria** 1819–1901, *on being shown a chart of the line of succession*

Satisfaction ····➤ Discontent

A book of verses underneath the bough,
A jug of wine, a loaf of bread—and Thou
Beside me singing in the wilderness—
And wilderness were paradise enow.
> **Edward Fitzgerald** 1809–83

These are the days when men of all social disciplines and
all political faiths seek the comfortable and the
accepted…in minor modification of the scriptural
parable, the bland lead the bland.
> **J. K. Galbraith** 1908-

If one cannot catch the bird of paradise, better take a wet
hen.
> **Nikita Khrushchev** 1894–1971

So long as the great majority of men are not deprived of
either property or honour, they are satisfied.
> **Niccolò Machiavelli** 1469–1527

Satisfaction

He is well paid that is well satisfied.
William Shakespeare 1564–1616

As long as I have a want, I have a reason for living. Satisfaction is death.
George Bernard Shaw 1856–1950

Content is disillusioning to behold: what is there to be content about?
Virginia Woolf 1882–1941

Science ····▶ Life Sciences, Technology

When I find myself in the company of scientists, I feel like a shabby curate who has strayed by mistake into a drawing room full of dukes.
W. H. Auden 1907–73

Anybody who is not shocked by this subject has failed to understand it.
Niels Bohr 1885–1962, *of quantum mechanics*

Basic research is what I am doing when I don't know what I am doing.
Werner von Braun 1912–77

The aim of science is not to open the door to infinite wisdom, but to set a limit to infinite error.
Bertolt Brecht 1898–1956

The scientific method, as far as it is a method, is nothing more than doing one's damnedest with one's mind, no holds barred.
Percy Williams Bridgeman 1882–1961

The essence of science: ask an impertinent question, and you are on the way to a pertinent answer.
Jacob Bronowski 1908–74

If an elderly but distinguished scientist says that something is possible he is almost certainly right, but if he says that it is impossible he is very probably wrong.

Arthur C. Clarke 1917–

In science the credit goes to the man who convinces the world, not to the man to whom the idea first occurs.

Francis Darwin 1848–1925

It is more important to have beauty in one's equations than to have them fit experiment.

Paul Dirac 1902–84

I ask you to look both ways. For the road to a knowledge of the stars leads through the atom; and important knowledge of the atom has been reached through the stars.

Arthur Eddington 1882–1944

The grand aim of all science [is] to cover the greatest number of empirical facts by logical deduction from the smallest possible number of hypotheses or axioms.

Albert Einstein 1879–1955

The great tragedy of Science—the slaying of a beautiful hypothesis by an ugly fact.

T. H. Huxley 1825–95

If we assume that the last breath of, say, Julius Caesar has by now become thoroughly scattered through the atmosphere, then the chances are that each of us inhales one molecule of it with every breath we take.

James Jeans 1877–1946, *now usually quoted as 'the dying breath of Socrates'*

It may be so, there is no arguing against facts and experiments.

Isaac Newton 1642–1727, *when told of an experiment which appeared to destroy his theory*

Science

The physicists have known sin; and this is a knowledge which they cannot lose.
     J. Robert Oppenheimer 1904–67

Where observation is concerned, chance favours only the prepared mind.
     Louis Pasteur 1822–95

A new scientific truth does not triumph by convincing its opponents and making them see the light, but rather because its opponents eventually die, and a new generation grows up that is familiar with it.
     Max Planck 1858–1947

Science is built up of facts, as a house is built of stones; but an accumulation of facts is no more a science than a heap of stones is a house.
     Henri Poincaré 1854–1912

Nature, and Nature's laws lay hid in night.
God said, *Let Newton be!* and all was light.
     Alexander Pope 1688–1744

Aristotle maintained that women have fewer teeth than men; although he was twice married, it never occurred to him to verify this statement by examining his wives' mouths.
     Bertrand Russell 1872–1970

All science is either physics or stamp collecting.
     Ernest Rutherford 1871–1937

We haven't got the money, so we've got to think!
     Ernest Rutherford 1871–1937

Science is for the cultivation of religion, not for worldly enjoyment.
     Sadi c.1213–91

It did not last: the Devil howling 'Ho!
Let Einstein be!' restored the status quo.
   J. C. Squire 1884–1958, *responding to Pope's lines on Newton*

It is much easier to make measurements than to know
exactly what you are measuring.
   J. W. N. Sullivan 1886–1937

Neutrinos, they are very small
They have no charge and have no mass
And do not interact at all.
   John Updike 1932–

Scotland

There are few more impressive sights in the world than a
Scotsman on the make.
   J. M. Barrie 1860–1937

Scotland, land of the omnipotent No.
   Alan Bold 1943–

My heart's in the Highlands, my heart is not here;
My heart's in the Highlands a-chasing the deer.
   Robert Burns 1759–96

Scots, wha hae wi' Wallace bled,
Scots, wham Bruce has aften led,
Welcome to your gory bed,—
Or to victorie.
   Robert Burns 1759–96

From the lone shieling of the misty island
Mountains divide us, and the waste of seas—
Yet still the blood is strong, the heart is Highland,
And we in dreams behold the Hebrides!
   John Galt 1779–1839

Scotland

The noblest prospect which a Scotchman ever sees, is the
high road that leads him to England!
Samuel Johnson 1709–84

Who owns this landscape?
The millionaire who bought it or
the poacher staggering downhill in the early morning
with a deer on his back?
Norman McCaig 1910–96

If one wanted a rough-and-ready generalization to express
the difference between a Glasgow man and an Edinburgh
man, one might say that every Edinburgh man considers
himself a little better than his neighbour, and every
Glasgow man just as good as his neighbour.
Edwin Muir 1887–1959

O Caledonia! stern and wild,
Meet nurse for a poetic child!
Sir Walter Scott 1771–1832

Stands Scotland where it did?
William Shakespeare 1564–1616

O flower of Scotland, when will we see your like again,
that fought and died for your bit hill and glen
and stood against him, proud Edward's army,
and sent him homeward tae think again.
Roy Williamson 1936–90

Sculpture

Most statues seem sad and introspective,
they hold their breath between coming and going,
They lament their devoured, once shuddering stone.
Dannie Abse 1923–

Carving is interrelated masses conveying an emotion: a perfect relationship between the mind and the colour, light and weight which is the stone, made by the hand which feels.

Barbara Hepworth 1903–75

It's amazing what you can do with an E in A-level art, twisted imagination and a chainsaw.

Damien Hirst 1965– , *after winning the 1995 Turner Prize*

The marble not yet carved can hold the form
Of every thought the greatest artist has.

Michelangelo 1475–1564

The first hole made through a piece of stone is a revelation.

Henry Moore 1898–1986

The Sea

A willing foe and sea room.

Anonymous *naval toast in the time of Nelson*

They that go down to the sea in ships: and occupy their business in great waters.

Bible

Don't talk to me about naval tradition. It's nothing but rum, sodomy, and the lash.

Winston Churchill 1874–1965

Water, water, everywhere,
And all the boards did shrink;
Water, water, everywhere,
Nor any drop to drink.

Samuel Taylor Coleridge 1772–1834

He lived by the sea, died on it, and was buried in it.

Thomas Fuller 1608–61, *of Sir Francis Drake*

The Sea

No man will be a sailor who has contrivance enough to get himself into a jail; for being in a ship is being in a jail, with the chance of being drowned...A man in a jail has more room, better food, and commonly better company.

Samuel Johnson 1709-84

It is an interesting biological fact that all of us have in our veins the exact same percentage of salt in our blood that exists in the ocean, and therefore, we have salt in our blood, in our sweat, in our tears. We are tied to the ocean. And when we go back to the sea—whether it is to sail or to watch it—we are going back from whence we came.

John F. Kennedy 1917-63

I must go down to the sea again, to the lonely sea and the sky,
And all I ask is a tall ship and a star to steer her by.

John Masefield 1878-1967

The sea hates a coward!

Eugene O'Neill 1888-1953

The sea has such extraordinary moods that sometimes you feel this is the only sort of life—and 10 minutes later you're praying for death.

Prince Philip 1921-

Full fathom five thy father lies;
Of his bones are coral made:
Those are pearls that were his eyes:
Nothing of him that doth fade,
But doth suffer a sea-change
Into something rich and strange.

William Shakespeare 1564-1616

Rocked in the cradle of the deep.

Emma Hart Willard 1787-1870

Secrecy

I shall be but a short time tonight. I have seldom spoken
with greater regret, for my lips are not yet unsealed. Were
these troubles over I would make a case, and I guarantee
that not a man would go into the lobby against us.

Stanley Baldwin 1867–1947, *usually quoted as 'My lips are
sealed'*

When thou doest alms, let not thy left hand know what
thy right hand doeth.

Bible

Nothing attracts me like a closed door. I cannot let my
camera rest until I have pried it open.

Margaret Bourke-White 1906–71

The truth is out there.

Chris Carter 1957– , *catchphrase*; The X Files

The small man said to the other: 'Where does a wise man
hide a pebble?' And the tall man answered in a low voice:
'On the beach.'

G. K. Chesterton 1874–1936

I know that's a secret, for it's whispered every where.

William Congreve 1670–1729

For secrets are edged tools,
And must be kept from children and from fools.

John Dryden 1631–1700

I would not open windows into men's souls.

Elizabeth I 1533–1603

We dance round in a ring and suppose,
But the Secret sits in the middle and knows.

Robert Frost 1874–1963

Secrecy

Once the toothpaste is out of the tube, it is awfully hard to get it back in.

H. R. Haldeman 1929– , *comment on the Watergate affair*

Love and a cough cannot be hid.

George Herbert 1593–1633

It is public scandal that constitutes offence, and to sin in secret is not to sin at all.

Molière 1622–73

The necessity of procuring good intelligence is apparent and need not be further urged.

George Washington 1732–99

The Self

Some thirty inches from my nose
The frontier of my Person goes,
And all the untilled air between
Is private *pagus* or demesne.

W. H. Auden 1907–73

Through the Thou a person becomes I.

Martin Buber 1878–1965

'You' your joys and your sorrows, your memories and ambitions, your sense of personal identity and free will, are in fact no more than the behaviour of a vast assembly of nerve cells and their associated molecules.

Francis Crick 1916–2004

I am the master of my fate:
I am the captain of my soul.

W. E. Henley 1849–1903

If I am not for myself who is for me; and being for my own self what am I?

Hillel 'The Elder' c.60 BC–AD c.9

It is not contrary to reason to prefer the destruction of
the whole world to the scratching of my finger.
David Hume 1711-76

I am not a number, I am a free man!
Patrick McGoohan 1928–   et al. *Number Six, in* The Prisoner

The self is hateful.
Blaise Pascal 1623-62

Thus God and nature linked the gen'ral frame,
And bade self-love and social be the same.
Alexander Pope 1688-1744

Personal isn't the same as important.
Terry Pratchett 1948–

Who is it that can tell me who I am?
William Shakespeare 1564-1616

It is easy—terribly easy—to shake a man's faith in
himself. To take advantage of that to break a man's spirit
is devil's work.
George Bernard Shaw 1856-1950

Rose is a rose is a rose is a rose, is a rose.
Gertrude Stein 1874-1946

If a man does not keep pace with his companions,
perhaps it is because he hears a different drummer. Let
him step to the music which he hears, however measured
or far away.
Henry David Thoreau 1817-62

Do I contradict myself?
Very well then I contradict myself,
(I am large, I contain multitudes.)
Walt Whitman 1819-92

Self-Knowledge

Know thyself.
Anonymous *inscribed on the temple of Apollo at Delphi*

The image of myself which I try to create in my own
mind in order that I may love myself is very different
from the image which I try to create in the minds of
others in order that they may love me.
W. H. Auden 1907–73

Why beholdest thou the mote that is in thy brother's eye,
but considerest not the beam that is in thine own eye?
Bible

O wad some Pow'r the giftie gie us
To see oursels as others see us!
It wad frae mony a blunder free us,
And foolish notion.
Robert Burns 1759–96

How little do we know that which we are!
How less what we may be!
Lord Byron 1788–1824

I do not know whether I was then a man dreaming I was
a butterfly, or whether I am now a butterfly dreaming I
am a man.
Chuang-tzu (or Zhuangzi) c.369–286 BC

I do not know myself, and God forbid that I should.
Johann Wolfgang von Goethe 1749–1832

All our knowledge is, ourselves to know.
Alexander Pope 1688–1744

A man who does not trust himself will never really trust
anybody.
Cardinal de Retz 1613–79

This above all: to thine own self be true,
And it must follow, as the night the day,
Thou canst not then be false to any man.
William Shakespeare 1564–1616

There are few things more painful than to recognise one's own faults in others.
John Wells 1936–

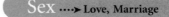

Sex ·····▶ Love, Marriage

That [sex] was the most fun I ever had without laughing.
Woody Allen 1935–

Don't knock masturbation. It's sex with someone I love.
Woody Allen 1935–

On bisexuality: It immediately doubles your chances for a date on Saturday night.
Woody Allen 1935–

Give me chastity and continency—but not yet!
St Augustine of Hippo AD 354–430

This trivial and vulgar way of coition; it is the foolishest act a wise man commits in all his life, nor is there any thing that will more deject his cooled imagination, when he shall consider what an odd and unworthy piece of folly he hath committed.
Sir Thomas Browne 1605–82

It doesn't matter what you do in the bedroom as long as you don't do it in the street and frighten the horses.
Mrs Patrick Campbell 1865–1940

The pleasure is momentary, the position ridiculous, and the expense damnable.
Lord Chesterfield 1694–1773

Sex

I have never yet seen anyone whose desire to build up his moral power was as strong as sexual desire.

Confucius 551–479 BC

Licence my roving hands, and let them go,
Behind, before, above, between, below.
O my America, my new found land,
My kingdom, safeliest when with one man manned.

John Donne 1572–1631

I'll have what she's having.

Nora Ephron 1941– , *said by woman to waiter, seeing Sally acting an orgasm*

Personally I know nothing about sex because I've always been married.

Zsa Zsa Gabor 1919–

But did thee feel the earth move?

Ernest Hemingway 1899–1961

When I hear his steps outside my door I lie down on my bed, close my eyes, open my legs, and think of England.

Lady Hillingdon 1857–1940

I'll come no more behind your scenes, David; for the silk stockings and white bosoms of your actresses excite my amorous propensities.

Samuel Johnson 1709–84

The only unnatural sex act is that which you cannot perform.

Alfred Kinsey 1894–1956

'Tisn't beauty, so to speak, nor good talk necessarily. It's just It. Some women'll stay in a man's memory if they once walked down a street.

Rudyard Kipling 1865–1936

The Duke returned from the wars today and did pleasure me in his top-boots.

Sarah, Duchess of Marlborough 1660–1744

Not tonight, Josephine.
Napoleon I 1769–1821

Delight of lust is gross and brief
And weariness treads on desire.
Petronius d. AD 65

Love is two minutes fifty-two seconds of squishing noises.
Johnny Rotten 1957–

Is it not strange that desire should so many years outlive
performance?
William Shakespeare 1564–1616

Someone asked Sophocles, 'How is your sex-life now? Are
you still able to have a woman?' He replied, 'Hush, man;
most gladly indeed am I rid of it all, as though I had
escaped from a mad and savage master.'
Sophocles c.496–406 BC

Is that a gun in your pocket, or are you just glad to
see me?
Mae West 1892–1980

Sickness ····▶ Medicine

A man's illness is his private territory and, no matter how
much he loves you and how close you are, you stay an
outsider. You are healthy.
Lauren Bacall 1924–

She is not sailing into the dark: the voyage is over, and
under the dark escort of Alzheimer's she has arrived
somewhere.
John Bayley 1925– , *of his wife Iris Murdoch*

If a lot of cures are suggested for a disease, it means that
the disease is incurable.
Anton Chekhov 1860–1904

Sickness

It's all about losing your brain without losing your mind.
Michael J. Fox 1961– , *on his fight against Parkinson's disease*

People mean well and do not see how distancing insistent cheeriness is, how it denies another's reality, denies a sick person the space or right to be sick and in pain.
Marilyn French 1929–

My final word, before I'm done,
Is 'Cancer can be rather fun'.
Thanks to the nurses and Nye Bevan
The NHS is quite like heaven
Provided one confronts the tumour
With a sufficient sense of humour.
J. B. S. Haldane 1892–1964

Did God who gave us flowers and trees,
Also provide the allergies?
E. Y. Harburg 1898–1981

Human nature seldom walks up to the word 'cancer'.
Rudyard Kipling 1865–1936

Illness is not something a person *has*; it's another way of *being*.
Jonathan Miller 1934–

The desire to take medicine is perhaps the greatest feature which distinguishes man from animals.
William Osler 1849–1919

Cured yesterday of my disease,
I died last night of my physician.
Matthew Prior 1664–1721

I now begin the journey that will lead me into the sunset of my life.
Ronald Reagan 1911–2004, *statement to the American people revealing that he had Alzheimer's disease*

Diseases desperate grown,
By desperate appliances are relieved
Or not at all.
William Shakespeare 1564–1616

I enjoy convalescence. It is the part that makes illness
worth while.
George Bernard Shaw 1856–1950

The biggest disease today is not leprosy or tuberculosis,
but rather the feeling of being unwanted, uncared for and
deserted by everybody.
Mother Teresa 1910–97

To know ourselves diseased, is half our cure.
Edward Young 1683–1765

Silence

Silence is the virtue of fools.
Francis Bacon 1561–1626

If we had a keen vision and feeling of all ordinary human
life, it would be like hearing the grass grow and the
squirrel's heart beat, and we should die of that roar
which lies on the other side of silence.
George Eliot 1819–80

Elected Silence, sing to me
And beat upon my whorlèd ear.
Gerard Manley Hopkins 1844–89

Thou still unravished bride of quietness,
Thou foster-child of silence and slow time.
John Keats 1795–1821

People talking without speaking
People hearing without listening...
'Fools,' said I, 'You do not know

Silence

Silence like a cancer grows.'
Paul Simon 1942–

Singing ····▸ Music

Today if something is not worth saying, people sing it.
Pierre-Augustin Caron de Beaumarchais 1732–99

The exercise of singing is delightful to Nature, and good
to preserve the health of man. It doth strengthen all parts
of the breast, and doth open the pipes.
William Byrd 1543–1623

Swans sing before they die: 'twere no bad thing
Should certain persons die before they sing.
Samuel Taylor Coleridge 1772–1834

Every tone [of the songs of the slaves] was a testimony
against slavery, and a prayer to God for deliverance from
chains.
Frederick Douglass c.1818–95

In writing songs I've learned as much from Cézanne as I
have from Woody Guthrie.
Bob Dylan 1941–

If a man were permitted to make all the ballads, he need
not care who should make the laws of a nation.
Andrew Fletcher of Saltoun 1655–1716

Opera is when a guy gets stabbed in the back and, instead
of bleeding, he sings.
Ed Gardner 1901–63

You think that's noise—you ain't heard nuttin' yet!
Al Jolson 1886–1950, *in a café, competing with the din from a
neighbouring building site*

The Skies

An unalterable and unquestioned law of the musical world required that the German text of French operas sung by Swedish artists should be translated into Italian for the clearer understanding of English-speaking audiences.
Edith Wharton 1862–1937

The Skies

Beautiful! Beautiful! Magnificent desolation.
Buzz Aldrin 1930– , *on landing on the moon*

Slowly, silently, now the moon
Walks the night in her silver shoon.
Walter de la Mare 1873–1956

Busy old fool, unruly sun,
Why dost thou thus,
Through windows, and through curtains call on us?
John Donne 1572–1631

Eppur si muove.
But it does move.
Galileo Galilei 1564–1642, *after his recantation, that the earth moves around the sun*

Look at the stars! look, look up at the skies!
O look at all the fire-folk sitting in the air!
The bright boroughs, the circle-citadels there!
Gerard Manley Hopkins 1844–89

…The evening star,
Love's harbinger.
John Milton 1608–74

The eternal silence of these infinite spaces [the heavens] terrifies me.
Blaise Pascal 1623–62

The Skies

The moon's an arrant thief,
And her pale fire she snatches from the sun.
William Shakespeare 1564-1616

I have loved the stars too fondly to be fearful of the
  night.
Sarah Williams

Sleep ····▸ Dreams

The sleep of a labouring man is sweet.
Bible

…The cool kindliness of sheets, that soon
Smooth away trouble; and the rough male kiss
Of blankets.
Rupert Brooke 1887-1915

When you're lying awake with a dismal headache, and
  repose is taboo'd by anxiety,
I conceive you may use any language you choose to
  indulge in, without impropriety.
W. S. Gilbert 1836-1911

Sleep is when all the unsorted stuff comes flying out as
from a dustbin upset in a high wind.
William Golding 1911-93

What hath night to do with sleep?
John Milton 1608-74

And so to bed.
Samuel Pepys 1633-1703

Methought I heard a voice cry, 'Sleep no more!
Macbeth does murder sleep,' the innocent sleep,
Sleep that knits up the ravelled sleave of care.
William Shakespeare 1564-1616

In winter I get up at night
And dress by yellow candle-light.
In summer, quite the other way,—
I have to go to bed by day.
Robert Louis Stevenson 1850–94

Early to rise and early to bed makes a male healthy and
wealthy and dead.
James Thurber 1894–1961

Tired Nature's sweet restorer, balmy sleep!
Edward Young 1683–1765

Society

Hunger allows no choice
To the citizen or the police;
We must love one another or die.
W. H. Auden 1907–73

We started off trying to set up a small anarchist
community, but people wouldn't obey the rules.
Alan Bennett 1934–

The greatest happiness of the greatest number is the
foundation of morals and legislation.
Jeremy Bentham 1748–1832

Society is indeed a contract…it becomes a partnership
not only between those who are living, but between those
who are living, those who are dead, and those who are to
be born.
Edmund Burke 1729–97

No man is an Island, entire of it self.
John Donne 1572–1631

Society

Only in the state does man have a rational
existence…Man owes his entire existence to the state, and
has his being within it alone.
   G. W. F. Hegel 1770–1831

In a consumer society there are inevitably two kinds of
slaves: the prisoners of addiction and the prisoners of
envy.
   Ivan Illich 1926–

From each according to his abilities, to each according to
his needs.
   Karl Marx 1818–83

The city is not a concrete jungle, it is a human zoo.
   Desmond Morris 1928–

There is no such thing as Society. There are individual
men and women, and there are families.
   Margaret Thatcher 1925–

The Social Contract is nothing more or less than a vast
conspiracy of human beings to lie to and humbug
themselves and one another for the general Good. Lies
are the mortar that bind the savage individual man into
the social masonry.
   H. G. Wells 1866–1946

Solitude

He who is unable to live in society, or who has no need
because he is sufficient for himself, must be either a beast
or a god.
   Aristotle 384–322 BC

He [Barrymore] would quote from Genesis the text which
says, 'It is not good for man to be alone,' and then add,
'But O my God, what a relief.'
   John Barrymore 1882–1942

Solitude

It is not good that the man should be alone; I will make him an help meet for him.
Bible

To fly from, need not be to hate, mankind.
Lord Byron 1788-1824

I am monarch of all I survey,
My right there is none to dispute.
William Cowper 1731-1800

I want to be alone.
Greta Garbo 1905-90

If you are idle, be not solitary; if you are solitary, be not idle.
Samuel Johnson 1709-84

Down to Gehenna or up to the Throne,
He travels the fastest who travels alone.
Rudyard Kipling 1865-1936

All the lonely people, where do they all come from?
John Lennon 1940-80 and **Paul McCartney** 1942-

Ships that pass in the night, and speak each other in
  passing;
Only a signal shown and a distant voice in the darkness;
So on the ocean of life we pass and speak one another,
Only a look and a voice; then darkness again and a
  silence.
Henry Wadsworth Longfellow 1807-82

A man should keep for himself a little back shop, all his own, quite unadulterated, in which he establishes his true freedom and chief place of seclusion and solitude.
Montaigne 1533-92

Never less alone than when alone.
Samuel Rogers 1763-1855

Solitude

Man goes into the noisy crowd to drown his own clamour of silence.
Rabindranath Tagore 1861–1941

Laugh and the world laughs with you;
Weep, and you weep alone;
For the sad old earth must borrow its mirth,
But has trouble enough of its own.
Ella Wheeler Wilcox 1855–1919

Sorrow ····▸ Bereavement, Suffering

Sob, heavy world,
Sob as you spin
Mantled in mist, remote from the happy.
W. H. Auden 1907–73

O my son Absalom, my son, my son Absalom! would God I had died for thee, O Absalom, my son, my son!
Bible

By the waters of Babylon we sat down and wept: when we remembered thee, O Sion.
Bible

I tell you, hopeless grief is passionless.
Elizabeth Barrett Browning 1806–61

We do not expect people to be deeply moved by what is not unusual. That element of tragedy which lies in the very fact of frequency, has not yet wrought itself into the coarse emotion of mankind.
George Eliot 1819–80

Nothing that can be said can begin to take away the anguish and pain of these moments. Grief is the price we pay for love.
Elizabeth II 1926–

How small and selfish is sorrow. But it bangs one about until one is senseless.
Queen Elizabeth, the Queen Mother 1900–2002

He felt the loyalty we all feel to unhappiness—the sense that that is where we really belong.
Graham Greene 1904–91

Now laughing friends deride tears I cannot hide,
So I smile and say 'When a lovely flame dies,
Smoke gets in your eyes.'
Otto Harbach 1873–1963

Grief is a species of idleness.
Samuel Johnson 1709–84

Tragedy ought really to be a great kick at misery.
D. H. Lawrence 1885–1930

No one ever told me that grief felt so like fear.
C. S. Lewis 1898–1963

Small sorrows speak; great ones are silent.
Seneca ('the Younger') c.4 BC–AD 65

When sorrows come, they come not single spies,
But in battalions.
William Shakespeare 1564–1616

Give sorrow words: the grief that does not speak
Whispers the o'er-fraught heart, and bids it break.
William Shakespeare 1564–1616

Tears, idle tears, I know not what they mean,
Tears from the depth of some divine despair.
Alfred, Lord Tennyson 1809–92

Sunt lacrimae rerum et mentem mortalia tangunt.
There are tears shed for things and mortality touches the heart.
Virgil 70–19 BC

Sorrow

Total grief is like a minefield. No knowing when one will
touch the tripwire.
Sylvia Townsend Warner 1893–1978

For of all sad words of tongue or pen,
The saddest are these: 'It might have been!'
John Greenleaf Whittier 1807–92

Speechmaking ····▶ Conversation

I do not object to people looking at their watches when I
am speaking. But I strongly object when they start
shaking them to make certain they are still going.
Lord Birkett 1883–1962

Grasp the subject, the words will follow.
Cato the Elder 234–149 BC

And adepts in the speaking trade
Keep a cough by them ready made.
Charles Churchill 1731–64

He [Lord Charles Beresford] is one of those orators of
whom it was well said, 'Before they get up, they do not
know what they are going to say; when they are speaking,
they do not know what they are saying; and when they
have sat down, they do not know what they have said.'
Winston Churchill 1874–1965

When you have nothing to say, say nothing.
Charles Caleb Colton c.1780–1832

Humming, Hawing and Hesitation are the three Graces of
contemporary Parliamentary oratory.
Julian Critchley 1930–2000

When asked what was first in oratory, [he] replied to his questioner, 'action,' what second, 'action,' and again third, 'action'.
Demosthenes c.384—c.322 BC

What worse change can any one bring against an orator than that his words and his sentiments do not tally?
Demosthenes c.384—c.322 BC

Public speaking is like the winds of the desert: it blows constantly without doing any good.
Faisal

Human speech is like a cracked kettle on which we tap crude rhythms for bears to dance to, while we long to make music that will melt the stars.
Gustave Flaubert 1821–80

The finest eloquence is that which gets things done and the worst is that which delays them.
David Lloyd George 1863–1945

But all was false and hollow; though his tongue
Dropped manna, and could make the worse appear
The better reason.
John Milton 1608–74

I do not much dislike the matter, but
The manner of his speech.
William Shakespeare 1564–1616

Friends, Romans, countrymen, lend me your ears.
William Shakespeare 1564–1616

If I reprehend any thing in this world, it is the use of my oracular tongue, and a nice derangement of epitaphs!
Richard Brinsley Sheridan 1751–1816

Speechmaking

Do you remember that in classical times when Cicero had
finished speaking, the people said, 'How well he spoke',
but when Demosthenes had finished speaking, they said,
'Let us march.'

Adlai Stevenson 1900–65

What can be said at all can be said clearly; and whereof
one cannot speak thereof one must be silent.

Ludwig Wittgenstein 1889–1951

The reason why we have two ears and only one mouth is
that we may listen the more and talk the less.

Zeno 333–261 BC

Sport

Sports do not build character. They reveal it.

Haywood Hale Broun 1918–

As the race wore on…his oar was dipping into the water
nearly *twice* as often as any other.

Desmond Coke 1879–1931, *usually misquoted as 'All rowed fast,
but none so fast as stroke'*

The important thing in life is not the victory but the
contest; the essential thing is not to have won but to have
fought well.

Baron Pierre de Coubertin 1863–1937, *on the Olympic Games*

There is plenty of time to win this game, and to thrash
the Spaniards too.

Francis Drake c.1540–96, *receiving news of the Armada while
playing bowls on Plymouth Hoe*

Nice guys. Finish last.

Leo Durocher 1906–91, *usually quoted as 'Nice guys finish last'*

I hated the easy assumption that girls had to be slower
than boys.

Dawn Fraser 1937–

I skated for pure enjoyment. That's how I wanted my Olympic moment to be.
Sarah Hughes 1985–

We all get cut and we all get stitched up. We get stud marks down our bodies, we break bones and we lose teeth. We play rugby.
Martin Johnson 1970–

Only two things does he [the modern citizen] anxiously wish for—bread and circuses.
Juvenal AD c.60–c.130

The flannelled fools at the wicket or the muddied oafs at the goals.
Rudyard Kipling 1865–1936

Men—athletes especially—have to be like King Kong. When we lose, we can't cry and we can't pout.
Carl Lewis 1961–

Chaos umpire sits,
And by decision more embroils the fray.
John Milton 1608–74

Sport…fosters international hostility and leads the audience, no doubt from boredom, to assault and do grievous bodily harm while watching it.
John Mortimer 1923–

Play up! play up! and play the game!
Henry Newbolt 1862–1938

Eclipse first, the rest nowhere.
Dennis O'Kelly c.1720–87, *comment on a horse race*

Serious sport has nothing to do with fair play. It is bound up with hatred, jealousy, boastfulness, and disregard of all the rules.
George Orwell 1903–50

Sport

For when the One Great Scorer comes to mark against
    your name,
He writes—not that you won or lost—but how you
    played the Game.
    Grantland Rice 1880–1954

To play billiards well is a sign of an ill-spent youth.
    Charles Roupell

Sure, winning isn't everything. It's the only thing.
    Henry 'Red' Sanders

Spring

In fact, it is about five o'clock in an evening that the first
hour of spring strikes—autumn arrives in the early
morning, but spring at the close of a winter day.
    Elizabeth Bowen 1899–1973

Whan that Aprill with his shoures soote
The droghte of March hath perced to the roote.
    Geoffrey Chaucer c.1343–1400

April is the cruellest month, breeding
Lilacs out of the dead land.
    T. S. Eliot 1888–1965

And since to look at things in bloom
Fifty springs are little room,
About the woodlands I will go
To see the cherry hung with snow.
    A. E. Housman 1859–1936

Work seethes in the hands of spring,
That strapping dairymaid.
    Boris Pasternak 1890–1960

Statistics

[The War Office kept three sets of figures:] one to mislead the public, another to mislead the Cabinet, and the third to mislead itself.
	Herbert Asquith 1852–1928

Statistics are the triumph of the quantitative method, and the quantitative method is the victory of sterility and death.
	Hilaire Belloc 1870–1953

A witty statesman said, you might prove anything by figures.
	Thomas Carlyle 1795–1881

Long and painful experience has taught me one great principle in managing business for other people, viz., if you want to inspire confidence, *give plenty of statistics.*
	Lewis Carroll 1832–98

There are three kinds of lies: lies, damned lies and statistics.
	Benjamin Disraeli 1804–81

From the fact that there are 400,000 species of beetles on this planet, but only 8,000 species of mammals, he [Haldane] concluded that the Creator, if He exists, has a special preference for beetles.
	J. B. S. Haldane 1892–1964

We are just statistics, born to consume resources.
	Horace 65–8 BC

He uses statistics as a drunken man uses lampposts—for support rather than for illumination.
	Andrew Lang 1844–1912

Statistics

If your experiment needs statistics, you ought to have done a better experiment.
Ernest Rutherford 1871–1937

Counting counts only when we have learnt how to count what counts.
Alan Ryan 1940–

The so-called science of poll-taking is not a science at all but a mere necromancy. People are unpredictable by nature, and although you can take a nation's pulse, you can't be sure that the nation hasn't just run up a flight of stairs.
E. B. White 1899–1985

Style ····▸ Brevity

Have something to say, and say it as clearly as you can. That is the only secret of style.
Matthew Arnold 1822–88

Style is the man.
Comte de Buffon 1707–88

Words easy to be understood do often hit the mark; when high and learned ones do only pierce the air.
John Bunyan 1628–88

The Mandarin style…is beloved by literary pundits, by those who would make the written word as unlike as possible to the spoken one.
Cyril Connolly 1903–74

Style is life! It is the very life-blood of thought!
Gustave Flaubert 1821–80

When we see a natural style, we are quite surprised and delighted, for we expected to see an author and we find a man.

Blaise Pascal 1623-62

True wit is Nature to advantage dressed,
What oft was thought, but ne'er so well expressed.

Alexander Pope 1688-1744

Too many flowers…too little fruit.

Sir Walter Scott 1771-1832, *of Felicia Hemans's literary style*

Proper words in proper places, make the true definition of a style.

Jonathan Swift 1667-1745

'Feather-footed through the plashy fen passes the questing vole'…'Yes,' said the Managing Editor. 'That must be good style.'

Evelyn Waugh 1903-66

I don't wish to sign my name, though I am afraid everybody will know who the writer is: one's style is one's signature always.

Oscar Wilde 1854-1900

Success ····▶ Failure, Winning

'Tis not in mortals to command success,
But we'll do more, Sempronius; we'll deserve it.

Joseph Addison 1672-1719

For what shall it profit a man, if he shall gain the whole world, and lose his own soul?

Bible

Success

Pourvu que ça dure!
Let's hope it lasts!
> **Laetitia Bonaparte** 1750–1836, *on her son Napoleon becoming Emperor, 1804*

The conduct of a losing party never appears right: at least it never can possess the only infallible criterion of wisdom to vulgar judgements—success.
> **Edmund Burke** 1729–97

Veni, vidi, vici.
I came, I saw, I conquered.
> **Julius Caesar** 100–44 BC

I have climbed to the top of the greasy pole.
> **Benjamin Disraeli** 1804–81

If *A* is a success in life, then *A* equals *x* plus *y* plus *z*. Work is *x*; *y* is play; and *z* is keeping your mouth shut.
> **Albert Einstein** 1879–1955

Success is relative:
It is what we can make of the mess we have made of things.
> **T. S. Eliot** 1888–1965

For a writer, success is always temporary, success is only a delayed failure. And it is incomplete.
> **Graham Greene** 1904–91

The moral flabbiness born of the exclusive worship of the bitch-goddess *success*.
> **William James** 1842–1910

In most things success depends on knowing how long it takes to succeed.
> **Montesquieu** 1689–1755

Success makes life easier. It doesn't make *living* easier.
> **Bruce Springsteen** 1949–

All you need in this life is ignorance and confidence; then success is sure.
Mark Twain 1835–1910

It is not enough to succeed. Others must fail.
Gore Vidal 1925–

Suffering ····> Sympathy

Justice inclines her scales so that wisdom comes at the price of suffering.
Aeschylus c.525–456 BC

Children's talent to endure stems from their ignorance of alternatives.
Maya Angelou 1928–

Even the dreadful martyrdom must run its course
Anyhow in a corner, some untidy spot
Where the dogs go on with their doggy life and the
    torturer's horse
Scratches its innocent behind on a tree.
W. H. Auden 1907–73

Nothing happens to anybody which he is not fitted by nature to bear.
Marcus Aurelius AD 121–80

Some people like being burdened. It gives them an interest.
Beryl Bainbridge 1933–

Where mass hunger reigns, we cannot speak of peace.
Willy Brandt 1913–92

The number of casualties will be more than any of us can bear.
Rudolph Giuliani 1944– , *in the aftermath of the terrorist attacks of 11 September 2001*

Suffering

To each his suff'rings, all are men,
Condemned alike to groan;
The tender for another's pain,
Th' unfeeling for his own.
Thomas Gray 1716–71

If suffer we must, let's suffer on the heights.
Victor Hugo 1802–85

Scars have the strange power to remind us that our past
is real.
Cormac McCarthy 1933–

It is not true that suffering ennobles the character;
happiness does that sometimes, but suffering, for the
most part, makes men petty and vindictive.
W. Somerset Maugham 1874–1965

What does not kill me makes me stronger.
Friedrich Nietzsche 1844–1900

The worst is not,
So long as we can say, 'This is the worst.'
William Shakespeare 1564–1616

He jests at scars, that never felt a wound.
William Shakespeare 1564–1616

I am a man
More sinned against than sinning.
William Shakespeare 1564–1616

Nothing begins, and nothing ends,
That is not paid with moan;
For we are born in other's pain,
And perish in our own.
Francis Thompson 1859–1907

Those who have courage to love should have courage to
suffer.
Anthony Trollope 1815–82

O you who have borne even heavier things, God will
grant an end to these too.
Virgil 70–19 BC

Too long a sacrifice
Can make a stone of the heart.
W. B. Yeats 1865–1939

Summer

Sumer is icumen in,
Lhude sing cuccu!
Groweth sed, and bloweth med,
And springeth the wude nu.
Anonymous *'Cuckoo Song'* (*c.1250*)

June is bustin' out all over.
Oscar Hammerstein II 1895–1960

Summer time an' the livin' is easy,
Fish are jumpin' an' the cotton is high.
Du Bose Heyward 1885–1940 and **Ira Gershwin** 1896–1983

The way to ensure summer in England is to have it
framed and glazed in a comfortable room.
Horace Walpole 1717–97

The Supernatural

Up the airy mountain,
Down the rushy glen,
We daren't go a-hunting,
For fear of little men.
William Allingham 1824–89

The Supernatural

From ghoulies and ghosties and long-leggety beasties
And things that go bump in the night,
Good Lord, deliver us!
Anonymous *The Cornish or West Country Litany*

I always knew the living talked rot, but it's nothing to the rot the dead talk.
Margot Asquith 1864–1945

Then a spirit passed before my face; the hair of my flesh stood up.
Bible

For we wrestle not against flesh and blood, but against principalities, against powers, against the rulers of the darkness of this world, against spiritual wickedness in high places.
Bible

Black magic operates most effectively in preconscious, marginal areas. Casual curses are the most effective.
William S. Burroughs 1914–97

The twilight is the crack between the worlds. It is the door to the unknown.
Carlos Castaneda *c.*1925–98

There is no such thing as magic, only acting.
Paul Daniels 1938–

THE FAT BOY: I wants to make your flesh creep.
Charles Dickens 1812–70

There are fairies at the bottom of our garden!
Rose Fyleman 1877–1957

Superstition is the poetry of life.
Johann Wolfgang von Goethe 1749–1832

All argument is against it; but all belief is for it.
Samuel Johnson 1709–84, *of the existence of ghosts*

Mr Geller may have psychic powers by means of which he can bend spoons; if so, he appears to be doing it the hard way.
James Randi 1928–

Double, double toil and trouble;
Fire burn and cauldron bubble.
William Shakespeare 1564–1616

Superstition sets the whole world in flames; philosophy quenches them.
Voltaire 1694–1778

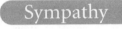
Sympathy

Nobody can tell what I suffer! But it is always so. Those who do not complain are never pitied.
Jane Austen 1775–1817

For pitee renneth soone in gentil herte.
Geoffrey Chaucer c.1343–1400

O divine Master, grant that I may not so much seek
To be consoled as to console;
To be understood as to understand.
St Francis of Assisi 1181–1226

Our sympathy is cold to the relation of distant misery.
Edward Gibbon 1737–94

But yet the pity of it, Iago! O! Iago, the pity of it, Iago!
William Shakespeare 1564–1616

If you see anybody fallen by the wayside and lying in the ditch, it isn't much good climbing into the ditch and lying by his side.
Dick Sheppard 1880–1937

Sympathy

When times get rough,
And friends just can't be found
Like a bridge over troubled water
I will lay me down.
   Paul Simon 1942-

Taxes

To tax and to please, no more than to love and to be
wise, is not given to men.
   Edmund Burke 1729-97

Read my lips: no new taxes.
   George Bush 1924-

The art of taxation consists in so plucking the goose as to
obtain the largest possible amount of feathers with the
smallest possible amount of hissing.
   Jean-Baptiste Colbert 1619-83

In this world nothing can be said to be certain, except
death and taxes.
   Benjamin Franklin 1706-90

All taxes must, at last, fall upon agriculture.
   Edward Gibbon 1737-94

Only the little people pay taxes.
   Leona Helmsley c.1920- , *reported at her trial for tax evasion*

Excise. A hateful tax levied upon commodities.
   Samuel Johnson 1709-84

Taxation without representation is tyranny.
   James Otis 1725-83

Income Tax has made more Liars out of the American
people than Golf.
   Will Rogers 1879-1935

There is no art which one government sooner learns of another than that of draining money from the pockets of the people.
Adam Smith 1723–90

It is the part of the good shepherd to shear his flock, not skin it.
Tiberius 42 BC–AD 37, *to governors who recommended burdensome taxes*

Pecunia non olet.

Money has no smell.
Vespasian AD 9–79, *quashing an objection to a tax on public lavatories*

The art of government is to make two-thirds of a nation pay all it possibly can pay for the benefit of the other third.
Voltaire 1694–1778

Teaching ····▶ Education

A teacher affects eternity; he can never tell where his influence stops.
Henry Brooks Adams 1838–1918

There is no such whetstone, to sharpen a good wit and encourage a will to learning, as is praise.
Roger Ascham 1515–68

For precept must be upon precept, precept upon precept; line upon line, line upon line; here a little, and there a little.
Bible

Be a governess! Better be a slave at once!
Charlotte Brontë 1816–55

Teaching

A man who reviews the old so as to find out the new is qualified to teach others.
Confucius 551–479 BC

I hope you enjoy the absence of pupils…the total oblivion of them for definite intervals is a necessary condition for doing them justice at the proper time.
James Clerk Maxwell 1831–79

We teachers can only help the work going on, as servants wait upon a master.
Maria Montessori 1870–1952

Men must be taught as if you taught them not,
And things unknown proposed as things forgot.
Alexander Pope 1688–1744

For every person who wants to teach there are approximately thirty who don't want to learn—much.
W. C. Sellar 1898–1951 and **R. J. Yeatman** 1898–1968

Homines dum docent discunt.
Even while they teach, men learn.
Seneca ('the Younger') c.4 BC–AD 65

He who can, does. He who cannot, teaches.
George Bernard Shaw 1856–1950

Give me a girl at an impressionable age, and she is mine for life.
Muriel Spark 1918–

Delightful task! to rear the tender thought,
To teach the young idea how to shoot.
James Thomson 1700–48

Knowledge has to be sucked into the brain, not pushed into it.
Victor Weisskopf 1908–2002

Technology ····▶ Inventions

Science finds, industry applies, man conforms.
   Anonymous *guidebook to 1933 Chicago World's Fair*

Give me but one firm spot on which to stand, and I will move the earth.
   Archimedes c.287–212 BC, *on the action of a lever*

I sell here, Sir, what all the world desires to have—POWER.
   Matthew Boulton 1728–1809, *speaking to Boswell of his engineering works*

Any sufficiently advanced technology is indistinguishable from magic.
   Arthur C. Clarke 1917–

For a successful technology, reality must take precedence over public relations, for nature cannot be fooled.
   Richard Phillips Feynman 1918–88

Technology…the knack of so arranging the world that we need not experience it.
   Max Frisch 1911–91

Technology happens. It's not good, it's not bad. Is steel good or bad?
   Andrew Grove 1936–

The thing with high-tech is that you always end up using scissors.
   David Hockney 1937–

This is not the age of pamphleteers. It is the age of the engineers. The spark-gap is mightier than the pen.
   Lancelot Hogben 1895–1975

Technology

One machine can do the work of fifty ordinary men. No machine can do the work of one extraordinary man.
Elbert Hubbard 1859–1915

Communism is Soviet power plus the electrification of the whole country.
Lenin 1870–1924

The new electronic interdependence recreates the world in the image of a global village.
Marshall McLuhan 1911–80

The medium is the message.
Marshall McLuhan 1911–80

When this circuit learns your job, what are you going to do?
Marshall McLuhan 1911–80

When you see something that is technically sweet, you go ahead and do it and you argue about what to do about it only after you have had your technical success. That is the way it was with the atomic bomb.
J. Robert Oppenheimer 1904–67

One servant is worth a thousand gadgets.
Joseph Alois Schumpeter 1883–1950

It has been said that an engineer is a man who can do for ten shillings what any fool can do for a pound.
Nevil Shute 1899–1960

Her own mother lived the latter years of her life in the horrible suspicion that electricity was dripping invisibly all over the house.
James Thurber 1894–1961

The Britain that is going to be forged in the white heat of this revolution will be no place for restrictive practices or for outdated methods on either side of industry.

Harold Wilson 1916–95, *usually quoted as 'the white heat of the technological revolution'*

Television

Television…thrives on unreason, and unreason thrives on television…[It] strikes at the emotions rather than the intellect.

Robin Day 1923–2000

Television has brought back murder into the home—where it belongs.

Alfred Hitchcock 1899–1980

Television is simultaneously blamed, often by the same people, for worsening the world and for being powerless to change it.

Clive James 1939–

Television brought the brutality of war into the comfort of the living room. Vietnam was lost in the living rooms of America—not the battlefields of Vietnam.

Marshall McLuhan 1911–80

Television is actually closer to reality than anything in books. The madness of TV is the madness of human life.

Camille Paglia 1947–

Television has made dictatorship impossible, but democracy unbearable.

Shimon Peres 1923–

Television

He who prides himself on giving what he thinks the public wants is often creating a fictitious demand for lower standards which he will then satisfy.
   Lord Reith 1889–1971

Nation shall speak peace unto nation.
   Montague John Rendall 1862–1950, *motto of the BBC*

Television today has replaced the theatre of the 20th century, the novels of the 19th, the Bible of the 17th, the folktales of the village, the bedtime stories parents told their children.
   Jonathan Sacks 1948–

Like having your own licence to print money.
   Roy Thomson 1894–1976, *on the profitability of commercial television in Britain*

Never miss a chance to have sex or appear on television.
   Gore Vidal 1925–

I hate television. I hate it as much as peanuts. But I can't stop eating peanuts.
   Orson Welles 1915–85

Television contracts the imagination and radio expands it.
   Terry Wogan 1938–

Temptation

Watch and pray, that ye enter not into temptation: the spirit indeed is willing but the flesh is weak.
   Bible

For the good that I would I do not: but the evil which I would not, that I do.
   Bible

From all the deceits of the world, the flesh, and the devil,
Good Lord, deliver us.
Book of Common Prayer 1662

What's done we partly may compute,
But know not what's resisted.
Robert Burns 1759–96

Who was it said a temptation resisted is a true measure
of character? Certainly no one in Beverly Hills.
Joan Collins 1933–

The Lord above made liquor for temptation—but
With a little bit of luck…
When temptation comes you'll give right in!
Alan Jay Lerner 1918–86

This extraordinary pride in being exempt from
temptation that you have not yet risen to the level of!
Eunuchs boasting of their chastity!
C. S. Lewis 1898–1963

If we are to be punished for the sins we have committed,
at least we should be praised for our yearning for the sins
we have not committed.
Jawaharlal Nehru 1889–1964

Is this her fault or mine?
The tempter or the tempted, who sins most?
William Shakespeare 1564–1616

There are several good protections against temptations,
but the surest is cowardice.
Mark Twain 1835–1910

I can resist everything except temptation.
Oscar Wilde 1854–1900

Tennis

Tennis

I call tennis the McDonald's of sport—you go in, they make a quick buck out of you, and you're out.
Pat Cash 1965-

New Yorkers love it when you spill your guts out there. Spill your guts at Wimbledon and they make you stop and clean it up.
Jimmy Connors 1952-

You cannot be serious!
John McEnroe 1959- , *said to tennis umpire at Wimbledon*

Do what you love and love what you do and everything else is detail.
Martina Navratilova 1956-

When we have matched our rackets to these balls,
We will in France, by God's grace, play a set
Shall strike his father's crown into the hazard.
William Shakespeare 1564-1616

If you can keep playing tennis when somebody is shooting a gun down the street, that's concentration. I didn't grow up playing at the country club.
Serena Williams 1981-

Thanks

They say late thanks are ever best.
Francis Bacon 1561-1626

A joyful and pleasant thing it is to be thankful.
Bible

When I'm not thanked at all, I'm thanked enough,
I've done my duty, and I've done no more.
Henry Fielding 1707-54

For this relief much thanks.
William Shakespeare 1564–1616

My father spent the last 20 years of his life writing letters. If someone thanked him for a present, he thanked them for thanking him and there was no end to the exchange but death.
Evelyn Waugh 1903–66

The Theatre

I go to the theatre to be entertained, I want to be taken out of myself, I don't want to see lust and rape and incest and sodomy and so on, I can get all that at home.
Alan Bennett 1934–

There's no business like show business.
Irving Berlin 1888–1989

Things on stage should be as complicated and as simple as in life. People dine, just dine, while their happiness is made and their lives are smashed. If in Act 1 you have a pistol hanging on the wall, then it must fire in the last act.
Anton Chekhov 1860–1904

Shakespeare is so tiring. You never get a chance to sit down unless you're a king.
Josephine Hull ?1886–1957

It's a sound you can't get in the movies or television…the sound of a wonderful, deep silence that means you've hit them where they live.
Shelley Winters 1922–

Thinking ····▸ Ideas, The Mind

To change your mind and to follow him who sets you right is to be nonetheless the free agent that you were before.

Marcus Aurelius AD 121–80

Never express yourself more clearly than you think.

Niels Bohr 1885–1962

Cogito, ergo sum.
I think, therefore I am.

René Descartes 1596–1650

It is a capital mistake to theorize before you have all the evidence. It biases the judgement.

Arthur Conan Doyle 1859–1930

What was once thought can never be unthought.

Friedrich Dürrenmatt 1921–

Reasons are not like garments, the worse for wearing.

Robert Devereux, 2nd Earl of Essex 1566–1601

I'll not listen to reason…Reason always means what someone else has got to say.

Elizabeth Gaskell 1810–65

Logical consequences are the scarecrows of fools and the beacons of wise men.

T. H. Huxley 1825–95

I'm Irish. We think sideways.

Spike Milligan 1918–2002

Doublethink means the power of holding two contradictory beliefs in one's mind simultaneously, and accepting both of them.

George Orwell 1903–50

I don't mind your thinking slowly: I mind your
publishing faster than you think.
Wolfgang Pauli 1900–58

You can't think rationally on an empty stomach, and a
whole lot of people can't do it on a full stomach either.
Lord Reith 1889–1971

How comes it to pass, then, that we appear such cowards
in reasoning, and are so afraid to stand the test of
ridicule?
Lord Shaftesbury 1671–1713

Yond Cassius has a lean and hungry look;
He thinks too much: such men are dangerous.
William Shakespeare 1564–1616

The real question is not whether machines think but
whether men do.
B. F. Skinner 1904–90

The important thing is not to think much but to love
much.
St Teresa of Ávila 1512–82

Time

Every instant of time is a pinprick of eternity.
Marcus Aurelius AD 121–80

VLADIMIR: That passed the time.
ESTRAGON: It would have passed in any case.
VLADIMIR: Yes, but not so rapidly.
Samuel Beckett 1906–89

Time is a great teacher but unfortunately it kills all its
pupils.
Hector Berlioz 1803–69

Time

I am Time grown old to destroy the world,
Embarked on the course of world annihilation.
   Bhagavad Gita 250 BC–AD 250

To every thing there is a season, and a time to every
purpose under the heaven:
A time to be born, and a time to die...
A time to weep, and a time to laugh; a time to mourn,
and a time to dance.
   Bible

Men talk of killing time, while time quietly kills them.
   Dion Boucicault 1820–90

What's not destroyed by Time's devouring hand?
Where's Troy, and where's the Maypole in the Strand?
   James Bramston c.1694–1744

I recommend to you to take care of minutes: for hours
will take care of themselves.
   Lord Chesterfield 1694–1773

I shall use the phrase 'time's arrow' to express this one-
way property of time which has no analogue in space.
   Arthur Eddington 1882–1944

The distinction between past, present and future is only
an illusion, however persistent.
   Albert Einstein 1879–1955

I have measured out my life with coffee spoons.
   T. S. Eliot 1888–1965

Time is...Time was...Time is past.
   Robert Greene c.1560–92

Time, you old gipsy man,
Will you not stay,
Put up your caravan
Just for one day?
   Ralph Hodgson 1871–1962

In the long run we are all dead.
John Maynard Keynes 1883–1946

Nothing puzzles me more than time and space; and yet nothing troubles me less, as I never think about them.
Charles Lamb 1775–1834

But at my back I always hear
Time's wingèd chariot hurrying near:
And yonder all before us lie
Deserts of vast eternity.
Andrew Marvell 1621–78

Tempus edax rerum.
Time the devourer of everything.
Ovid 43 BC–AD c.17

Even such is Time, which takes in trust
Our youth, our joys, and all we have,
And pays us but with age and dust.
Walter Ralegh c.1552–1618

Half our life is spent trying to find something to do with the time we have rushed through life trying to save.
Will Rogers 1879–1935

Three o'clock is always too late or too early for anything you want to do.
Jean-Paul Sartre 1905–80

Ah! the clock is always slow;
It is later than you think.
Robert W. Service 1874–1958

To-morrow, and to-morrow, and to-morrow,
Creeps in this petty pace from day to day,
To the last syllable of recorded time;
And all our yesterdays have lighted fools
The way to dusty death.
William Shakespeare 1564–1616

Time

Time hath, my lord, a wallet at his back,
Wherein he puts alms for oblivion.
William Shakespeare 1564–1616

As if you could kill time without injuring eternity.
Henry David Thoreau 1817–62

Time is
Too slow for those who wait,
Too swift for those who fear,
Too long for those who grieve,
Too short for those who rejoice;
But for those who love,
Time is eternity.
Henry Van Dyke 1852–1933

Sed fugit interea, fugit inreparabile tempus.
But meanwhile it is flying, irretrievable time is flying.
Virgil 70–19 BC

Time, like an ever-rolling stream,
Bears all its sons away.
Isaac Watts 1674–1748

The Town ····> The Country

We do not look in great cities for our best morality.
Jane Austen 1775–1817

If you would be known, and not know, vegetate in a
village; if you would know, and not be known, live in a
city.
Charles Caleb Colton c.1780–1832

Slums may well be breeding-grounds of crime, but
middle-class suburbs are incubators of apathy and
delirium.
Cyril Connolly 1903–74

Transience

The materials of city planning are sky, space, trees, steel and cement in that order and in that hierarchy.
Le Corbusier 1887–1965

I come from suburbia...and I don't ever want to go back. It's the one place in the world that's further away than anywhere else.
Frederic Raphael 1931–

The modern city is a place for banking and prostitution and very little else.
Frank Lloyd Wright 1867–1959

Transience

Sic transit gloria mundi.
Thus passes the glory of the world.
Anonymous *said at the coronation of a new Pope, while flax is burned*

All flesh is as grass, and all the glory of man as the flower of grass. The grass withereth, and the flower thereof falleth away.
Bible

He who binds to himself a joy
Doth the winged life destroy
But he who kisses the joy as it flies
Lives in Eternity's sunrise.
William Blake 1757–1827

The reputation which the world bestows
is like the wind, that shifts now here now there,
its name changed with the quarter whence it blows.
Dante Alighieri 1265–1321

Look thy last on all things lovely,
Every hour.
Walter de la Mare 1873–1956

Transience

Gather ye rosebuds while ye may,
Old Time is still a-flying:
And this same flower that smiles to-day,
To-morrow will be dying.
    Robert Herrick 1591–1674

Like that of leaves is a generation of men.
    Homer 8th century BC

Travel

Travel, in the younger sort, is a part of education; in the
elder, a part of experience. He that travelleth into a
country before he hath some entrance into the language,
goeth to school, and not to travel.
    Francis Bacon 1561–1626

See one promontory (said Socrates of old), one
mountain, one sea, one river, and see all.
    Robert Burton 1577–1640

Men travel faster now, but I do not know if they go to
better things.
    Willa Cather 1873–1947

What on earth good accrues from going to the North and
South Poles? I never could understand—no one is going
there when they can go to Monte Carlo!
    John Arbuthnot Fisher 1841–1920

Worth seeing, yes; but not worth going to see.
    Samuel Johnson 1709–84, *of the Giant's Causeway*

Of all noxious animals, too, the most noxious is a tourist.
And of all tourists the most vulgar, ill-bred, offensive and
loathsome is the British tourist.
    Francis Kilvert 1840–79

A good traveller is one who does not know where he is going to, and a perfect traveller does not know where he came from.
Lin Yutang 1895–1976

Whenever I prepare for a journey I prepare as though for death. Should I never return, all is in order.
Katherine Mansfield 1888–1923

A man travels the world in search of what he needs and returns home to find it.
George Moore 1852–1933

In the middle ages people were tourists because of their religion, whereas now they are tourists because tourism is their religion.
Robert Runcie 1921–2000

To travel hopefully is a better thing than to arrive, and the true success is to labour.
Robert Louis Stevenson 1850–94

I always love to begin a journey on Sundays, because I shall have the prayers of the church, to preserve all that travel by land, or by water.
Jonathan Swift 1667–1745

There is no land unhabitable nor sea innavigable.
Robert Thorne d. 1527

Trust and Treachery

I think the greatest of all human virtues is loyalty. It embraces all the best of the human character: courage, faith, love and charity.
Douglas Bader 1910–82

He that is surety for a stranger shall smart for it.
Bible

Trust and Treachery

Just for a handful of silver he left us,
Just for a riband to stick in his coat.

Robert Browning 1812–89, *of Wordsworth accepting the Laureateship*

Anyone can rat, but it takes a certain amount of ingenuity to re-rat.

Winston Churchill 1874–1965, *on rejoining the Conservatives twenty years after leaving them for the Liberals*

I know what it is to be a subject, and what to be a Sovereign. Good neighbours I have had, and I have met with bad: and in trust I have found treason.

Elizabeth I 1533–1603

Anyone who hasn't experienced the ecstasy of betrayal knows nothing about ecstasy at all.

Jean Genet 1910–86

Treason doth never prosper, what's the reason?
For if it prosper, none dare call it treason.

John Harington 1561–1612

And I said to the man who stood at the gate of the year:
'Give me a light that I may tread safely into the unknown.'
   And he replied:
   'Go out into the darkness and put your hand into the Hand of God. That shall be to you better than light and safer than a known way.'

Minnie Louise Haskins 1875–1957, *quoted by George VI in his Christmas broadcast, 1939*

It is better to suffer wrong than to do it, and happier to be sometimes cheated than not to trust.

Samuel Johnson 1709–84

Quis custodiet ipsos custodes?
Who is to guard the guards themselves?

Juvenal AD c.60–c.130

To betray, you must first belong.
  Kim Philby 1912–88

But I'm always true to you, darlin', in my fashion.
Yes I'm always true to you, darlin', in my way.
  Cole Porter 1891–1964

> *Equo ne credite, Teucri,*
Quidquid est, timeo Danaos et dona ferentes.

Do not trust the horse, Trojans. Whatever it is, I fear the
  Greeks even when they bring gifts.
  Virgil 70–19 BC

Having watched the form of our traitors for a number of
years, I cannot think that espionage can be recommended
as a technique for building an impressive civilization. It's
a lout's game.
  Rebecca West 1892–1983

Truth ····▶ Lies

The truth is often a terrible weapon of aggression. It is
possible to lie, and even to murder, for the truth.
  Alfred Adler 1870–1937

The truth which makes men free is for the most part the
truth which men prefer not to hear.
  Herbert Agar 1897–1980

Plato is dear to me, but dearer still is truth.
  Aristotle 384–322 BC

It contains a misleading impression, not a lie. It was
being economical with the truth.
  Robert Armstrong 1927–

What is truth? said jesting Pilate; and would not stay for
an answer.
  Francis Bacon 1561–1626

Truth

This is hard to answer, so I'll tell the truth.
David Ben-Gurion 1886–1973

And ye shall know the truth, and the truth shall make you free.
Bible

Great is Truth, and mighty above all things.
Bible (Apocrypha)

A truth that's told with bad intent
Beats all the lies you can invent.
William Blake 1757–1827

One of the favourite maxims of my father was the distinction between the two sorts of truths, profound truths recognized by the fact that the opposite is also a profound truth, in contrast to trivialities where opposites are obviously absurd.
Niels Bohr 1885–1962

'Tis strange—but true; for truth is always strange;
Stranger than fiction.
Lord Byron 1788–1824

What I tell you three times is true.
Lewis Carroll 1832–98

It is commonly said, and more particularly by Lord Shaftesbury, that ridicule is the best test of truth.
Lord Chesterfield 1694–1773

When you have eliminated the impossible, whatever remains, *however improbable*, must be the truth.
Arthur Conan Doyle 1859–1930

Nothing is too wonderful to be true, if it be consistent with the laws of nature, and in such things as these, experiment is the best test of such consistency.
Michael Faraday 1791–1867

An exaggeration is a truth that has lost its temper.
Kahlil Gibran 1883–1931

Truth is not merely what we are thinking, but also why, to whom and under what circumstances we say it.
Václav Havel 1936–

True and False are attributes of speech, not of things. And where speech is not, there is neither Truth nor Falsehood.
Thomas Hobbes 1588–1679

It is the customary fate of new truths to begin as heresies and to end as superstitions.
T. H. Huxley 1825–95

In lapidary inscriptions a man is not upon oath.
Samuel Johnson 1709–84

Honesty is praised and left to shiver.
Juvenal AD c.60–c.130

It is one thing to show a man that he is in error, and another to put him in possession of truth.
John Locke 1632–1704

The presence of those seeking the truth is infinitely to be preferred to those who think they've found it.
Terry Pratchett 1948–

But, my dearest Agathon, it is truth which you cannot contradict; you can without any difficulty contradict Socrates.
Socrates 469–399 BC

There was things which he stretched, but mainly he told the truth.
Mark Twain 1835–1910

I can't tell a lie, Pa; you know I can't tell a lie. I did cut it with my hatchet.
George Washington 1732–99

Truth

The truth is rarely pure, and never simple.
    Oscar Wilde 1854–1900

A thing is not necessarily true because a man dies for it.
    Oscar Wilde 1854–1900

The United States

Good Americans, when they die, go to Paris.
    Thomas Gold Appleton 1812–84

America! America!
God shed His grace on thee
And crown thy good with brotherhood
From sea to shining sea!
    Katherine Lee Bates 1859–1929

God bless America,
Land that I love,
Stand beside her and guide her
Thru the night with a light from above.
    Irving Berlin 1888–1989

We are a nation of communities…a brilliant diversity
spread like stars, like a thousand points of light in a
broad and peaceful sky.
    George Bush 1924–

Isn't this a billion dollar country?
    Charles Foster 1828–1904, *responding to a Democratic gibe about a 'million dollar Congress'*

Yes, America is gigantic, but a gigantic mistake.
    Sigmund Freud 1856–1939

Go West, young man, and grow up with the country.
    Horace Greeley 1811–72

Give me your tired, your poor,
Your huddled masses yearning to breathe free.
Emma Lazarus 1849–87

There can be no fifty-fifty Americanism in this country.
There is room here for only 100 per cent. Americanism,
only for those who are Americans and nothing else.
Theodore Roosevelt 1858–1919

I like to be in America!
OK by me in America!
Ev'rything free in America
For a small fee in America!
Stephen Sondheim 1930–

Overpaid, overfed, oversexed, and over here.
Tommy Trinder 1909–89, *of American troops in Britain during the Second World War*

America is a vast conspiracy to make you happy.
John Updike 1932–

The United States themselves are essentially the greatest
poem.
Walt Whitman 1819–92

America is God's Crucible, the great Melting-Pot where
all the races of Europe are melting and re-forming!
Israel Zangwill 1864–1926

The Universe

Had I been present at the Creation, I would have given
some useful hints for the better ordering of the universe.
Alfonso 'the Wise', King of Castile 1221–84, *on studying the Ptolemaic system*

'Gad! she'd better!'
Thomas Carlyle 1795–1881, *on hearing that Margaret Fuller 'accept[ed] the universe'*

The Universe

The eternal mystery of the world is its comprehensibility...The fact that it is comprehensible is a miracle.

Albert Einstein 1879–1955, *usually quoted as 'The most incomprehensible fact about the universe is that it is comprehensible'*

Now, my own suspicion is that the universe is not only queerer than we suppose, but queerer than we *can* suppose.

J. B. S. Haldane 1892–1964

If we find the answer to that [why it is that we and the universe exist], it would be the ultimate triumph of human reason—for then we would know the mind of God.

Stephen Hawking 1942–

This, now, is the judgement of our scientific age—the third reaction of man upon the universe! This universe is not hostile, nor yet is it friendly. It is simply indifferent.

John H. Holmes 1879–1964

There is a coherent plan to the universe, though I don't know what it's a plan for.

Fred Hoyle 1915–2001

From the intrinsic evidence of his creation, the Great Architect of the Universe now begins to appear as a pure mathematician.

James Jeans 1877–1946

How is it that hardly any major religion has looked at science and concluded, 'This is better than we thought! The Universe is much bigger than our prophets said, grander, more subtle, more elegant'?

Carl Sagan 1934–96

There are more things in heaven and earth, Horatio,
Than are dreamt of in your philosophy.
   William Shakespeare 1564–1616

The world is everything that is the case.
   Ludwig Wittgenstein 1889–1951

Keep violence in the mind
Where it belongs.
   Brian Aldiss 1925–

Pale Ebenezer thought it wrong to fight,
But Roaring Bill (who killed him) thought it right.
   Hilaire Belloc 1870–1953

All they that take the sword shall perish with the sword.
   Bible

I say violence is necessary. It is as American as cherry pie.
   H. Rap Brown 1943–

         Who overcomes
By force, hath overcome but half his foe.
   John Milton 1608–74

If you strike a child take care that you strike it in anger,
even at the risk of maiming it for life. A blow in cold
blood neither can nor should be forgiven.
   George Bernard Shaw 1856–1950

Where force is necessary, there it must be applied boldly,
decisively and completely. But one must know the
limitations of force; one must know when to blend force
with a manoeuvre, a blow with an agreement.
   Leon Trotsky 1879–1940

411

Violence

The quietly pacifist peaceful
always die
to make room for men
who shout.
Alice Walker 1944-

Wales

It profits a man nothing to give his soul for the whole
world…But for Wales—!
Robert Bolt 1924-95

Who dare compare the English, the most degraded of all
the races under heaven, with the Welsh?
Giraldus Cambrensis 1146?-1220?

Wales, Wales, sweet are thy hills and vales,
Thy speech, thy song,
To thee belong,
O may they live ever in Wales.
Evan James

Everyday when I wake up, I thank the Lord I'm Welsh.
Cerys Matthews 1969-

Though it appear a little out of fashion,
There is much care and valour in this Welshman.
William Shakespeare 1564-1616

The land of my fathers. My fathers can have it.
Dylan Thomas 1914-53

The Welsh remain the only race whom you can vilify
without being called a racist.
A. N. Wilson 1950-

When war enters a country
It produces lies like sand.
   Anonymous

We make war that we may live in peace.
   Aristotle 384–322 BC

The bomber will always get through. The only defence is
in offence, which means that you have to kill more
women and children more quickly than the enemy if you
want to save yourselves.
   Stanley Baldwin 1867–1947

Not worth the healthy bones of a single Pomeranian
grenadier.
   Otto von Bismarck 1815–98, *of possible German involvement
   in the Balkans*

This policy cannot succeed through speeches, and
shooting-matches, and songs; it can only be carried out
through blood and iron.
   Otto von Bismarck 1815–98

C'est magnifique, mais ce n'est pas la guerre.
It is magnificent, but it is not war.
   Pierre Bosquet 1810–61, *on the charge of the Light Brigade at
   Balaclava, 1854*

They have gone too long without a war here. Where is
morality to come from in such a case, I ask? Peace is
nothing but slovenliness, only war creates order.
   Bertolt Brecht 1898–1956

As you know, God is usually on the side of the big
squadrons against the small.
   Comte de Bussy-Rabutin 1618–93

War

In war, whichever side may call itself the victor, there are no winners, but all are losers.

Neville Chamberlain 1869–1940

We shall fight on the beaches, we shall fight on the landing grounds, we shall fight in the fields and in the streets, we shall fight in the hills; we shall never surrender.

Winston Churchill 1874–1965

Let us therefore brace ourselves to our duty, and so bear ourselves that, if the British Empire and its Commonwealth lasts for a thousand years, men will still say, 'This was their finest hour.'

Winston Churchill 1874–1965

Never in the field of human conflict was so much owed by so many to so few.

Winston Churchill 1874–1965

Laws are silent in time of war.

Cicero 106–43 BC

War is nothing but a continuation of politics with the admixture of other means.

Karl von Clausewitz 1780–1831, *commonly rendered 'War is the continuation of politics by other means'*

Everything is very simple in war, but the simplest thing is difficult. These difficulties accumulate and produce a friction which no man can imagine exactly who has not seen war.

Karl von Clausewitz 1780–1831

War is too serious a matter to entrust to military men.

Georges Clemenceau 1841–1929

ROBERT DUVALL: I love the smell of napalm in the morning. It smells like victory.

Francis Ford Coppola 1939–

War is the most exciting and dramatic thing in life. In fighting to the death you feel terribly relaxed when you manage to come through.

Moshe Dayan 1915–81

I am not only a pacifist but a militant pacifist. I am willing to fight for peace. Nothing will end war unless the people themselves refuse to go to war.

Albert Einstein 1879–1955

There never was a good war, or a bad peace.

Benjamin Franklin 1706–90

If we are attacked we can only defend ourselves with guns not with butter.

Joseph Goebbels 1897–1945

Would you rather have butter or guns?…preparedness makes us powerful. Butter merely makes us fat.

Hermann Goering 1893–1946

War is hell, and all that, but it has a good deal to recommend it. It wipes out all the small nuisances of peace-time.

Ian Hay 1876–1952

Always mystify, mislead, and surprise the enemy, if possible.

Thomas Jonathan 'Stonewall' Jackson 1824–63, *his strategic motto during the Civil War*

Among the calamities of war may be jointly numbered the diminution of the love of truth, by the falsehoods which interest dictates and credulity encourages.

Samuel Johnson 1709–84, *possibly the source of 'When war is declared, Truth is the first casualty'; attributed also to Hiram Johnson*

It is well that war is so terrible. We should grow too fond of it.

Robert E. Lee 1807–70

War

He knew that the essence of war is violence, and that moderation in war is imbecility.

Lord Macaulay 1800–59

Rule 1, on page 1 of the book of war, is: 'Do not march on Moscow'...[Rule 2] is: 'Do not go fighting with your land armies in China.'

Field Marshal Montgomery 1887–1976

Probably the battle of Waterloo *was* won on the playing-fields of Eton, but the opening battles of all subsequent wars have been lost there.

George Orwell 1903–50

My subject is War, and the pity of War.
The Poetry is in the pity.

Wilfred Owen 1893–1918

Little girl...Sometime they'll give a war and nobody will come.

Carl Sandburg 1878–1967

Once more unto the breach, dear friends, once more;
Or close the wall up with our English dead!
In peace there's nothing so becomes a man
As modest stillness and humility:
But when the blast of war blows in our ears,
Then imitate the action of the tiger.

William Shakespeare 1564–1616

There is many a boy here to-day who looks on war as all glory, but, boys, it is all hell.

General Sherman 1820–91

War is capitalism with the gloves off.

Tom Stoppard 1937–

The battle of Waterloo was won on the playing fields of Eton.

Duke of Wellington 1769–1852

Next to a battle lost, the greatest misery is a battle gained.
Duke of Wellington 1769–1852

Wealth ····▶ Money

Riches are a good handmaid, but the worst mistress.
Francis Bacon 1561–1626

It is easier for a camel to go through the eye of a needle, than for a rich man to enter into the kingdom of God.
Bible

Greed is all right…Greed is healthy. You can be greedy and still feel good about yourself.
Ivan F. Boesky 1937–

The man who dies…rich dies disgraced.
Andrew Carnegie 1835–1919

Let me tell you about the very rich. They are different from you and me.
F. Scott Fitzgerald 1896–1940, *to which Ernest Hemingway replied, 'Yes, they have more money'*

In every well-governed state, wealth is a sacred thing; in democracies it is the only sacred thing.
Anatole France 1844–1924

We are all Adam's children but silk makes the difference.
Thomas Fuller 1654–1734

The greater the wealth, the thicker will be the dirt.
J. K. Galbraith 1908–

If you can actually count your money, then you are not really a rich man.
J. Paul Getty 1892–1976

Wealth

We are not here to sell a parcel of boilers and vats, but the potentiality of growing rich, beyond the dreams of avarice.

Samuel Johnson 1709–84, *at the sale of Thrale's brewery*

Will the people in the cheaper seats clap your hands? All the rest of you, if you'll just rattle your jewellery.

John Lennon 1940–80, *at a Royal Variety Performance*

Let us be frank about it: most of our people have never had it so good.

Harold Macmillan 1894–1986

I spend my life ministering to the swinish luxury of the rich.

William Morris 1834–96

Having money is rather like being a blonde. It is more fun but not vital.

Mary Quant 1934–

A kiss on the hand may be quite continental,
But diamonds are a girl's best friend.

Leo Robin 1900–84

The chief enjoyment of riches consists in the parade of riches.

Adam Smith 1723–90

How many things I can do without!

Socrates 469–399 BC, *on looking at a multitude of goods exposed for sale*

It was very prettily said, that we may learn the little value of fortune by the persons on whom heaven is pleased to bestow it.

Richard Steele 1672–1729

I've been rich and I've been poor: rich is better.

Sophie Tucker 1884–1966

Rainy days—
silkworms droop
on mulberries.
Matsuo Basho 1644-94

The rain, it raineth on the just
And also on the unjust fella:
But chiefly on the just, because
The unjust steals the just's umbrella.
Lord Bowen 1835-94

Every time it rains, it rains
Pennies from heaven.
Don't you know each cloud contains
Pennies from heaven?
Johnny Burke 1908-64

The frost performs its secret ministry,
Unhelped by any wind.
Samuel Taylor Coleridge 1772-1834

I believe we should all behave quite differently if we lived
in a warm, sunny climate all the time.
Noël Coward 1899-1973

This is a London particular...A fog, miss.
Charles Dickens 1812-70

A woman rang to say she heard there was a hurricane on
the way. Well don't worry, there isn't.
Michael Fish 1944- , *weather forecast on the night before
serious gales in southern England*

Children are dumb to say how hot the day is,
How hot the scent is of the summer rose.
Robert Graves 1895-1985

Weather

When two Englishmen meet, their first talk is of the weather.
Samuel Johnson 1709–84

It is impossible to live in a country which is continually under hatches…Rain! Rain! Rain!
John Keats 1795–1821

No one can tell me,
Nobody knows,
Where the wind comes from,
Where the wind goes.
A. A. Milne 1882–1956

The first fall of snow is not only an event, but it is a magical event. You go to bed in one kind of world and wake up to find yourself in another quite different, and if this is not enchantment, then where is it to be found?
J. B. Priestley 1894–1984

The fog comes
on little cat feet.
Carl Sandburg 1878–1967

So foul and fair a day I have not seen.
William Shakespeare 1564–1616

There is no such thing as bad weather. All weather is good because it is God's.
St Teresa of Ávila 1512–82

The best sun we have is made of Newcastle coal.
Horace Walpole 1717–97

It was the wrong kind of snow.
Terry Worrall *explaining disruption on British Rail*

Weddings

If it were not for the presents, an elopement would be preferable.
George Ade 1866–1944

Now you will feel no rain, for each of you will be shelter for the other. Now you will feel no cold, for each of you will be warmth for the other.
Anonymous *from the saying known as the 'Apache Blessing'*

As the bridegroom rejoiceth over the bride.
Bible

Wilt thou love her, comfort her, honour, and keep her in sickness and in health; and, forsaking all other, keep thee only unto her, so long as ye both shall live?
Book of Common Prayer 1662

And as a rose new-plucked from Venus' thorn,
So doth a bride her bridegroom's bed adorn…
And as a rose in Venus' bosom worn,
So doth a bridegroom his bride's bed adorn.
Thomas Campion 1567–1620

It's pretty easy. Just say 'I do' whenever anyone asks you a question.
Richard Curtis 1956– , *advice to a prospective bridegroom*

I'm getting married in the morning,
Ding dong! The bells are gonna chime.
Pull out the stopper;
Let's have a whopper;
But get me to the church on time!
Alan Jay Lerner 1918–86

The young bride was the idol, the amusement, the victim of the evening.
Alessandro Manzoni 1785–1873

Weddings

Fair Concord, ever abide by their couch, and to so well-matched a pair may Venus ever be propitious.
Martial AD C.40–C.104

          The trouble
with being best man is, you don't get a chance to
    prove it.
Les A. Murray 1938–

Happy is the bride that the sun shines on.
Proverb

What woman, however old, has not the bridal-favours
and raiment stowed away, and packed in lavender, in the
inmost cupboards of her heart?
William Makepeace Thackeray 1811–63

Her veil blows across my face
as we cling together in the porch.
Propped on the mantelpiece,
The photograph distils our ecstasy.
Hugo Williams 1942–

Winning

The race is not to the swift, nor the battle to the strong.
Bible

You ask, what is our aim? I can answer in one word:
Victory, victory at all costs, victory in spite of all terror;
victory, however long and hard the road may be; for
without victory, there is no survival.
Winston Churchill 1874–1965

Victory has a hundred fathers, but no-one wants to
recognise defeat as his own.
Count Galeazzo Ciano 1903–44

Winning is everything. The only ones who remember you
when you come second are your wife and your dog.
   Damon Hill 1960–

The moment of victory is much too short to live for that
and nothing else.
   Martina Navratilova 1956–

The gods are on the side of the stronger.
   Tacitus AD c.56–after 117

We are not interested in the possibilities of defeat; they
do not exist.
   Queen Victoria 1819–1901

Winter

The English winter—ending in July,
To recommence in August.
   Lord Byron 1788–1824

No shade, no shine, no butterflies, no bees,
No fruits, no flowers, no leaves, no birds,—
November!
   Thomas Hood 1799–1845

The most serious charge which can be brought against
New England is not Puritanism but February.
   Joseph Wood Krutch 1893–1970

Winter is icummen in,
Lhude sing Goddamm,
Raineth drop and staineth slop,
And how the wind doth ramm!
   Ezra Pound 1885–1972

Winter

O, Wind,
If Winter comes, can Spring be far behind?
Percy Bysshe Shelley 1792–1822

Let no man boast himself that he has got through the perils of winter till at least the seventh of May.
Anthony Trollope 1815–82

Woman's Role ····▶ Men and Women

If all men are born free, how is it that all women are born slaves?
Mary Astell 1668–1731

The freedom women were supposed to have found in the Sixties largely boiled down to easy contraception and abortion: things to make life easier for men, in fact.
Julie Burchill 1960–

I could have stayed home and baked cookies and had teas. But what I decided was to fulfil my profession, which I entered before my husband was in public life.
Hillary Rodham Clinton 1947–

The worker is the slave of capitalist society, the female worker is the slave of that slave.
James Connolly 1868–1916

One is not born a woman: one becomes one.
Simone de Beauvoir 1908–86

Today the problem that has no name is how to juggle work, love, home and children.
Betty Friedan 1921–

I didn't fight to get women out from behind the vacuum cleaner to get them onto the board of Hoover.
Germaine Greer 1939–

My mother said it was simple to keep a man, you must be a maid in the living room, a cook in the kitchen and a whore in the bedroom. I said I'd hire the other two and take care of the bedroom bit.

Jerry Hall

A woman's preaching is like a dog's walking on his hinder legs. It is not done well; but you are surprised to find it done at all.

Samuel Johnson 1709-84

The first blast of the trumpet against the monstrous regiment of women.

John Knox c.1505-72

But if God had wanted us to think just with our wombs, why did He give us a brain?

Clare Booth Luce 1903-87

Feminism is the most revolutionary idea there has ever been. Equality for women demands a change in the human psyche more profound then anything Marx dreamed of. It means valuing parenthood as much as we value banking.

Polly Toynbee 1946-

The Queen is most anxious to enlist every one who can speak or write to join in checking this mad, wicked folly of 'Woman's Rights', with all its attendant horrors, on which her poor feeble sex is bent, forgetting every sense of womanly feeling and propriety.

Queen Victoria 1819-1901

I do not wish them [women] to have power over men; but over themselves.

Mary Wollstonecraft 1759-97

Women

The weaker sex, to piety more prone.
William Alexander, Earl of Stirling c.1567–1640

All the privilege I claim for my own sex…is that of loving
longest, when existence or when hope is gone.
Jane Austen 1775–1817

Who can find a virtuous woman? for her price is far
above rubies.
Bible

Good women always think it is their fault when someone
else is being offensive. Bad women never take the blame
for anything.
Anita Brookner 1928–

In her first passion woman loves her lover,
In all the others all she loves is love.
Lord Byron 1788–1824

Women, then, are only children of a larger growth.
Lord Chesterfield 1694–1773

The prime truth of woman, the universal mother…that if
a thing is worth doing, it is worth doing badly.
G. K. Chesterton 1874–1936

She knows her man, and when you rant and swear,
Can draw you to her *with a single hair*.
John Dryden 1631–1700

The happiest women, like the happiest nations, have no
history.
George Eliot 1819–80

What does a woman want?
Sigmund Freud 1856–1939

Women are people who shop. Shopping is the festival of the female oppressed.
Germaine Greer 1939–

Being a woman is of special interest only to aspiring male transsexuals. To actual women, it is merely a good excuse not to play football.
Fran Lebowitz 1946–

She's the sort of woman who lives for others—you can always tell the others by their hunted expression.
C. S. Lewis 1898–1963

A woman will always sacrifice herself if you give her the opportunity. It is her favourite form of self-indulgence.
W. Somerset Maugham 1874–1965

Woman was God's second blunder.
Friedrich Nietzsche 1844–1900

Woman is the nigger of the world.
Yoko Ono 1933–

Slamming their doors, stamping their high heels, banging their irons and saucepans—the eternal flaming racket of the female.
John Osborne 1929–

The greatest glory of a woman is to be least talked about by men.
Pericles c.495–429 BC

Every woman adores a Fascist,
The boot in the face, the brute
Brute heart of a brute like you.
Sylvia Plath 1932–63

Women

She floats, she hesitates; in a word, she's a woman.
Jean Racine 1639–99

O Woman! in our hours of ease,
Uncertain, coy, and hard to please...
When pain and anguish wring the brow,
A ministering angel thou!
Sir Walter Scott 1771–1832

Frailty, thy name is woman!
William Shakespeare 1564–1616

Vitality in a woman is a blind fury of creation.
George Bernard Shaw 1856–1950

Here's to the maiden of bashful fifteen
Here's to the widow of fifty
Here's to the flaunting, extravagant quean;
And here's to the housewife that's thrifty.
Richard Brinsley Sheridan 1751–1816

The great and almost only comfort about being a woman
is that one can always pretend to be more stupid than
one is and no one is surprised.
Freya Stark 1893–1993

We are becoming the men we wanted to marry.
Gloria Steinem 1934–

From birth to 18 a girl needs good parents. From 18 to 35,
she needs good looks. From 35 to 55, good personality.
From 55 on, she needs good cash.
Sophie Tucker 1884–1966

When once a woman has given you her heart, you can
never get rid of the rest of her body.
John Vanbrugh 1664–1726

Words ····> Language, Meaning

Acronyms are your allies. They sound impressive while conveying no information. Use them liberally.
Scott Adams 1957–

The Greeks had a word for it.
Zoë Akins 1886–1958

Words are the tokens current and accepted for conceits, as moneys are for values.
Francis Bacon 1561–1626

There is no use indicting words, they are no shoddier than what they peddle.
Samuel Beckett 1906–89

'When *I* use a word,' Humpty Dumpty said in a rather scornful tone, 'it means just what I choose it to mean—neither more nor less.'
Lewis Carroll 1832–98

It cannot in the opinion of His Majesty's Government be classified as slavery in the extreme acceptance of the word without some risk of terminological inexactitude.
Winston Churchill 1874–1965

A man who could make so vile a pun would not scruple to pick a pocket.
John Dennis 1657–1734

> Words strain,
Crack and sometimes break, under the burden,
Under the tension, slip, slide, perish,
Decay with imprecision, will not stay in place,
Will not stay still.
T. S. Eliot 1888–1965

Words

The chief merit of language is clearness, and we know that nothing detracts so much from this as do unfamiliar terms.
Galen 129–99 AD

Dialect words—those terrible marks of the beast to the truly genteel.
Thomas Hardy 1840–1928

And once sent out, a word takes wing beyond recall.
Horace 65–8 BC

Lexicographer. A writer of dictionaries, a harmless drudge.
Samuel Johnson 1709–84

I am not yet so lost in lexicography as to forget that words are the daughters of earth, and that things are the sons of heaven. Language is only the instrument of science, and words are but the signs of ideas.
Samuel Johnson 1709–84

Words are, of course, the most powerful drug used by mankind.
Rudyard Kipling 1865–1936

In my youth there were words you couldn't say in front of a girl; now you can't say 'girl'.
Tom Lehrer 1928–

Woord is but wynd; leff woord and tak the dede.
John Lydgate c.1370–c.1451

Parents can plant magic in a child's mind through certain words spoken with some thrilling quality of voice, some uplift of the heart and spirit.
Robert MacNeil 1931–

Syllables govern the world.
John Selden 1584–1654

In a world full of audio visual marvels, may words matter to you and be full of magic.
Godfrey Smith 1926–

Work ····▶ Careers

In the sweat of thy face shalt thou eat bread.
Bible

For the labourer is worthy of his hire.
Bible

Work is love made visible.
Kahlil Gibran 1883–1931

That state is a state of slavery in which a man does what he likes to do in his spare time and in his working time that which is required of him.
Eric Gill 1882–1940

I have long been of the opinion that if work were such a splendid thing the rich would have kept more of it for themselves.
Bruce Grocott 1940–

I like work: it fascinates me. I can sit and look at it for hours. I love to keep it by me: the idea of getting rid of it nearly breaks my heart.
Jerome K. Jerome 1859–1927

Why should I let the toad *work*
Squat on my life?
Can't I use my wit as a pitchfork
And drive the brute off?
Philip Larkin 1922–85

Blessèd are the horny hands of toil!
James Russell Lowell 1819–91

Work

Work expands so as to fill the time available for its completion.
C. Northcote Parkinson 1909–93

We spend our midday sweat, our midnight oil;
We tire the night in thought, the day in toil.
Francis Quarles 1592–1644

It's true hard work never killed anybody, but I figure why take the chance?
Ronald Reagan 1911–2004

If you have great talents, industry will improve them: if you have but moderate abilities, industry will supply their deficiency.
Joshua Reynolds 1723–92

Which of us…is to do the hard and dirty work for the rest—and for what pay? Who is to do the pleasant and clean work, and for what pay?
John Ruskin 1819–1900

One of the symptoms of approaching nervous breakdown is the belief that one's work is terribly important, and that to take a holiday would bring all kinds of disaster.
Bertrand Russell 1872–1970

The labour we delight in physics pain.
William Shakespeare 1564–1616

Work was like a stick. It had two ends. When you worked for the knowing you gave them quality; when you worked for a fool you simply gave him eye-wash.
Alexander Solzhenitsyn 1918–

Work to survive, survive by consuming, survive to consume: the hellish cycle is complete.
Raoul Vaneigem 1934–

Writing ·····▶ Literature, Style

If you can't annoy somebody with what you write, I think there's little point in writing.
Kingsley Amis 1922–95

Let other pens dwell on guilt and misery. I quit such odious subjects as soon as I can.
Jane Austen 1775–1817

Writers, like teeth, are divided into incisors and grinders.
Walter Bagehot 1826–77

Manuscripts don't burn.
Mikhail Bulgakov 1891–1940

Beneath the rule of men entirely great
The pen is mightier than the sword.
Edward Bulwer-Lytton 1803–73

When in doubt have a man come through the door with a gun in his hand.
Raymond Chandler 1888–1959

A writer must be as objective as a chemist: he must abandon the subjective line; he must know that dung-heaps play a very reasonable part in a landscape, and that evil passions are as inherent in life as good ones.
Anton Chekhov 1860–1904

They shut me up in prose—
As when a little girl
They put me in the closet—
Because they liked me 'still'.
Emily Dickinson 1830–86

We must beat the iron while it is hot, but we may polish it at leisure.
John Dryden 1631–1700

Writing

The writer's only responsibility is to his art. He will be completely ruthless if he is a good one...If a writer has to rob his mother, he will not hesitate; the *Ode on a Grecian Urn* is worth any number of old ladies.
   William Faulkner 1897–1962

The test of a round character is whether it is capable of surprising in a convincing way. If it never surprises, it is flat. If it does not convince, it is flat pretending to be round.
   E. M. Forster 1879–1970

Only connect!...Only connect the prose and the passion.
   E. M. Forster 1879–1970

The business of the poet and novelist is to show the sorriness underlying the grandest things, and the grandeur underlying the sorriest things.
   Thomas Hardy 1840–1928

The most essential gift for a good writer is a built-in, shock-proof shit detector. This is the writer's radar and all great writers have had it.
   Ernest Hemingway 1899–1961

I am a camera with its shutter open, quite passive, recording, not thinking.
   Christopher Isherwood 1904–86

No man but a blockhead ever wrote, except for money.
   Samuel Johnson 1709–84

Read over your compositions, and where ever you meet with a passage which you think is particularly fine, strike it out.
   Samuel Johnson 1709–84

A writer's ambition should be...to trade a hundred
contemporary readers for ten readers in ten years' time
and for one reader in a hundred years.
Arthur Koestler 1905-83

When my sonnet was rejected, I exclaimed, 'Damn the
age; I will write for Antiquity!'
Charles Lamb 1775-1834

If you try to nail anything down in the novel, either it
kills the novel, or the novel gets up and walks away with
the nail.
D. H. Lawrence 1885-1930

There is no need for the writer to eat a whole sheep to be
able to tell you what mutton tastes like. It is enough if he
eats a cutlet. But he should do that.
W. Somerset Maugham 1874-1965

Things unattempted yet in prose or rhyme.
John Milton 1608-74

       What in me is dark
Illumine, what is low raise and support;
That to the height of this great argument
I may assert eternal providence,
And justify the ways of God to men.
John Milton 1608-74

If you steal from one author, it's plagiarism; if you steal
from many, it's research.
Wilson Mizner 1876-1933

The last thing one knows in constructing a work is what
to put first.
Blaise Pascal 1623-62

But those who cannot write, and those who can,
All rhyme, and scrawl, and scribble, to a man.
Alexander Pope 1688-1744

Writing

And, as imagination bodies forth
The forms of things unknown, the poet's pen
Turns them to shapes, and gives to airy nothing
A local habitation and a name.
    William Shakespeare 1564–1616

Writing is not a profession but a vocation of
unhappiness.
    Georges Simenon 1903–89

Not that the story need be long, but it will take a long
while to make it short.
    Henry David Thoreau 1817–62

I have written my work, not as an essay which is to win
the applause of the moment, but as a possession for all
time.
    Thucydides c.455–c.400 BC

The composition of a tragedy requires *testicles*.
    Voltaire 1694–1778, *on being asked why no woman had ever
written 'a tolerable tragedy'*

I come from a backward place: your duty is supplied by
life around you. One guy plants bananas; another plants
cocoa; I'm a writer, I plant lines. There's the same clarity
of occupation, and the sense of devotion.
    Derek Walcott 1930–

A woman must have money and a room of her own if
she is to write fiction.
    Virginia Woolf 1882–1941

Never forget what I believe was observed to you by
Coleridge, that every great and original writer, in
proportion as he is great and original, must himself create
the taste by which he is to be relished.
    William Wordsworth 1770–1850

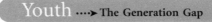

Youth ····▶ The Generation Gap

I'm not young enough to know everything.
J. M. Barrie 1860–1937

Youth is something very new: twenty years ago no one mentioned it.
Coco Chanel 1883–1971

It is better to waste one's youth than to do nothing with it at all.
Georges Courteline 1858–1929

20 to 40 is the fillet steak of life. After that it's all short cuts.
Philip Larkin 1922–85

A boy's will is the wind's will
And the thoughts of youth are long, long thoughts.
Henry Wadsworth Longfellow 1807–82

Youth is vivid rather than happy, but memory always remembers the happy things.
Bernard Lovell 1913–

Whom the gods love dies young.
Menander 342–c.292 BC

O Adolescence, O Adolescence,
I wince before thine incandescence.
Thy constitution young and hearty
Is too much for this aged party.
Ogden Nash 1902–71

The atrocious crime of being a young man…I shall neither attempt to palliate nor deny.
William Pitt 1708–78

Being young is greatly overestimated…Any failure seems so total. Later on you realize you can have another go.
Mary Quant 1934–

Youth

My salad days,
When I was green in judgement.
William Shakespeare 1564–1616

The force that through the green fuse drives the flower
Drives my green age.
Dylan Thomas 1914–53

The only way to stay young is to avoid old people.
James D. Watson 1928–

Heaven lies about us in our infancy!
Shades of the prison-house begin to close
Upon the growing boy.
William Wordsworth 1770–1850

Index of Authors

Abbott, George
  Lifestyles

Abse, Dannie
  Men, Sculpture

Accius
  Government

Acheson, Dean
  Britain,
  Bureaucracy,
  Careers

Acton, Lord
  Power

Adams, Abigail
  Character, Fashion

Adams, Douglas
  Advice, Life, Music

Adams, Franklin P.
  Elections,
  Middle Age

Adams, Henry Brooks
  Education,
  Experience,
  Meaning, Morality,
  Teaching

Adams, John
  Democracy,
  Government,
  Letters, Politics,
  Presidency

Adams, Michael
  Canada

Adams, Phillip
  Leisure

Adams, Scott
  Words

Adamson, Harold
  Crises

Addison, Joseph
  Business, Future,
  Gardens,
  Happiness,
  Patriotism, Success

Ade, George
  Weddings

Adenauer, Konrad
  Character

Adler, Alfred
  Truth

Adorno, Theodor
  Poetry

Aeschylus
  Suffering

Aesop
  Prayer

Agar, Herbert
  Truth

Agate, James
  Certainty

Agathon
  Past

Agee, James
  Nature

Akins, Zoë
  Words

Alain
  Ideas

Alcott, Louisa May
  Christmas, Mothers

Aldington, Richard
  Patriotism

Aldiss, Brian
  Violence

Aldrin, Buzz
  Skies

Alexander, Cecil Frances
  Animals, Class

Alexander, Tsar II
  Revolution

Alexander, William, Earl of Stirling
  Women

Alfonso 'the Wise', King of Castile
  Universe

Ali, Muhammad
  Boxing

Ali ibn-Abi-Talib
  Enemies

Allen, Fred
  Management

Allen, Woody
  Death, Sex

Allingham, William
  Supernatural

Ambrose, St
  Behaviour

American Declaration of Independence
  Human Rights

Ames, Fisher
  Government

Amies, Hardy
  Clothes

Amis, Kingsley
  Men and Women,
  Writing

Amis, Martin
  Middle Age

Anacharsis
  Law

Andersen, Hans Christian
  Birth

Andrewes, Bishop Lancelot
  Church

Index of Authors

Angelou, Maya
Suffering

Anka, Paul
Lifestyles

Anonymous
*Army, Bereavement,
Business,
Computers, Crises,
Determination,
Economics,
Education, Effort,
Elections,
Experience, Fame,
Foolishness,
Friendship, God,
Gossip, Human
Rights, Ideas,
Intelligence,
Journalism, Justice,
Knowledge, Liberty,
Lies, Madness,
Mathematics,
Moderation, Music,
Past, Race, Sea,
Self-Knowledge,
Summer,
Supernatural,
Technology,
Transience, War,
Weddings*

Anouilh, Jean
Deceit, France, Love

Apelles
Drawing

**Apollinaire,
Guillaume**
Custom, Invention

**Appleton, Thomas
Gold**
United States

Arbus, Diane
Photography

Arbuthnot, Dr
Law

Archilochus
Knowledge

Archimedes
*Invention,
Technology*

Arden, Elizabeth
Money

Arendt, Hannah
Evil, Revolution

Aristotle
*Friendship,
Goodness, Ideas,
Knowledge, Nature,
Politics, Solitude,
Truth, War*

Armour, Richard
Food

Armstrong, Louis
Music

Armstrong, Neil
Achievement

Armstrong, Robert
Truth

Arnald-Amaury
Cynicism

Arnold, Matthew
*Autumn, Belief,
Leadership,
Memory, Middle
Age, Perfection,
Poetry, Style*

Asaf, George
Anxiety

Ascham, Roger
Education, Teaching

Asher, Jane
Housework

Ashford, Daisy
Middle Age

Asimov, Isaac
Health

Asquith, Herbert
Statistics

Asquith, Margot
Supernatural

Astell, Mary
Woman's Role

Astley, Jacob
Prayer

Astor, Nancy
Drink

Atkinson, Brooks
Democracy, Past

Atkinson, Rowan
Cars

**Attenborough,
David**
Animals

Attlee, Clement
Democracy, Politics

Atwood, Margaret
Prayer

Aubrey, John
Reading

**Auctoritates
Aristotelis**
Argument

Auden, W. H.
*Appearance,
Behaviour,
Bereavement,
Books, Evil, Failure,
Generation Gap,
Habit, Heart,
Humour,
Intelligence, Letters,
Names,
Photography,
Poetry, Railways,
Science, Self, Self-
Knowledge, Society,
Sorrow, Suffering*

**Augustine, St of
Hippo**
*Evil, Justice,
Lifestyles,
Moderation, Sex*

Aung San Suu Kyi
Men and Women

Aurelius, Marcus
*Suffering, Thinking,
Time*

Index of Authors

Austen, Jane
Conversation, Gifts, Gossip, Happiness, Hospitality, Humour, Idleness, Literature, Marriage, Men, Perfection, Pleasure, Sympathy, Town, Women, Writing

Awdry, Revd W.
Railways

Ayer, A. J.
Opinion

Ayres, Pam
Medicine

Bacall, Lauren
Sickness

Bacon, Francis
Ability, Action, Advice, Anger, Beauty, Belief, Books, Certainty, Change, Children, Dance, Death, Diplomacy, Education, Fame, Family, Friendship, Gardens, Houses, Indifference, Invention, Knowledge, Life, Marriage, Medicine, Misfortune, Money, Nature, Old Age, Parents, Power, Revenge, Royalty, Silence, Thanks, Travel, Truth, Wealth, Words

Bacon, Francis
Friendship

Bacon, Roger
Mathematics

Baden-Powell, Lord
Planning

Bader, Douglas
Trust

Baez, Joan
Opinion

Bagehot, Walter
Bureaucracy, Journalism, Languages, Leadership, Pleasure, Politicians, Royalty, Writing

Bailey, David
Photography

Bainbridge, Beryl
Suffering

Bairnsfather, Bruce
Advice

Baldwin, James
Money, Poverty

Baldwin, Stanley
Parting, Secrecy, War

Ballard, J. G.
Honours

Banks, Joseph
Australia

Bannister, Roger
Exercise

Barnard, Frederick R.
Language

Barnes, Julian
Books, Children, Love

Barnum, Phineas T.
Foolishness

Barrett, Matt
Debt

Barrie, J. M.
Belief, Charm, Death, Festivals, Memory, Practicality, Scotland, Youth

Barry, Sebastian
Ireland

Barrymore, John
Solitude

Barthes, Roland
Cars

Baruch, Bernard
Old Age

Barzun, Jacques
Life

Basho, Matsuo
Autumn, Weather

Bates, Katherine Lee
United States

Battle of Maldon, The
Determination

Baudelaire, Charles
Class, Invention, Progress

Baxter, Richard
Behaviour

Bayley, John
Sickness

Beamer, Todd
Action

Beaumarchais, Pierre-Augustin Caron de
Human Race, Humour, Singing

Beaverbrook, Lord
Invention

Beckett, Samuel
Boredom, Failure, Habit, Human Race, Time, Words

Becon, Thomas
Drink

Bede, The Venerable
History, Life

Beecham, Thomas
Music

Index of Authors

Beerbohm, Max
Dreams,
Imagination,
Philosophy

Beethoven, Ludwig van
Cookery, Fate

Beeton, Mrs
Management

Behan, Brendan
Fame

Behn, Aphra
Money, Poverty

Bellah, James Warner *see*
Goldbeck, Willis and
Bellah, James Warner

Bellarmine, Cardinal Robert
Memory

Belloc, Hilaire
Class, Cookery,
Doubt, Elections,
Life Sciences,
Misfortune,
Pleasure, Statistics,
Violence

Benchley, Robert
Quotations

Benenson, Peter
Action

Ben-Gurion, David
Truth

Benn, Tony
Belief, Future,
Honours,
Photography

Bennett, Alan
Behaviour, Memory,
Morality, Royalty,
Society, Theatre

Bennett, Arnold
Idealism, Marriage

Bennett, Brian *see*
Welch, Bruce and
Bennett, Brian

Bensley, Connie
Body

Bentham, Jeremy
Animals, Human
Rights, Poetry,
Punishment, Society

Bentley, Edmund Clerihew
Biography

Beresford, Lord Charles
Apology

Bergman, Ingrid
Lovers

Berkeley, Bishop George
Mathematics

Berlin, Irving
Christmas, Dance,
Good Looks, Love,
Theatre, United
States

Berlin, Isaiah
Liberty

Berlioz, Hector
Time

Bernal, J. D.
Life Sciences

Bernanos, Georges
Hell, Prayer

Berra, Yogi
Baseball, Ending,
Future

Berryman, John
Boredom, Fear

Betjeman, John
Christmas,
Education,
Environment

Bevan, Aneurin
Journalism,
Moderation,
Politicians

Beveridge, William Henry
Progress

Bevin, Ernest
Enemies

Bhagavad Gita
Time

Bhutto, Benazir
Power

Bible
Absence,
Achievement, Anger,
Animals, Argument,
Beauty, Beginning,
Belief, Bereavement,
Birth, Body, Books,
Brevity, Careers,
Chance, Change,
Charity, Children,
Christmas,
Cooperation, Death,
Debt, Despair,
Doubt, Drink,
Earth, Ending,
Enemies,
Environment, Envy,
Equality, Evil,
Fame, Family, Fate,
Foolishness,
Forgiveness,
Gardens, Gifts,
God, Greatness,
Hatred, Heaven,
Hope, Hospitality,
Hypocrisy, Idealism,
Idleness,
Indifference,
Journalism, Justice,
Knowledge,
Language,
Leadership, Life,
Lifestyles, Love,
Lovers, Manners,
Marriage, Medicine,
Misfortune, Money,

Index of Authors

*Murder, Old Age,
Parents, Peace,
Pollution, Poverty,
Prayer, Present,
Pride, Progress,
Punishment,
Religion, Revenge,
Sea, Secrecy, Self-
Knowledge, Sleep,
Solitude, Sorrow,
Success,
Supernatural,
Teaching,
Temptation,
Thanks, Time,
Transience, Trust,
Truth, Violence,
Wealth, Weddings,
Winning, Women,
Work*

Bible (Apocrypha)
*Business, Medicine,
Truth*

Bidault, Georges
Mistakes

Bierce, Ambrose
Pollution

Biko, Steve
Power

Billings, Josh
Knowledge

Binchy, Maeve
Festivals

Binyon, Laurence
Autumn

Bion
Cruelty

Birkett, Lord
Speechmaking

Bishop, Elizabeth
Dreams, Earth

Bismarck, Otto von
*Europe,
Politics, War*

Blacker, Valentine
Practicality

**Blackstone,
William**
Justice

Blair, Tony
*Action, Certainty,
Crime,
Determination,
Education,
Leadership, Religion*

Blake, Eubie
Old Age

Blake, William
*Anger, Animals,
Cruelty, England,
Environment,
Goodness,
Imagination,
Knowledge, Love,
Poetry, Transience,
Truth*

**Blanchflower,
Danny**
Football

Bliss, Arthur
Old Age

Blix, Hans
Danger

**Blücher, Gebhard
Lebrecht**
London

Blythe, Ronald
Management

Boesky, Ivan F.
Wealth

Boethius
Misfortune

Bogart, John B.
Journalism

Bohr, Niels
*Belief, Future,
Science, Thinking,
Truth*

Bold, Alan
Scotland

**Bolingbroke, Henry
St John, 1st
Viscount**
Mistakes

Bolívar, Simón
Revolution

Böll, Heinrich
Happiness

Bolt, Robert
Wales

Bonaparte, Laetitia
Success

**Bonhoeffer,
Dietrich**
Character

Bono
Ireland

**Book of Common
Prayer**
*Conscience, Death,
Environment,
Languages,
Marriage, Night,
Peace, Temptation,
Weddings*

Boren, James H.
Bureaucracy

Borges, Jorge Luis
Night

Borgia, Cesare
Ambition

Borrow, George
Literature

Bosquet, Pierre
War

Boswell, James
Manners

Boucicault, Dion
Time

**Boulay, Antoine de
la Meurthe**
Mistakes

Boulez, Pierre
Revolution

Index of Authors

Boulton, Matthew
Technology

Bourke-White, Margaret
Secrecy

Bowen, Elizabeth
Absence, Envy, Experience, Fate, Spring

Bowen, Lord
Justice, Weather

Bowie, David
Heroes

Boy George
Character

Brackett, Charles and Wilder, Billy
Cinema

Bradford, John
Chance

Bradley, F. H.
Philosophy

Bradman, Don
Cricket

Bradshaw, John
Revolution

Bramah, Ernest
Conversation

Bramston, James
Time

Branagh, Kenneth
Friendship

Brando, Marlon
Acting

Brandt, Willy
Suffering

Braque, Georges
Art

Brasher, Christopher
Drugs

Braun, Werner von
Science

Brecht, Bertolt
Clothes, Goodness, Heroes, Morality, Revolution, Science, War

Brenan, Gerald
Boredom, Leisure

Brenner, Sydney
Computers

Brews, Margery
Lovers

Bridgeman, Percy Williams
Science

Bridger, Roy
Progress

Bright, John
Government

Brillat-Savarin, Anthelme
Cookery, Eating, Invention

Brockbank, Russell
Europe

Brodrick, St John
Manners

Brokaw, Tom
Fishing

Bronowski, Jacob
Action, Cruelty, Science

Brontë, Charlotte
Teaching

Brontë, Emily
Courage, Friendship, Lovers

Brooke, Rupert
Death, Flowers, History, Past, Sleep

Brookner, Anita
Mothers, Women

Brooks, Gwendolyn
Present

Brooks, J.
Animals

Brophy, Brigid
Cruelty

Broun, Haywood Hale
Sport

Brown, Gordon
Fathers

Brown, H. Rap
Violence

Brown, Lew
Life

Brown, T. E.
Gardens

Brown, Thomas
Hatred

Browne, Sir Thomas
Dreams, Human Race, Medicine, Nature, Praise, Sex

Browning, Elizabeth Barrett
Lovers, Prayer, Sorrow

Browning, Robert
Ambition, Beauty, Birds, Choice, Cynicism, Determination, England, Ignorance, Optimism, Perfection, Trust

Bruce, Lenny
Drugs

Brummell, Beau
Clothes

Brundtland, Gro Harlem
Environment

Bruno, Frank
Boxing

Buber, Martin
Self

Buchan, John
Happiness

Buchman, Frank
Economics

Index of Authors

Buffon, Comte de
Genius, Style

Bulgakov, Mikhail
Writing

Bulwer-Lytton, Edward
Friendship, Reading, Writing

Bunyan, John
Pride, Punishment, Style

Burchill, Julie
Woman's Role

Burgess, Anthony
Presidency

Burke, Edmund
Ambition, Cooperation, Custom, Danger, Determination, Europe, Evil, Family, Fear, Future, Human Rights, Law, Liberty, Politicians, Politics, Practicality, Society, Success, Taxes

Burke, Johnny
Weather

Burns, John
England

Burns, Robert
Animals, Chance, Cruelty, Drink, Eating, Equality, Friendship, Honours, Love, Lovers, Meeting, Memory, Scotland, Self-Knowledge, Temptation

Burroughs, William S.
Drugs, Evil, Supernatural

Burton, Robert
Poetry, Religion, Travel

Busenbaum, Hermann
Morality

Bush, Barbara
Presidency

Bush, George
Boredom, Family, Food, Idealism, Taxes, United States

Bush, George W.
Achievement, Planning

Bussy-Rabutin, Comte de
War

Butler, Nicholas Murray
Knowledge

Butler, Samuel
Cynicism, Hypocrisy, Opinion

Butler, Samuel
Art, Canada, Conscience, Dogs, Language, Life Sciences, Praise

Butler, William
Food

Byatt, A. S.
Books

Byrd, William
Singing

Byron, Lord
Censorship, Criticism, Dance, Dogs, Fame, Hatred, Hospitality, Lies, Literature, Marriage, Men and Women, Nature, Pleasure, Religion, Revenge, Self-Knowledge,

Solitude, Truth, Winter, Women

Cabell, James Branch
Pessimism

Caesar, Julius
Ambition, Behaviour, Choice, Success

Caine, Michael
Class

Callimachus
Books

Calonne, Charles Alexandre de
Effort

Camara, Helder
Poverty

Cameron, James
Parting

Cameron, Simon
Politicians

Campbell, Mrs Patrick
Marriage, Sex

Campbell, Roy
Human Race

Campbell, Thomas
Country

Campion, Thomas
Weddings

Camus, Albert
Charm, Goodness, Imagination, Lies, Morality, Revolution

Canetti, Elias
Dreams

Canning, George
Friendship, Patriotism

Cantona, Eric
Journalism

Capa, Robert
Photography

Index of Authors

Capone, Al
Crime

Capp, Al
Art

Capra, Frank
Cinema

Caracciolo, Francesco
England

Carey, George
Church

Carlyle, Thomas
Biography, Civilization, France, History, Idleness, Libraries, Statistics, Universe

Carnegie, Andrew
Wealth

Carr, Emily
Drawing

Carroll, Lewis
Beginning, Behaviour, Belief, Books, Conversation, Effort, Gifts, Justice, Language, Manners, Meaning, Names, Philosophy, Present, Reality, Statistics, Truth, Words

Carson, Rachel
Pollution

Carter, Chris
Secrecy

Carter, Henry
Australia

Carter, Howard
Invention

Cartier, Jacques
Canada

Cartier-Bresson, Henri
Photography

Cartwright, John
Democracy

Casals, Pablo
Old Age

Cash, Pat
Tennis

Cassandre, A. M.
Advertising

Castaneda, Carlos
Supernatural

Castle, Barbara
Determination

Castro, Fidel
Economics

Cather, Willa
Management, Travel

Catherine, Empress the Great
Forgiveness

Cato the Elder
Speechmaking

Catullus
Parting

Cavell, Edith
Patriotism

Ceauşescu, Nicolae
Enemies

Cecil, Lord Hugh
Retirement

Celan, Paul
Poetry

Centlivre, Susannah
Money

Cervantes
Eating, Painting

Cézanne, Paul
Drawing

Chamberlain, Joseph
Politics

Chamberlain, Neville
Peace, War

Chamfort, Nicolas-Sébastien
Humour, Intelligence, Love, Poverty

Chandler, Raymond
Crime, Language, Writing

Chanel, Coco
Europe, Fashion, Youth

Channon, Henry 'Chips'
Diaries

Chaplin, Charlie
Acting, Cinema

Chapman, Graham et al.
Change, Death, Progress

Charles I
Apology, Royalty

Charles V, Emperor
Languages

Charles, Hugh see Parker, Ross and Charles, Hugh

Charles, Prince of Wales
Architecture

Chatwin, Bruce
Exercise

Chaucer, Geoffrey
Behaviour, Birds, Education, Good Looks, Hypocrisy, Murder, Spring, Sympathy

Chekhov, Anton
Friendship, Good Looks, Hatred, Pollution, Sickness, Theatre, Writing

Chesterfield, Lord
Advice, Behaviour, Chance,

Index of Authors

Conversation,
Enemies, Idleness,
Knowledge,
Manners, Religion,
Sex, Time, Truth,
Women

Chesterton, G. K.
Crime, Custom,
God, Ideas, Ireland,
Knowledge,
Literature,
Prejudice, Railways,
Secrecy, Women

Chevalier, Maurice
Old Age

Child, Lydia Maria
Festivals

Choiseul, Duc de
Politicians

Chomsky, Noam
Computers,
Language

Chuang-tzu (or Zhuangzi)
Self-Knowledge

Church, Francis Pharcellus
Christmas

Churchill, Charles
Envy, Hypocrisy,
Patriotism,
Speechmaking

Churchill, Lord Randolph
Ireland,
Mathematics

Churchill, Winston
Achievement,
Animals,
Architecture, Babies,
Britain, Courage,
Democracy,
Diplomacy, Drink,
Ending, Europe,
Food, Future,
Honours, Language,

Politicians,
Quotations,
Revenge, Sea,
Speechmaking,
Trust, War,
Winning, Words

Ciano, Count Galeazzo
Winning

Cibber, Colley
Fashion, Marriage

Cicero
Behaviour, Law,
Mistakes, Money,
Philosophy, War

Cioran, E. M.
Idleness

Clare, John
Present

Clark, Alan
Bureaucracy,
Character,
Politicians, Politics

Clarke, Arthur C.
Earth, Science,
Technology

Clarke, John
Home

Clausewitz, Karl von
War

Clayton, Tubby
Charity

Cleaver, Eldridge
Conversation,
Management

Clemenceau, Georges
Old Age, War

Clinton, Bill
Drugs, Life
Sciences, Meaning,
Morality

Clinton, Hillary Rodham
Children, Marriage,

Woman's Role

Clough, Arthur Hugh
Crime,
Determination,
Envy, Fear, Murder

Cobbett, William
London

Cockburn, Claud
Journalism, Reality

Cocteau, Jean
Books

Coetzee, J. M.
Dreams

Cohen, John
Language

Cohen, Leonard
Body, Canada,
Pessimism

Coke, Desmond
Sport

Coke, Edward
Business, Houses

Colbert, Jean-Baptiste
Government, Taxes

Coleridge, Samuel Taylor
Babies, Chance,
Men and Women,
Night, Poetry,
Politics, Pollution,
Prayer, Sea,
Singing, Weather

Collins, Joan
Medicine,
Temptation

Colman, George, the Elder and Garrick, David
Love

Colton, Charles Caleb
Examinations,
Praise,

Index of Authors

Colton, Charles Caleb (*cont.*)
Speechmaking, Town

Comden, Betty and **Green, Adolph**
Ending

Compton, Denis
Cricket

Compton-Burnett, Ivy
Men and Women, Poverty

Confucius
Education, Human Race, Sex, Teaching

Congreve, William
Good Looks, Gossip, Love, Music, Revenge, Secrecy

Connolly, Billy
Fishing, Marriage

Connolly, Cyril
Charm, Criticism, Memory, Men and Women, Style, Town

Connolly, James
Woman's Role

Connors, Jimmy
Tennis

Conrad, Joseph
Action, Ambition, Management

Conran, Shirley
Housework, Planning

Constable, John
Beauty, Painting

Constant, Benjamin
Art

Constitution of the United States
Punishment

Cook, James
Ambition

Cook, Peter
Pleasure

Coolidge, Calvin
Civilization, Determination

Cooper, Alice
Lifestyles

Cope, Wendy
Lovers, Poetry

Coppola, Francis Ford
War

Corneille, Pierre
Danger

Cornford, Francis M.
Lies

Cornuel, Mme
Heroes

Cory, William
Boats

Cosby, Bill
Marriage

Coubertin, Baron Pierre de
Sport

Coué, Émile
Medicine

Coupland, Douglas
Careers

Courteline, Georges
Youth

Cousteau, Jacques
Pollution

Coward, Noël
Acting, Class, England, Leisure, Music, Weather

Cowper, William
Change, Country, God, Pleasure, Solitude

Crabbe, George
Habit, Poverty

Crashaw, Richard
Marriage

Creighton, Bishop Mandell
Goodness

Crick, Francis
Life Sciences, Self

Crisp, Quentin
Biography, Housework

Critchley, Julian
Speechmaking

Cromwell, Oliver
Achievement, Mistakes, Painting, Parting

Cronenberg, David
Fear

Crossman, Richard
Bureaucracy

Crowley, Aleister
Lifestyles

Cumberland, Bishop Richard
Idleness

cummings, e. e.
Body, Progress

Cunningham, Allan
Boats

Cuomo, Mario
Politics

Cupitt, Don
Christmas

Curie, Marie
Family

Curran, John Philpot
Liberty

Curtis, Richard
Weddings

Curtiz, Michael
Cinema

Index of Authors

Cyprian, St
Church

Dali, Salvador
Ambition

Daniels, Paul
Supernatural

Dante Alighieri
*Conscience, Gossip,
Hell, Love, Middle
Age, Misfortune,
Peace, Transience*

**Danton, Georges
Jacques**
Courage

Darrow, Clarence
Presidency

Darwin, Charles
*Animals,
Appearance,
Language, Life
Sciences, Nature*

Darwin, Francis
Science

David, Elizabeth
Cookery

Davies, Sir John
Dance

Davies, Robertson
*Biography, Canada,
Luck*

Davies, Scrope
Madness

Davies, W. H.
Birds, Leisure

Davis, Sammy Jnr.
Prejudice

Davis, Thomas
Hospitality

Dawkins, Richard
Death, Life Sciences

**Dawson,
Christopher**
Evil

Day, Robin
Television

Dayan, Moshe
War

**de Beauvoir,
Simone**
Woman's Role

de Bernières, Louis
Heart, Love

Debray, Régis
Politics

Decatur, Stephen
Patriotism

Defoe, Daniel
*Anxiety, Church,
Custom, Evil,
Poverty*

Degas, Edgar
Art, Genius

de Gaulle, Charles
*Canada,
Censorship,
Diplomacy, France*

Delafield, E. M.
Leisure

de la Mare, Walter
*Eating, Meeting,
Skies, Transience*

**de Leon, Walter
and Jones, Paul M.**
Life

Delius, Frederick
Music

Della Femina, Jerry
Advertising

de Mille, Agnes
Dance

Demosthenes
Speechmaking

Dempsey, Jack
Boxing

Deneuve, Catherine
Men, Photography

Deng Xiaoping
Practicality

Dennis, John
Words

**De Quincey,
Thomas**
Drugs, Murder

Descartes, René
*Mind, Practicality,
Thinking*

**Destouches,
Philippe Néricault**
Absence

De Vries, Peter
Eating

Dewar, James
Prejudice

Dewar, Lord
Cars

Diamond, John
Health

**Diana, Princess of
Wales**
Royalty

Dickens, Charles
*Babies,
Bureaucracy,
Business, Chance,
Christmas, Class,
Education, Food,
Knowledge, Law,
Letters, Love,
Money, Optimism,
Pride, Protest,
Supernatural,
Weather*

Dickinson, Emily
Parting, Writing

**Diefenbaker, John
G.**
Old Age

**Dillon, Wentworth,
Earl of Roscommon**
Reading

DiMaggio, Joe
Baseball

Dinesen, Isak
Human Race

Diogenes
Cynicism

Index of Authors

Dionysius of Halicarnassus
History

Dirac, Paul
Science

Disraeli, Benjamin
Apology, Careers, Change, Democracy, Education, Experience, Government, Human Race, Justice, Lies, Peace, Politics, Progress, Royalty, Statistics, Success

Donleavy, J. P.
Discontent

Donne, John
Animals, Death, Imagination, Letters, Love, Prayer, Sex, Skies, Society

Dostoevsky, Fedor
Beauty

Douglas, Lord Alfred
Love

Douglas, Keith
Misfortune

Douglas, O.
Letters, Quotations

Douglass, Frederick
Human Rights, Race, Singing

Dowson, Ernest
Memory

Doyle, Arthur Conan
Country, Crime, Genius, Imagination, Intelligence, Libraries, Thinking, Truth

Drake, Francis
Achievement, Sport

Drayton, Michael
Journalism, Parting

Drucker, Peter F.
Pollution

Dryden, John
Anger, Discontent, Exercise, Genius, Happiness, Love, Men, Mistakes, Secrecy, Women, Writing

Du Bellay, Joachim
France

Dubos, René
Prejudice

Du Deffand, Mme
Achievement

Dumas, Alexandre
Cooperation

Dumas, Alexandre
Marriage

Dumouriez, General
Experience

Duncan, Ronald
Animals

Duport, James
Madness

Duras, Marguerite
Fear

Durocher, Leo
Sport

Durrell, Lawrence
Church

Dürrenmatt, Friedrich
Thinking

Dury, Ian
Body

Dworkin, Andrea
Birth

Dylan, Bob
Failure, Generation

Gap, Heroes, Money, Singing

Earhart, Amelia
Courage, Flight, Luck

Eastman, George
Photography

Eddington, Arthur
Chance, Science, Time

Edison, Thomas Alva
Genius

Edmund, St of Abingdon
Education

Edward VIII
Royalty

Edwards, John
Management

Edwards, Jonathan
Death

Ehrenreich, Barbara
Exercise

Ehrmann, Max
Peace

Einstein, Albert
Chance, Future, God, Intelligence, Mathematics, Practicality, Prejudice, Religion, Science, Success, Time, Universe, War

Eisenhower, Dwight D.
Army, Peace, Planning, Presidency

Eisenstaedt, Alfred
Photography

Elgar, Edward
Art, Music

Index of Authors

Eliot, George
Despair, Discontent, Elections, Gifts, Gossip, Humour, Lovers, Mothers, Pride, Silence, Sorrow, Women

Eliot, T. S.
Beginning, Cats, Death, Ending, Experience, Fear, Forgiveness, Hell, Knowledge, Morality, Old Age, Poetry, Pollution, Reality, Spring, Success, Time, Words

Elizabeth I
Forgiveness, Government, Royalty, Secrecy, Trust

Elizabeth II
France, Misfortune, Royalty, Sorrow

Elizabeth, Queen, the Queen Mother
Sorrow

Ellis, Alice Thomas
Character, Family

Ellis, Havelock
Pollution

Elton, Ben
Leadership

Elyot, Thomas
Football

Emerson, Ralph Waldo
Ability, Achievement, Ambition, Babies, Biography, Danger, Education, Flowers, Friendship, Gardens, Greatness, Heroes, Honour,

Hospitality, Justice, Language, Languages, Quotations

Empson, William
Literature

Engels, Friedrich see Marx, Karl and Engels, Friedrich

Ephron, Nora
Sex

Epicurus
Death

Epstein, Julius J. et al.
Friendship, Lovers, Meeting

Erhard, Ludwig
Europe

Ertz, Susan
Boredom

Essex, Robert Devereux, 2nd Earl of
Thinking

Estienne, Henri
Generation Gap

Eubank, Chris
Housework

Euclid
Mathematics

Eulalia, Infanta of Spain
Royalty

Euripides
Fate, Hypocrisy, Knowledge, Marriage

Fadiman, Clifton
Food

Faisal
Speechmaking

Falkland, Lucius Cary, Viscount
Change

Faraday, Michael
Invention, Truth

Farquhar, George
Poverty

Faulkner, William
Drink, Writing

Fawkes, Guy
Revolution

Fenton, James
Quotations

Ferdinand I, Emperor
Justice

Fermi, Enrico
Ignorance

Feynman, Richard Phillips
Technology

Field, Frank
Certainty

Fielding, Henry
Envy, Gossip, Thanks

Fields, Dorothy
Determination, Optimism

Fields, W. C.
Elections, Foolishness, Humour

Firth, Colin
Names

Fish, Michael
Weather

Fisher, John Arbuthnot
Travel

Fitzgerald, Edward
Day, Drink, Flowers, Past, Present, Satisfaction

Fitzgerald, F. Scott
Despair, Intelligence, Middle Age, Wealth

Index of Authors

Fitzsimmons, Robert
Boxing

Flaubert, Gustave
Art, Enemies, Parting, Poetry, Speechmaking, Style

Flecker, James Elroy
Knowledge

Fleming, Ian
Chance

Fletcher, Andrew of Saltoun
Singing

Florian, Jean-Pierre Claris de
Love

Foley, J.
Army

Forbes, Miss C. F.
Clothes

Ford, Gerald
Government

Ford, Henry
Choice, Evil, Exercise, History

Forgy, Howell
Practicality

Forster, E. M.
Creativity, Criticism, Cynicism, Death, Democracy, Gossip, Literature, Luck, Manners, Patriotism, Railways, Writing

Forsyth, Frederick
Memory

Foster, Charles
United States

Fotheringham, Allan
Canada

Fox, Charles James
Revolution

Fox, Michael J.
Sickness

Fox, Theodore
Medicine

France, Anatole
Government, Lies, Prejudice, Wealth

Francis, St of Assisi
Sympathy

Frank, Anne
Diaries

Franklin, Benjamin
Advice, Business, Cooperation, Hope, Human Race, Invention, Taxes, War

Fraser, Dawn
Sport

Frederick the Great
Government, Prejudice

Freeman, E. A.
History

French, Marilyn
Family, Housework, Sickness

Freud, Sigmund
Body, Dreams, Life, United States, Women

Friedan, Betty
Woman's Role

Friedman, Milton
Economics

Frisch, Max
Technology

Frost, David
Parents

Frost, Robert
Birthdays, Careers, Change, Choice, Determination,

Happiness, Home, Poetry, Politics, Secrecy

Fry, Christopher
Goodness

Fry, Elizabeth
Punishment

Fuller, John
Lovers

Fuller, R. Buckminster
Earth

Fuller, Thomas
Architecture, Sea

Fuller, Thomas
Gardens, Luck, Wealth

Fyleman, Rose
Supernatural

Gabor, Zsa Zsa
Hatred, Sex

Gaitskell, Hugh
Country, Europe

Galbraith, J. K.
Crises, Economics, Mistakes, Mountains, Politics, Satisfaction, Wealth

Galen
Words

Galileo Galilei
Mathematics, Skies

Gallagher, Noel
Drugs

Galloway, George
Protest

Galsworthy, John
Beauty

Galt, John
Scotland

Gandhi, Mahatma
Civilization, Country

Garbo, Greta
Solitude

Index of Authors

Gardiner, Richard
  Gardens
Gardner, Ed
  Singing
Garrick, David
  Cookery
Garrick, David see
Colman, George, the
Elder and Garrick,
David
Gaskell, Elizabeth
  Men, Thinking
Gauguin, Paul
  Art
Gay, John
  *Choice, Deceit,
  Marriage*
Geddes, Eric
  Revenge
Geldof, Bob
  Health, Race
Genet, Jean
  Trust
George II
  Madness
George V
  Patriotism
George VI
  Diplomacy
George, Eddie
  Retirement
Gershwin, Ira see
Heyward, Du Bose
and Gershwin, Ira
Gervais, Ricky and
Merchant, Stephen
  Management
Gesta Romanorum
  Lifestyles
Getty, J. Paul
  Business, Wealth
Gibbon, Edward
  *Country, History,
  Languages, London,
  Punishment,*

*Religion, Sympathy,
Taxes*
Gibran, Kahlil
  *Marriage, Parents,
  Truth, Work*
Gide, André
  Love
Gigli, Beniamino
  Retirement
Gilbert, W. S.
  *Certainty, Elections,
  Equality, Language,
  Meaning, Men,
  Pride, Punishment,
  Railways, Sleep*
Gill, A. A.
  Hospitality
Gill, Eric
  Work
**Gilman, Charlotte
Perkins**
  Housework
Giovanni, Nikki
  Mistakes
**Giraldus
Cambrensis**
  Wales
Giraudoux, Jean
  Law, Poetry
Giuliani, Rudolph
  Suffering
Gladstone, W. E.
  *Crises, Democracy,
  Economics, Future,
  Government*
Gloucester, Duke of
  Books
Godard, Jean-Luc
  Cinema
Godwin, William
  Crises
Goebbels, Joseph
  Protest, War
Goering, Hermann
  Race, War

**Goethe, Johann
Wolfgang von**
  *Art, Character,
  Discontent, Effort,
  Fame, Lifestyles,
  Love, Mathematics,
  Old Age, Reality,
  Self-Knowledge,
  Supernatural*
Goldbeck, Willis
and **Bellah, James
Warner**
  Journalism
Golding, William
  Sleep
Goldsmith, Oliver
  Law, Life, Marriage
Goldwater, Barry
  Moderation
Goldwyn, Sam
  *Certainty,
  Cinema, Law*
Gorky, Maxim
  Art
Gould, Stephen Jay
  Greatness
Goya
  Dreams
Grace, W. G.
  Cricket
Graham, D. M.
  Patriotism
Graham, Martha
  Dance
Grahame, Kenneth
  Boats, Cars
Grant, Ulysses S.
  Law
Grass, Günter
  Protest
Graves, Robert
  Weather
Gray, John Chipman
  Housework

Index of Authors

Gray, Thomas
Children, Fame, Ignorance, Night, Suffering

Greeley, Horace
United States

Green, Adolph *see* Comden, Betty and Green, Adolph

Greene, Graham
Goodness, Happiness, Indifference, Lies, Reading, Sorrow, Success

Greene, Robert
Time

Greer, Germaine
Football, Good Looks, Men and Women, Woman's Role, Women

Gregg, Hubert
London

Gregory, Dick
Baseball

Grellet, Stephen
Goodness

Grey, Lord of Fallodon
Civilization

Griffith-Jones, Mervyn
Censorship

Grocott, Bruce
Work

Grossmith, George and Grossmith, Weedon
Home, Misfortune

Grossmith, Weedon *see* Grossmith, George and Grossmith, Weedon

Grove, Andrew
Business, Technology

Guest, Edgar A.
Houses

Gurney, Dorothy Frances
Gardens

Haddon, Mark
Mathematics

Hakuin
Cooperation

Haldane, J. B. S.
Life Sciences, Mathematics, Sickness, Statistics, Universe

Haldeman, H. R.
Secrecy

Hale, Edward Everett
Politicians

Hale, Nathan
Patriotism

Halifax, George Savile, Marquess of
Punishment

Halifax, Lord
Anger

Hall, Jerry
Woman's Role

Hamilton, Alex
Character

Hamilton, William
Mind

Hammerstein II, Oscar
Hope, Meeting, Music, Summer

Hand, Learned
Names

Hansberry, Lorraine
Race

Harbach, Otto
Sorrow

Harburg, E. Y.
Medicine, Sickness

Hardy, Godfrey Harold
Mathematics

Hardy, Thomas
Appearance, History, Luck, Pessimism, Words, Writing

Hare, Maurice Evan
Fate

Harington, John
Trust

Harlech, Lord
Britain

Harman, Lord Justice
Business

Harris, Joel Chandler
Luck

Harris, Rolf
Retirement

Harris, Thomas and Tally, Ted
Eating

Harrison, Tony
Lovers

Hart, Lorenz
Behaviour, Lovers

Harte, Bret
Luck

Hartley, L. P.
Past

Haskins, Minnie Louise
Trust

Index of Authors

Hattersley, Roy
  Football, Politicians
Havel, Václav
  Hope, Nature,
  Protest, Truth
Hawking, Stephen
  Mathematics,
  Universe
Hay, Ian
  Humour, War
Hazlitt, William
  Country, Hatred,
  Manners, Names,
  Prejudice
Head, Bessie
  Race
Heaney, Seamus
  Ireland
Hearst, William
Randolph
  Journalism
Hegel, G. W. F.
  Philosophy, Reality,
  Society
Heine, Heinrich
  Censorship
Heisenberg,
Werner
  Mistakes
Heller, Joseph
  Madness, Peace
Hellman, Lillian
  Conscience,
  Cynicism
Helmsley, Leona
  Taxes
Héloïse
  Lovers
Helvétius
  Prejudice
Hemingway, Ernest
  Courage, Sex,
  Writing
Henley, W. E.
  Determination, Self

Henri IV
  Cynicism, Poverty
Henry, O.
  Deceit
Henry, Patrick
  Liberty
Hepworth, Barbara
  Drawing, Sculpture
Heraclitus
  Change, Character
Herbert, A. P.
  Country, Marriage
Herbert, George
  Hope, Secrecy
Herman, Henry *see*
Jones, Henry Arthur
and Herman, Henry
Herodotus
  Custom
Herrick, Robert
  Clothes, Marriage,
  Transience
Hervey, Lord
  Lies
Hesiod
  Effort
Hesse, Hermann
  Hatred
Heston, Charlton
  Apology
Hewart, Lord
  Justice
Hewitt, C. W.
  Cars
Heyward, Du Bose
and **Gershwin, Ira**
  Summer
Hicks, J. R.
  Business
Hicks, Seymour
  Old Age
Hightower, Jim
  Moderation
Hill, Aaron
  Courage

Hill, Damon
  Winning
Hill, Joe
  Revolution
Hillary, Edmund
  Mountains
Hillel 'The Elder'
  Self
Hillingdon, Lady
  Sex
Hilton, James
  Old Age
Hippocrates
  Art, Medicine
Hippocrates
  Manners, Medicine
Hirst, Damien
  Sculpture
Hitchcock, Alfred
  Acting, Cinema,
  Fear, Television
Hitler, Adolf
  Leadership, Lies
Hobbes, Thomas
  Life, Opinion,
  Truth
Hockney, David
  Criticism, Painting,
  Technology
Hodgkin, Howard
  Painting
Hodgson, Ralph
  Animals, Time
Hogben, Lancelot
  Technology
Holiday, Billie
  Drugs
Holland, Henry
Scott
  Death
Holmes, John H.
  Universe

Index of Authors

Holmes, Oliver Wendell
Conversation, Festivals

Home, Lord
Fishing

Homer
Death, Gifts, Transience

Hood, Thomas
Poverty, Winter

Hope, A. D.
Australia

Hope, Anthony
Children

Hope, Bob
Birthdays, Golf, Money

Hopkins, Gerard Manley
Beauty, Birds, Despair, Environment, Mind, Pollution, Prayer, Silence, Skies

Horace
Anger, Birthdays, Brevity, Crises, Death, Effort, Fame, Foolishness, Hope, Hospitality, Literature, Mistakes, Moderation, Money, Nature, Patriotism, Poetry, Present, Statistics, Words

Hornby, Nick
Cynicism, Fathers, Football

Horne, Donald Richmond
Australia

Housman, A. E.
Drink, Nature,

Past, Prejudice, Spring

Howells, William Dean
Hospitality

Hoyle, Fred
Universe

Hubbard, Elbert
Genius, Life, Technology

Hubbard, Frank McKinney ('Kin')
Revenge

Hughes, Sarah
Sport

Hughes, Thomas
Cricket

Hugo, Victor
France, Ideas, Suffering

Hull, Josephine
Theatre

Hume, Basil
Prayer

Hume, David
Beauty, Custom, Religion, Self

Hunt, G. W.
Patriotism

Hurd, Douglas
Idleness

Huxley, Aldous
Achievement, Apology, Change, Criticism, Education, Experience, Happiness, Manners

Huxley, Julian
God

Huxley, T. H.
Doubt, Science, Thinking, Truth

Hytner, Nicholas
Cinema

Ibarruri, Dolores
Liberty

Ibsen, Henrik
Clothes

Ice Cube
Fathers

Illich, Ivan
Society

Inge, Charles
Ability

Inge, Dean
Argument, Liberty, Power

Ingersoll, Robert G.
God

Ingham, Bernard
Government

Ingres, J. A. D.
Drawing

Irving, John
Memory

Irving, Washington
Conversation

Isaacson, Walter
Computers

Isherwood, Christopher
Writing

Issigonis, Alec
Management

Jackson, Jesse
Race

Jackson, Mahalia
Poverty

Jackson, Michael
Fathers

Jackson, Thomas Jonathan 'Stonewall'
War

Jacobs, Joe
Boxing

Jagger, Mick and Richards, Keith
Protest

Index of Authors

Jalal ad-Din ar-Rumi
Religion

James, Carwyn
Revenge

James, Clive
Television

James, Evan
Wales

James, Henry
Criticism, Day, Lifestyles, Literature

James, William
Lies, Success

Jarrell, Randall
Manners

Jean-Baptiste, Marianne
Britain

Jeans, James
Life Sciences, Science, Universe

Jefferson, Thomas
Anger, Civilization, Exercise, Gardens, Liberty, Morality, Politicians, Politics, Revolution

Jeffrey, Francis, Lord
Criticism

Jennings, Elizabeth
Animals

Jerome, Jerome K.
Idleness, Medicine, Work

Jerome, William
Home

Joad, C. E. M.
Meaning

John, Elton and Taupin, Bernie
Gifts

John Paul II, Pope
Church

Johnson, Amy
Flight

Johnson, Boris
Cars

Johnson, Lyndon Baines
Enemies, Intelligence

Johnson, Martin
Sport

Johnson, Philander Chase
Optimism

Johnson, Samuel
Achievement, Advertising, Behaviour, Biography, Careers, Change, Conversation, Criticism, Death, Effort, Equality, Evil, Fishing, Food, Friendship, Genius, Ignorance, Imagination, Intelligence, Justice, Knowledge, Language, Languages, Libraries, Lifestyles, London, Marriage, Music, Opinion, Patriotism, Philosophy, Poetry, Poverty, Praise, Reading, Scotland, Sea, Sex, Solitude, Sorrow, Supernatural, Taxes, Travel, Trust, Truth, War, Wealth, Weather, Woman's Role, Words, Writing

John XXIII, Pope
Church

Johst, Hanns
Civilization

Jolson, Al
Singing

Jones, Henry Arthur and Herman, Henry
Past

Jones, Paul M. *see de Leon, Walter and Jones, Paul M.*

Jones, Steve
Chance

Jonson, Ben
Lies, Religion

Joseph, Jenny
Idleness, Old Age

Jowett, Benjamin
Lies

Joyce, James
Ireland

Julian of Norwich
Optimism

Jung, Carl Gustav
Belief, Children, Cruelty, Drugs, Heart, Life, Middle Age

Justice, Donald
Middle Age

Juvenal
Children, Conversation, Evil, Health, Pleasure, Poverty, Punishment, Sport, Trust, Truth

Kalmar, Bert et al.
Honour, Parting

Kant, Immanuel
Happiness, Human Race, Morality

Kapuscinski, Ryszard
Effort

Index of Authors

Karan, Donna
  Fashion
Karr, Alphonse
  Change,
  Punishment
Keane, Fergal
  Babies
Keating, Paul
  Australia
Keating, Ronan
  Fame
Keats, John
  Autumn, Beauty,
  Death, Discontent,
  Dreams,
  Imagination,
  Invention, Love,
  Names, Philosophy,
  Pleasure, Poetry,
  Silence, Weather
Keenan, Brian
  Liberty
Keillor, Garrison
  Christmas, Men
Keller, Helen
  Language,
  Literature
Kennedy, John F.
  Beginning,
  Cooperation,
  Diplomacy, Liberty,
  Patriotism,
  Race, Sea
Kennedy, Joseph P.
  Determination
Kennedy, Robert
  Protest
Kerr, Jean
  Flight, Good Looks
Kerry, John
  Army
**Keynes, John
Maynard**
  Examinations,
  Government, Time

Khrushchev, Nikita
  Satisfaction
Kiam, Victor
  Business
Kierkegaard, Sören
  Life
Kilmer, Joyce
  Creativity
Kilvert, Francis
  Mountains, Travel
**King, Benjamin
Franklin**
  Pessimism
**King, Martin
Luther**
  Cooperation,
  Equality, Idealism,
  Justice, Protest,
  Race
King, Stephen
  Fear, Retirement
**King, William Lyon
Mackenzie**
  Canada
Kingsley, Charles
  Goodness,
  Punishment
Kinnock, Neil
  Patriotism
Kinsey, Alfred
  Sex
Kipling, Rudyard
  Army, Art, Cats,
  Character, Crises,
  Dogs, England,
  Gardens,
  Journalism,
  Knowledge,
  Madness, Men and
  Women, Mothers,
  Opinion, Sex,
  Sickness, Solitude,
  Sport, Words
Kissinger, Henry
  Management,
  Power

Klee, Paul
  Drawing, Painting
**Klopstock,
Friedrich**
  Meaning
Knox, John
  Woman's Role
Knox, Ronald
  Babies, Opinion
Koestler, Arthur
  God, Writing
Kohl, Helmut
  Europe
Koran, The
  Goodness
Kraus, Karl
  Cars
Kronecker, Leopold
  Mathematics
**Krutch, Joseph
Wood**
  Cats, Winter
Kuan Tao-sheng
  Marriage
Kubrick, Stanley
  Politics
Kundera, Milan
  Intelligence
la Bruyère, Jean de
  Life
**Laclos, Pierre
Choderlos de**
  Happiness
Lacroix, Christian
  Fashion
Laforgue, Jules
  Life
Lahr, John
  Advertising
Laing, R. D.
  Madness
Lamb, Charles
  Anger, Belief, Debt,
  Gardens, Gifts,
  Humour, Libraries,

Index of Authors

Meeting, Pleasure, Time, Writing

Lamont, Norman
Economics, Government

Lampedusa, Giuseppe di
Change

Lance, Bert
Management

Lang, Andrew
Statistics

Lang, Julia
Beginning

Lao Tzu
Beginning, Law

Larkin, Philip
Birthdays, Books, Boredom, Day, Happiness, Life, London, Old Age, Parents, Pessimism, Work, Youth

la Rochefoucauld, Duc de
Absence, Home, Hypocrisy, Love, Mind, Misfortune

Latimer, Hugh
Determination

Laurier, Wilfrid
Canada

Lawrence, D. H.
Australia, Autumn, Behaviour, Literature, Sorrow, Writing

Lazarus, Emma
United States

Leacock, Stephen
Advertising

Leary, Timothy
Computers, Lifestyles

Lebowitz, Fran
Conversation, Fame, Women

Lec, Stanislaw
Censorship, Progress

Le Corbusier
Houses, Town

Lee, Nathaniel
Madness

Lee, Robert E.
War

Lehrer, Tom
Achievement, Life, Words

Lenin
Liberty, Politics, Progress, Technology

Lennon, John
Fame, Happiness, Wealth

Lennon, John and McCartney, Paul
Friendship, Lovers, Money, Old Age, Past, Peace, Solitude

Leonardo da Vinci
Life, Nature

Lerner, Alan Jay
Charm, Flowers, Men, Temptation, Weddings

Lespinasse, Julie de
Lovers

Lessing, Doris
Cats, Charm

Lessing, G. E.
Prayer

Leverhulme, Lord
Advertising

Levi, Primo
Cruelty

Levin, Bernard
Bureaucracy

Lévis, Duc de
Government

Lewis, Carl
Sport

Lewis, C. S.
Bereavement, Courage, Forgiveness, Future, Prayer, Sorrow, Temptation, Women

Lewis, Sinclair
Literature

Liberace
Criticism

Lichtenberg, Georg Christoph
Journalism

Lincoln, Abraham
Change, Criticism, Deceit, Democracy, Determination, Elections, Good Looks, Planning

Lindbergh, Charles
Flight

Lin Yutang
Travel

Lippmann, Walter
Leadership

Lively, Penelope
Languages

Livingstone, Ken
Economics, Elections, Politics

Livy
Failure

Lloyd George, David
Britain, Politics, Speechmaking

Locke, John
Mistakes, Opinion, Truth

Lodge, David
Children

Index of Authors

Long, H. Kingsley
see McArthur,
Alexander and Long,
H. Kingsley

**Longfellow, Henry
Wadsworth**
*Biography, Festivals,
God, Life, Night,
Solitude, Youth*

Longford, Lord
Old Age, Pride

Loos, Anita
Parting, Practicality

Lorenz, Edward N.
Chance

Louis, Joe
Boxing

Louis XIV
*Management,
Royalty*

Louis XVIII
Army, Manners

Lovelace, Ada
Computers

Lovelace, Richard
Honour, Liberty

Lovell, Bernard
Youth

**Lowell, James
Russell**
Work

Lowell, Robert
*Middle Age,
Pessimism*

Lowndes, William
Money

Lowry, Malcolm
Love

Luce, Clare Booth
Woman's Role

Lucretius
Creativity

**Lula da Silva, Luiz
Inácio**
Peace

Lurie, Alison
Life

Luther, Martin
God, Pleasure

Lutyens, Edwin
Mothers

Luxemburg, Rosa
Liberty

Lydgate, John
Words

Lyte, Henry Francis
Change

**McArthur,
Alexander and
Long, H. Kingsley**
Poverty

MacArthur, Ellen
Boats

Macaulay, Lord
*Imagination,
Liberty, Morality,
Pleasure,
Praise, War*

McCaig, Norman
Scotland

McCarthy, Cormac
Suffering

McCartney, Paul see
Lennon, John and
McCartney, Paul

McCormick, P. D.
Australia

**McCullough,
Colleen**
Middle Age

MacDiarmid, Hugh
Flowers

Macdonald, John A.
Misfortune

McEnroe, John
Tennis

McGinley, Phyllis
*Babies,
Conversation,
Generation Gap,*

Hospitality, Houses

**McGoohan, Patrick
et al.**
Self

McGough, Roger
Education, Flowers

McGregor, Jimmie
Football

**Machiavelli,
Niccolò**
*Government,
Revenge,
Satisfaction*

Maclaine, Shirley
Reality

**Maclaren,
Alexander**
Church

**MacLeish,
Archibald**
Poetry

McLuhan, Marshall
*Cars, Technology,
Television*

Macmillan, Harold
*Morality,
Politicians, Politics,
Power, Wealth*

MacNeice, Louis
*Birth, Marriage,
Music, Religion*

MacNeil, Robert
Words

Madan, Geoffrey
Belief

Madonna
Men

**Magee, John
Gillespie**
Flight

Magna Carta
Human Rights

Magritte, René
Mind

Index of Authors

Mahaffy, John Pentland
Ireland

Mahler, Gustav
Music

Mailer, Norman
Fashion, Heroes, Presidency

Major, John
Britain, Economics, Heart, Punishment

Malcolm X
Peace

Mallory, George Leigh
Mountains

Mancroft, Lord
Cricket

Mandela, Nelson
Diplomacy, Forgiveness, Hatred

Manikan, Ruby
Education

Mankiewicz, Joseph L.
Anxiety

Mann, Thomas
Bereavement, Conversation, Festivals

Mansfield, Katherine
Travel

Manzoni, Alessandro
Weddings

Mao Tse-tung
Politics, Power

Maradona, Diego
Football

Marie-Antoinette
Indifference

Marks, Leo
Lovers

Marlborough, Sarah, Duchess of
Sex

Marlowe, Christopher
Love, Religion

Marquis, Don
Misfortune, Optimism, Poetry

Marshall, Arthur
Life

Martial
Birthdays, Health, Lovers, Weddings

Martin, Dean
Drink

Marvell, Andrew
Gardens, Love, Time

Marvell, Holt
Memory

Marx, Groucho
Pride

Marx, Karl
Custom, History, Philosophy, Religion, Society

Marx, Karl and Engels, Friedrich
Class

Mary, Queen of Scots
Ending

Masefield, John
Boats, Sea

Massinger, Philip
Action

Mathew, James
Justice

Mathison, Melissa
Home

Matlovich, Leonard
Army

Matthews, Cerys
Wales

Maugham, W. Somerset
Food

Maugham, W. Somerset
Charity, Death, Hospitality, Love, Men and Women, Money, Morality, Mothers, Suffering, Women, Writing

Maurois, André
Old Age

Maxwell, James Clerk
Teaching

Mayakovsky, Vladimir
Poetry

Mayer, Louis B.
Cinema

Medici, Cosimo de'
Forgiveness

Melba, Nellie
Music

Melbourne, Lord
Art, Certainty, Education, Honours, Politicians, Religion

Melville, Herman
Censorship

Menander
Life, Youth

Mencken, H. L.
Conscience, Intelligence, Management, Men and Women

Menuhin, Yehudi
Babies

Menzies, Robert Gordon
Australia

Index of Authors

Mercer, Johnny
  Optimism
Merchant, Stephen
  see Gervais, Ricky and
  Merchant, Stephen
Meredith, George
  Certainty, Cookery
Meredith, Owen
  Genius
Merritt, Dixon Lanier
  Birds
Meynell, Viola
  Housework
Michelangelo
  Perfection,
  Sculpture
Mies van der Rohe, Ludwig
  Architecture
Mill, John Stuart
  Discontent,
  Happiness, Liberty
Millay, Edna St Vincent
  Bereavement
Miller, Arthur
  Business,
  Journalism
Miller, Jonathan
  Ability, Sickness
Milligan, Spike
  Money, Thinking
Milne, A. A.
  Birthdays,
  Christmas, Eating,
  Education, Ideas,
  Weather
Milton, John
  Action, Books,
  Change,
  Conversation,
  Dance, England,
  Evil, Fame, Heart,
  Hell, Hypocrisy,
  Men and Women,

Mind, Music,
  Opinion, Peace,
  Philosophy, Poetry,
  Skies, Sleep,
  Speechmaking,
  Sport, Violence,
  Writing
Mitchell, Adrian
  Poetry
Mitchell, Joni
  Life
Mitchell, Margaret
  Birth, Hope,
  Indifference
Mizner, Wilson
  Doubt, Practicality,
  Writing
Molière
  Criticism, Custom,
  Eating, Foolishness,
  Justice, Language,
  Medicine, Secrecy
Moltke, Helmuth von
  Planning
Montagu, Lady Mary Wortley
  Enemies
Montaigne
  Belief, Cats,
  Children,
  Housework, Ideas,
  Lifestyles, Love,
  Solitude
Montesquieu
  Birth, God, History,
  Success
Montessori, Maria
  Teaching
Montgomery, Field Marshal
  War
Moore, Clement C.
  Christmas
Moore, George
  Travel

Moore, Henry
  Sculpture
Moore, Marianne
  Ireland
Moore, Thomas
  Love, Memory
More, Sir Thomas
  Parting
Morgan, John Pierpont
  Law
Morris, Desmond
  Cruelty, Society
Morris, Estelle
  Examinations
Morris, William
  Houses, Wealth
Morrison, Toni
  Beauty, Choice,
  Old Age
Morrison, Van
  Music
Mortimer, John
  Ambition, Good
  Looks, Past, Sport
Mountbatten, Lord
  Bereavement
Mowlam, Mo
  Peace
Mozart, Wolfgang Amadeus
  Fathers, Music
Mugabe, Robert
  Cricket
Muggeridge, Malcolm
  Evil, Protest
Muir, Edwin
  Scotland
Muller, H. J.
  Human Race
Mumford, Lewis
  Generation Gap
Munch, Edvard
  Painting

Index of Authors

Murdoch, Iris
Flowers, Marriage, Mind

Murray, Les A.
Weddings

Muste, Rev. A. J.
Love

Nabokov, Vladimir
Railways, Reading

Napoleon I
Army, Courage, England, Europe, Failure, Past, Sex

Nash, Ogden
Cars, Cats, Children, Dogs, Drink, Family, Fathers, Festivals, Hospitality, Houses, Leisure, Middle Age, Parents, Youth

Navratilova, Martina
Tennis, Winning

Nehru, Jawaharlal
Temptation

Neill, A. S.
Examinations

Nelson, Horatio, Lord
England

Nemerov, Howard
Invention

Neruda, Pablo
Love

Nesbit, Edith
Children, Pleasure

Neumann, John von
Mathematics

Newbolt, Henry
Cricket, Sport

Newman, Cardinal
Belief

Newman, John Henry
Doubt

Newton, Isaac
Invention, Progress, Science

Nicholson, Vivian
Money

Nicolson, Harold
Diaries, Marriage

Niebuhr, Reinhold
Change

Niemöller, Martin
Cooperation

Nietzsche, Friedrich
Human Race, Humour, Lifestyles, Morality, Suffering, Women

Nightingale, Florence
Medicine

Nixon, Richard
Hatred, Presidency

Nobbs, David
Careers

Norris, Steven
Cars

North, Christopher
Law

Northcliffe, Lord
Censorship, Honours

Norton, Caroline
Death

Norworth, Jack
Baseball

Nyerere, Julius
Debt

Occam, William of
Philosophy

Ochs, Adolph S.
Journalism

Ogilvy, David
Advertising

O'Kelly, Dennis
Sport

Okpik, Abraham
Race

Oldfield, Bruce
Fashion

Olivier, Laurence
Acting

Omar, Caliph
Censorship

Onassis, Jacqueline Kennedy
Parents

Ondaatje, Michael
Heart

O'Neill, Eugene
Crime, Sea

Ono, Yoko
Women

Oppenheimer, J. Robert
Invention, Science, Technology

O'Rourke, P. J.
Debt

Ortega y Gasset, José
Environment

Orwell, George
Advertising, Appearance, Argument, Body, Censorship, Class, Equality, Future, Government, Liberty, Politics, Power, Prejudice, Sport, Thinking, War

Osborne, Dorothy
Letters

Osborne, John
Royalty, Women

Osler, Mirabel
Gardens

Index of Authors

Osler, William
Medicine, Sickness

O'Sullivan, John L.
Government

Otis, James
Taxes

O'Toole, Peter
Exercise

Ovid
Character,
Moderation,
Religion, Time

Owen, Wilfred
Army, Poetry, War

Paderewski, Ignacy Jan
Music

Paglia, Camille
Civilization,
Television

Paige, Leroy ('Satchel')
Exercise

Paine, Thomas
Belief, Patriotism,
Religion

Paley, William
Argument

Palmerston, Lord
Death, Meeting

Pankhurst, Emmeline
Argument

Papp, Laszlo
Boxing

Parker, Charlie
Music

Parker, Dorothy
Acting, Appearance,
Birth, Death, Gifts

Parker, Ross and Charles, Hugh
England, Meeting

Parkes, Henry
Australia

Parkinson, C. Northcote
Bureaucracy,
Management,
Money, Work

Parks, Rosa
Race

Parnell, Charles Stewart
Advice

Parsons, Tony
Poverty

Parton, Dolly
Appearance

Pascal, Blaise
Appearance,
Brevity, Death,
Heart, Human
Race, Self, Skies,
Style, Writing

Pasternak, Boris
Life, Spring

Pasteur, Louis
Science

Paterson, Craig
Presidency

Patton, George S.
Army, Planning

Pauli, Wolfgang
Thinking

Pavese, Cesare
Boredom

Payn, James
Misfortune

Payne, J. H.
Home

Peacock, Thomas Love
Humour, Marriage

Peake, Mervyn
Lifestyles

Pearson, Hesketh
Honours

Péguy, Charles
Liberty

Pelé
Football

Pembroke, Lord
Government

Pepys, Samuel
Punishment, Sleep

Peres, Shimon
Television

Pericles
Bereavement, Fame,
Women

Persons, Ted
Past

Pétain, Marshal
Biography

Peter, Laurence
Management

Petrarch
Love

Petronius
Death, Sex

Phelps, Edward John
Mistakes

Philby, Kim
Trust

Philip, Prince
Cookery,
Marriage, Sea

Picasso, Pablo
Drawing, Genius,
Painting

Pirsig, Robert M.
God, Mind

Pitt, William
Environment, Youth

Pitt, William
Europe

Pius VII, Pope
Diplomacy

Pius XII, Pope
Mistakes

Planck, Max
Science

Index of Authors

Plath, Sylvia
Bereavement, Birth,
Madness,
Perfection, Women

Plato
Justice,
Mathematics,
Religion

Pliny the Elder
Books, Invention,
Nature

Poincaré, Henri
Science

**Pompadour,
Madame de**
Revolution

Pompidou, Georges
Politicians

Pope, Alexander
Bereavement,
Brevity, Charity,
Children,
Conversation, Dogs,
Education,
Environment,
Foolishness,
Forgiveness,
Goodness,
Government,
Happiness, Heart,
Hope, Hospitality,
Human Race,
Intelligence,
Knowledge,
Mistakes, Opinion,
Praise, Reading,
Retirement, Science,
Self, Self-
Knowledge, Style,
Teaching, Writing

Popper, Karl
Prejudice

Porter, Cole
Country, Love,
Trust

Porter, Roy
Medicine

Portillo, Michael
Careers

Potter, Beatrix
Food

Potter, Dennis
Flight, Present,
Religion

Pound, Ezra
Literature, Middle
Age, Music, Winter

Poussin, Nicolas
Painting

Powell, Anthony
Character, Names,
Old Age

Powell, Enoch
Politicians

Pratchett, Terry
Advice,
Conversation, Self,
Truth

Priestley, J. B.
Class, Family,
Football, Weather

Prior, Matthew
Sickness

Pritchett, V. S.
Books

Protagoras
Human Race

Proust, Marcel
Day, Heaven,
Memory

Proverb
Absence,
Advertising, Ending,
Enemies, Exercise,
Health, Weddings

Publilius Syrus
Charity, Good
Looks

Pulitzer, Joseph
Journalism

Punch
Behaviour, Choice,

Diplomacy

Puzo, Mario
Choice, Law

Quant, Mary
Wealth, Youth

Quarles, Francis
Work

**Quiller-Couch,
Arthur**
Perfection

Rabelais, François
Children, Eating,
Knowledge,
Lifestyles

Rabin, Yitzhak
Peace

Racine, Jean
Women

**Rainborowe,
Thomas**
Human Rights

Ralegh, Walter
Ambition, Time

Raleigh, Walter
Examinations,
Quotations

Randi, James
Supernatural

Rantzen, Esther
Family

Raphael, Frederic
Town

Ratner, Gerald
Business

Raymond, Derek
Madness

Rayner, Claire
Happiness, Mothers

Reade, Charles
Habit

Reagan, Ronald
Character,
Leadership,
Management,
Sickness, Work

Index of Authors

Reger, Max
Criticism

Reith, Lord
*Prejudice,
Television, Thinking*

**Rendall, Montague
John**
Television

Renoir, Jean
Letters

Retz, Cardinal de
*Management, Self-
Knowledge*

Reynolds, Joshua
Work

Rhodes, Cecil
*Achievement,
England*

Rice, Grantland
Sport

Rice-Davies, Mandy
Lies

Richards, Keith
Drugs

Richards, Keith *see*
Jagger, Mick and
Richards, Keith

Richardson, Joely
Failure

Richardson, Ralph
Acting

Richter, Jean Paul
Birthdays

Rilke, Rainer Maria
Fate, Love

Ritz, César
Business

Rivarol, Antoine de
France

**Robespierre,
Maximilien**
Human Rights

Robin, Leo
Wealth

Robinson, Jancis
Drink

**Rochester, John
Wilmot, Earl of**
Courage

Roddick, Anita
*Appearance,
Business*

Rogers, Richard
Architecture

Rogers, Samuel
*Action, Marriage,
Solitude*

Rogers, Will
*Civilization, Heroes,
Humour, Ignorance,
Taxes, Time*

Roland, Mme
Liberty

**Rolle, Richard de
Hampole**
Class

Roosevelt, Eleanor
Behaviour, Pride

**Roosevelt, Franklin
D.**
*Economics, Fear,
Human Rights*

**Roosevelt,
Theodore**
*Army, Diplomacy,
Fathers, Journalism,
Presidency, United
States*

Rootes, Lord
Cars

Ross, Eric
Life

Rossetti, Christina
Memory

Rostand, Jean
*Life Sciences,
Murder*

Rosten, Leo
Children

Roth, Philip
Parents

**Rothschild,
Philippe de**
Dogs

Rotten, Johnny
Sex

Roupell, Charles
Sport

**Rousseau, Jean-
Jacques**
Liberty

Rowland, Helen
Foolishness, Men

Rowling, J. K.
*Ability, Morality,
Poverty*

Royden, Maude
Church

Rumbold, Richard
Democracy

Rumsfeld, Donald
*Advice, Criticism,
Europe, Ignorance,
Knowledge*

Runcie, Robert
Religion, Travel

Runyon, Damon
Money

Rushdie, Salman
Absence, Liberty

Rusk, Dean
Crises

Ruskin, John
*Beauty,
Cooperation,
Ignorance, Painting,
Work*

Russell, Bertrand
*Belief, Boredom,
Censorship, Cruelty,
Fathers, Leisure,
Mathematics,
Opinion, Progress,
Science, Work*

Index of Authors

Russell, William Howard
Army

Rutherford, Ernest
Science, Statistics

Ryan, Alan
Statistics

Sacks, Jonathan
Television

Sadi
Science

Sagan, Carl
Earth, Invention, Universe

Sagan, Françoise
Envy

Saint-Exupéry, Antoine de
Children, Fear, Love, Perfection

Saki
Clothes, Cookery, Leadership, Politicians

Salisbury, Lord
Charity, Elections

Sallust
Friendship

Samuel, Lord
Libraries

Sandburg, Carl
Babies, Language, Past, War, Weather

Sanders, Henry 'Red'
Sport

Santayana, George
Past

Sargent, John Singer
Painting

Sartre, Jean-Paul
Despair, Habit, Hell, Liberty, Time

Saunders, Cicely
Death

Sayers, Dorothy L.
Men and Women, Quotations

Scalpone, Al
Prayer

Scanlon, Hugh
Liberty

Schelling, Friedrich von
Architecture

Schiller, Friedrich von
Happiness, Intelligence

Schlesinger, Arthur M. Jr.
Presidency

Schnabel, Artur
Music

Schulberg, Budd
Ability

Schumacher, E. F.
Economics, Environment

Schumpeter, Joseph Alois
Technology

Schurz, Carl
Patriotism

Schwitters, Kurt
Painting

Scott, C. P.
Journalism

Scott, Robert Falcon
Experience

Scott, Sir Walter
Chance, Deceit, Indifference, Patriotism, Scotland, Style, Women

Scott-Maxwell, Florida
Parents

Searle, Ronald *see* Willans, Geoffrey and Searle, Ronald

Seeger, Pete
Experience

Segal, Erich
Love

Seinfeld, Jerry
Achievement

Sei Shōnagon
Enemies

Selden, John
Law, Pleasure, Words

Sellar, W. C. and Yeatman, R. J.
Examinations, History, Teaching

Seneca ('the Younger')
Death, Ignorance, Sorrow, Teaching

Service, Robert W.
Time

Sexton, Anne
Fathers, Old Age

Shackleton, Ernest
Effort

Shaftesbury, Lord
Religion

Shaftesbury, Lord
Thinking

Shakespeare, William
Acting, Action, Ambition, Anxiety, Appearance, Army, Bereavement, Careers, Chance, Character, Charity, Children, Choice, Clothes, Conscience, Conversation,

Index of Authors

Shakespeare, William (cont.)
  Courage, Cruelty, Custom, Danger, Day, Death, Debt, Determination, Diplomacy, Doubt, Dreams, Eating, Education, Effort, Ending, England, Envy, Equality, Evil, Failure, Fame, Family, Fate, Fathers, Fear, Flowers, Food, Friendship, Future, Generation Gap, Gifts, Goodness, Greatness, Heart, Honour, Hospitality, Human Race, Humour, Hypocrisy, Imagination, Indifference, Journalism, Justice, Language, Law, Leisure, Libraries, Life, Love, Lovers, Madness, Manners, Marriage, Meaning, Medicine, Meeting, Memory, Men, Misfortune, Moderation, Money, Morality, Murder, Music, Names, Nature, Old Age, Parting, Past, Peace, Perfection, Pollution, Praise, Prayer, Present, Reading, Royalty, Satisfaction, Scotland, Sea, Self, Self-Knowledge, Sex, Sickness, Skies, Sleep, Sorrow, Speechmaking, Suffering, Supernatural, Sympathy, Temptation, Tennis, Thanks, Thinking, Time, Universe, Wales, War, Weather, Women, Work, Writing, Youth

Shankly, Bill
  Football

Shaw, George Bernard
  Army, Art, Beauty, Choice, Cinema, Dance, Democracy, Determination, Drink, England, Fame, Forgiveness, Generation Gap, Goodness, Happiness, Hell, Honours, Ideas, Imagination, Indifference, Languages, Liberty, Life, Love, Marriage, Men and Women, Music, Parents, Patriotism, Photography, Poverty, Progress, Satisfaction, Self, Sickness, Teaching, Violence, Women

Shelley, Percy Bysshe
  Autumn, Dreams, Hell, Hope, Poetry, Royalty, Winter

Sheppard, Dick
  Sympathy

Sheridan, Philip Henry
  Prejudice

Sheridan, Richard Brinsley
  Acting, Manners, Speechmaking, Women

Sherman, General
  War

Shute, Nevil
  Technology

Sibelius, Jean
  Criticism

Sidney, Philip
  Charity, France, Humour, Poetry

Sieyès, Abbé Emmanuel Joseph
  Revolution

Signoret, Simone
  Marriage

Simenon, Georges
  Writing

Simon, Paul
  Silence, Sympathy

Simpson, N. F.
  Management

Sinatra, Frank
  Lifestyles

Skinner, B. F.
  Education, Thinking

Smart, Christopher
  Cats

Smiles, Samuel
  Eating, Management

Smith, Adam
  Business, Taxes, Wealth

Smith, Delia
  Food, Football

Smith, F. E.
  Ambition

Smith, Godfrey
  Words

Index of Authors

Smith, Iain Duncan
Determination

Smith, Logan Pearsall
Careers, Fashion, Hypocrisy, Reading

Smith, Stevie
Creativity, Death, Indifference, Past

Smith, Sydney
Books, Country, Criticism, Death, Food, Heaven, Houses, Lifestyles, Marriage, Mathematics, Poverty, Prayer, Protest

Socrates
Knowledge, Philosophy, Truth, Wealth

Solon
Happiness

Solzhenitsyn, Alexander
Censorship, Power, Work

Sondheim, Stephen
United States

Sontag, Susan
Reality

Soper, Donald
Church

Sophocles
Human Race, Life, Sex

Spark, Muriel
Middle Age, Teaching

Sparrow, John
Dogs

Spencer, Herbert
Crime, Foolishness, Perfection

Spencer, Lord
Honours

Spencer, Stanley
Painting

Spielberg, Steven
Past

Spock, Benjamin
Babies

Spring-Rice, Cecil
Patriotism

Springsteen, Bruce
Success

Spurgeon, C. H.
Lies

Squire, J. C.
Drink, Science

Staël, Mme de
Behaviour

Stalin, Joseph
Class, Death, Power

Stanley, Henry Morton
Meeting

Stark, Freya
Women

Steele, Richard
Letters, Reading, Wealth

Steffens, Lincoln
Revolution

Stein, Gertrude
Literature, Self

Steinbeck, John
Greatness, Lifestyles

Steinem, Gloria
Men and Women, Women

Steiner, George
Morality

Steiner, Peter
Computers

Stendhal
Literature

Stengel, Casey
Baseball

Stephens, James
Perfection

Sterne, Laurence
Determination, France, Ideas

Stevens, Anthony
Men and Women

Stevens, Wallace
Imagination, Music, Reality

Stevenson, Adlai
Liberty, Praise, Speechmaking

Stevenson, Robert Louis
Brevity, Eating, Food, Lies, Marriage, Sleep, Travel

Stewart, Ian
Life Sciences

Stewart, Martha
Cookery

Sting
Environment, Pride

Stone, Oliver *see* Weiser, Stanley and Stone, Oliver

Stoppard, Tom
Biography, Bureaucracy, Elections, Journalism, Knowledge, War

Stowell, Lord
Law

Strachey, Lytton
Biography

Stravinsky, Igor
Music

Strunsky, Simeon
Quotations

Suckling, John
Love

Index of Authors

Sullivan, J. W. N.
Science

Sullivan, Louis Henri
Architecture

Surtees, R. S.
Animals, Dance, Eating, Pleasure

Swenson, May
Children

Swift, Jonathan
Church, Criticism, Genius, Hospitality, Lies, Life Sciences, Old Age, Progress, Religion, Style, Travel

Szasz, Thomas
Forgiveness, Justice, Medicine

Szent-Györgyi, Albert von
Invention, Life Sciences

Tacitus
Peace, Winning

Tagore, Rabindranath
Prejudice, Solitude

Talleyrand, Charles-Maurice de
Ending, Moderation

Tally, Ted *see* Harris, Thomas and Tally, Ted

Tarantino, Quentin
Knowledge

Taupin, Bernie *see* John, Elton and Taupin, Bernie

Tawney, R. H.
Honours

Teale, Edwin Way
Autumn

Tebbit, Norman
Patriotism

Tecumseh
Race

Temple, William
Cricket

Tennyson, Alfred, Lord
Army, Belief, Birds, Change, Death, Determination, Europe, Festivals, Gardens, Honour, Honours, Love, Mistakes, Nature, Perfection, Prayer, Sorrow

Tenzing Norgay
Mountains

Terence
Human Race

Teresa, Mother
Sickness

Teresa, St of Ávila
God, Goodness, Housework, Thinking, Weather

Teresa, St of Lisieux
Heaven

Tertullian
Belief, Church

Thackeray, William Makepeace
Family, Men and Women, Weddings

Thatcher, Margaret
Charity, Choice, Determination, Europe, Home, Journalism, Leadership, Money, Society

Theroux, Paul
Manners

Thomas, Dylan
Death, Housework, Life, Old Age, Power, Wales, Youth

Thomas, Edward
Past

Thomas à Kempis
God, Goodness

Thompson, Francis
Suffering

Thomson, James
Britain, Teaching

Thomson, Roy
Television

Thoreau, Henry David
Birds, Clothes, Education, Life, Pollution, Self, Time, Writing

Thorne, Robert
Travel

Thucydides
Writing

Thurber, James
Humour, Sleep, Technology

Thurlow, Edward, 1st Baron
Conscience

Tiberius
Taxes

Tillich, Paul
Anxiety

Tipu Sultan
Heroes

Titus
Charity

Tocqueville, Alexis de
Class

Tolstoy, Leo
Body, Family, Hypocrisy

Index of Authors

Torke, Michael
Mind

Toussenel, A.
Dogs

Townshend, Pete
Generation Gap

Toynbee, Polly
Woman's Role

Travis, Merle
Poverty

Trevelyan, G. M.
France

Trillin, Calvin
Books

Trinder, Tommy
United States

Trollope, Anthony
Equality, Ideas,
Pride, Retirement,
Suffering, Winter

Trollope, Frances
Autumn

Trotsky, Leon
Civilization, Old
Age, Planning,
Violence

Trudeau, Pierre
Censorship

Truffaut, François
Protest

Truman, Harry S.
Economics,
Government,
Leadership,
Politicians

Trump, Donald
Business

Trump, Ivana
Revenge

Truth, Sojourner
Human Rights

Tsvetaeva, Marina
Bereavement,
Deceit, Lies

Tucker, Sophie
Wealth, Women

Tupper, Martin
Books

Turgenev, Ivan
Nature, Prayer

Tusa, John
Management

Twain, Mark
Anger, Books,
Custom, Doubt,
Festivals, Food,
Foolishness,
Generation Gap,
Golf, Gossip,
Honours, Human
Race, Invention,
Journalism,
Knowledge, Lies,
Prayer, Quotations,
Success,
Temptation, Truth

Twiggy
Middle Age

Tynan, Kenneth
Criticism

Tyson, Mike
Boxing

**Unamuno, Miguel
de**
Doubt

**Universal
Declaration of
Human Rights**
Human Rights

Updike, John
Boredom, England,
Fame, Parents,
Science, United
States

Ustinov, Peter
Computers,
Friendship, Parents,
Retirement

Valéry, Paul
Politics

Vanbrugh, John
Women

**Vanderbilt, William
H.**
Business

**van der Post,
Laurens**
Murder

Van Dyke, Henry
Hospitality, Houses,
Time

Vaneigem, Raoul
Work

Vaughan, Harry
Character

Vegetius
Peace

Versace, Gianni
Fashion

Vespasian
Taxes

Vicious, Sid
Music

Victoria, Queen
Birth, Children,
Humour, Royalty,
Winning, Woman's
Role

Vidal, Gore
Business, Lies,
Success, Television

Vidor, King
Marriage

**Viera Gallo, José
Antonio**
Politics

Vigneault, Gilles
Canada

Villon, François
Past

Virgil
Ability, Courage,
Experience, Love,

Index of Authors

Virgil (*cont.*)
Money, Night,
Sorrow, Suffering,
Time, Trust

Voltaire
Boredom, Canada,
Censorship, Change,
Democracy, God,
Government,
Management,
Optimism,
Perfection,
Practicality,
Supernatural,
Taxes, Writing

Walcott, Derek
Creativity, Writing

Walker, Alice
Earth, Life, Violence

**Wallace, William
Ross**
Mothers

Wallas, Graham
Meaning

Walpole, Horace
Fashion, Goodness,
Life, Summer,
Weather

Walpole, Robert
Politicians

Walton, Izaak
Fishing, Health

Walton, Sam
Business

**Warburton, Bishop
William**
Religion

Warhol, Andy
Fame

**Warner, Sylvia
Townsend**
Diaries, Food,
Misfortune, Sorrow

**Washington,
George**
Army, Secrecy,
Truth

Waterhouse, Keith
Manners

Watson, James D.
Youth

**Watson, Thomas
Snr.**
Business

Watts, Isaac
God, Idleness, Time

Waugh, Evelyn
Britain, England,
Manners, Style,
Thanks

Webster, Daniel
Ambition

Webster, John
Death, Discontent,
Fate

Wedgwood, Josiah
Race

Weil, Simone
Economics

Weinreich, Max
Language

**Weir, Robert
Stanley**
Canada

Weiser, Stanley and
Stone, Oliver
Eating, Economics

Weisskopf, Victor
Teaching

**Weissmuller,
Johnny**
Men and Women

Weizmann, Chaim
Luck

Welch, Bruce and
Bennett, Brian
Leisure

Weldon, Fay
Children, Honours,
Life, Parents

Welles, Orson
Cinema,
Civilization, Flight,
Television

**Wellington, Duke
of**
Army, Books,
Life, War

Wells, H. G.
History, Morality,
Society

Wells, John
Self-Knowledge

Wesker, Arnold
Censorship

Wesley, John
Church, Old Age,
Religion

West, Mae
Choice, Diaries,
Goodness, Humour,
Meeting, Men, Sex

West, Rebecca
Housework, Trust

**Westwood,
Vivienne**
Clothes

Wetherell, Charles
Biography

Wharton, Edith
Singing

Whately, Richard
Economics

**Whistler, James
McNeill**
Argument,
Criticism,
Examinations,
Painting,
Quotations

White, E. B.
Statistics

Index of Authors

White, T. H.
Education, Law

Whitehead, Alfred North
Ideas, Intelligence, Philosophy

Whitehorn, Katharine
Mothers

Whitman, Walt
Body, Charity, Creativity, Festivals, Self, United States

Whittier, John Greenleaf
Food, Sorrow

Whitton, Charlotte
Men and Women

Wiesel, Elie
Indifference

Wilberforce, Bishop Samuel
Life Sciences

Wilcox, Ella Wheeler
Religion, Solitude

Wilde, Oscar
Advice, Biography, Country, Cynicism, Diaries, England, Experience, Genius, Gossip, Hospitality, Idealism, Literature, Love, Marriage, Men and Women, Mistakes, Parents, Reality, Style, Temptation, Truth

Wilder, Billy *see* **Brackett, Charles and Wilder, Billy**

Wilder, Thornton
Bereavement

Wilensky, Robert
Computers

Will, George F.
Baseball

Willans, Geoffrey and Searle, Ronald
Christmas, Ignorance

Willard, Emma Hart
Sea

William III
Fate

Williams, Hugo
Fathers, Weddings

Williams, R. J. P.
Life Sciences

Williams, Rowan
Human Race

Williams, Sarah
Skies

Williams, Serena
Tennis

Williams, Shirley
Church

Williams, Tennessee
Determination, Human Race, Reality

Williams, William Carlos
Certainty

Williamson, Marianne
Fear

Williamson, Roy
Scotland

Wilson, A. N.
Wales

Wilson, Edward O.
Mind

Wilson, Harold
Crises, Politics, Technology

Wilson, McLandburgh
Pessimism

Wilson, Woodrow
Cinema, Democracy

Windsor, Barbara
Acting

Windsor, Duchess of
Body

Winters, Shelley
Theatre

Winterson, Jeanette
Lovers

Wittgenstein, Ludwig
Language, Philosophy, Speechmaking, Universe

Wodehouse, P. G.
Apology, Discontent, Family, Golf

Wogan, Terry
Television

Wolfe, Tom
Politics

Wollstonecraft, Mary
Mind, Parents, Woman's Role

Wolstenholme, Kenneth
Ending

Woods, Tiger
Race

Woolf, Virginia
Books, Misfortune, Satisfaction, Writing

Woollcott, Alexander
Pleasure

Index of Authors

Wordsworth, William
  Birth, Children, Death, England, Flowers, Goodness, Imagination, Knowledge, Leisure, London, Nature, Poetry, Revolution, Writing, Youth

Worrall, Terry
  Weather

Wotton, Henry
  Architecture, Bereavement, Diplomacy

Wright, Frank Lloyd
  Architecture, Town

Yāqūt
  Earth

Yeatman, R. J. *see* Sellar, W. C. and Yeatman, R. J.

Yeats, W. B.
  Change, Death, Heart, Idealism, Indifference, Ireland, Life, Love, Old Age, Perfection, Poetry, Suffering

Young, Edward
  Foolishness, Idleness, Quotations, Sickness, Sleep

Young, George W.
  Drink

Young, Neil
  Lifestyles

Zangwill, Israel
  United States

Zappa, Frank
  Journalism, Progress

Zeno
  Speechmaking

Zobel, Hiller B.
  Law